FIFTEEN MODERN AMERICAN POETS

FIFTEEN

MODERN AMERICAN POETS

Edited by GEORGE P. ELLIOTT

New York
Toronto

RINEHART & COMPANY, INC.

Acknowledgments

ELIZABETH BISHOP

All Miss Bishop's poems appearing in this anthology are from POEMS: NORTH & SOUTH—A COLD SPRING, copyright 1940, 1946, 1947, 1948, 1949, 1951, 1952, 1955 by Elizabeth Bishop. Reprinted by permission of Houghton Mifflin Company.

RICHARD EBERHART

This Fevers Me; For a Lamb; In a Hard Intellectual Light; Two Loves; When Golden Flies upon My Carcass Come; If I Could Only Live at the Pitch That Is near Madness; Rumination; Cover Me Over; A Meditation; Imagining How It Would Be to Be Dead; and *New Hampshire, February* are from SELECTED POEMS (1951) by Richard Eberhart, reprinted by permission of Oxford University Press, Inc.

Go to the Shine That's on a Tree; What If Remembrance?; Reality! Reality! What Is It?; The Horse Chestnut Tree; Seals, Terns, Time; Forms of the Human; and *The Human Being Is a Lonely Creature* are from UNDERCLIFF: POEMS 1946–1953 by Richard Eberhart, reprinted by permission of Oxford University Press, Inc.

Idols of Imagination, copyright by Yale University Press, is reprinted by permission of THE YALE REVIEW. *Cold Fall* is reprinted by permission of THE POET. *Sestina* is reprinted by permission of INTERIM. *The Day-Bed* is reprinted by permission of BOTTEGHE OSCURE

RANDALL JARRELL

A Girl in a Library; Seele im Raum; The Black Swan; The Orient Express; and *The Sleeping Beauty* are from THE SEVEN-LEAGUE CRUTCHES, copyright 1951 by Randall Jarrell. Reprinted by permission of Harcourt, Brace and Company, Inc.

The Märchen; Loss; and *A Ward in the States* are from LOSSES by Randall Jarrell, copyright 1948 by Harcourt, Brace and Company, Inc.

A Utopian Journey is reprinted from SELECTED POEMS by Randall Jarrell, by permission of Alfred A. Knopf, Inc. Copyright 1955 by Randall Jarrell.

90 North is from BLOOD FOR A STRANGER by Randall Jarrell, copyright 1942 by Harcourt, Brace and Company, Inc.

Acknowledgments

The Death of the Ball Turret Gunner; Losses; A Lullaby; Second Air Force; and *The Metamorphoses* are from LITTLE FRIEND, LITTLE FRIEND (1945). Reprinted by permission of Randall Jarrell.

ROBERT LOWELL

Colloquy in Black Rock; The Quaker Graveyard in Nantucket; Children of Light; The Drunken Fisherman; Between the Porch and the Altar; After the Surprising Conversions; Where the Rainbow Ends; Noli Me Tangere; and *Death from Cancer* are from LORD WEARY'S CASTLE, copyright 1944, 1946 by Robert Lowell. Reprinted by permission of Harcourt, Brace and Company, Inc.

Falling Asleep over the Aeneid and *Mother Marie Therese* are from THE MILLS OF THE KAVANAUGHS, copyright 1946, 1947, 1948, 1950, 1951 by Robert Lowell. Reprinted by permission of Harcourt, Brace and Company, Inc.

JOSEPHINE MILES

Herald; Lark; Lineman Calling; Driver Saying; Enlightenment; and *For Futures* are from Josephine Miles, LINES AT INTERSECTION, copyright 1939 by The Macmillan Company.

Government Injunction Restraining Harlem Cosmetic Co.; Appointment in Doctor's Office; Moonrise in City Park; Preliminary to Classroom Lecture; and *Polo Match, Sunday, 2 p.m.,* are from POEMS ON SEVERAL OCCASIONS by Josephine Miles. Copyright 1941 by New Directions.

Housewife; Opal; The Thoroughgoing; The Sympathizers; and *What Followed* are from LOCAL MEASURES, copyright 1946 by Josephine Miles. Reprinted by permission of Harcourt, Brace and Company, Inc.

Harvest Moon; Bombay; Statute; Kind; The Halt; Pride; The Day the Winds; Idea of Joy; Meeting; Education; Riddle; The Plastic Glass; Son; Sale; Belief; and *Reasons* are from PREFABRICATIONS. Reprinted by permission of the Indiana University Press.

Monkey and *The Savages* first appeared in the KENYON REVIEW, and *Mercury* in PERSPECTIVE. All three are reprinted by permission of Josephine Miles. *Confessed* is reprinted by permission of Josephine Miles.

HOWARD NEMEROV

The Frozen City and *A Chromium-Plated Hat* are from THE IMAGE AND THE LAW by Howard Nemerov, copyright 1947 by Henry Holt and Company, Inc. Reprinted by permission of the publishers.

A Poem of Margery Kempe; Sonnet at Easter; The Lives of Gulls and Children; and *The Ecstasies of Dialectic* are from GUIDE TO THE RUINS, copyright 1948, 1949, 1950 by Howard Nemerov. Reprinted by permission of Random House, Inc.

The Winter Lightning; The Pond; The Salt Garden; The Goose Fish; Young Woman; and *The Snow Globe* are from THE SALT GARDEN, copyright 1951, 1952, 1954, 1955 by Howard Nemerov. Reprinted by permission of Little, Brown & Co., and the Atlantic Monthly Press.

HYAM PLUTZIK

An Equation; The Begetting of Cain; Divisibility; Mr. Pollington Remembers a Poet; Identity; My Sister; He Inspects His Armory; Argumentum ad Hominem; On the Photograph of a Man I Never Saw; Exhortation to the Artists; and *Portrait* are from ASPECTS OF PROTEUS, copyright 1949 by Hyam Plutzik. Reprinted by permission of Harper & Brothers.

For T. S. E. Only first appeared in THE AMERICAN SCHOLAR; and *The Road* in the PRAIRIE SCHOONER (published by the University of Nebraska Press). The poems are reprinted by permission of these journals, respectively, as well as by permission of Hyam Plutzik.

The excerpts from *Horatio* are used by permission of Hyam Plutzik.

THEODORE ROETHKE

Root Cellar and *Dolor,* copyright 1943 by Modern Poetry Association, Inc. *Moss Gathering,* copyright 1946 by Editorial Publications, Inc. *Four for Sir John Davies: I. The Dance,* copyright 1952 by The Atlantic Monthly Company. The following are copyright by Theodore Roethke as of the dates indicated. *On the Road to Woodlawn,* 1941; *The Lost Son,* 1947; *Elegy for Jane,* 1950; *The Waking,* 1953; and *Four for Sir John Davies: II. The Partner,* 1952, *III. The Wraith* and *IV. The Vigil,* 1953. All these poems, as well as *Give Way, Ye Gates,* are from THE WAKING by Theodore Roethke. Reprinted by permission of Doubleday & Company, Inc.

The Song is reprinted from THE HUDSON REVIEW, VIII-1, Spring, 1955. Copyright 1955 by the The Hudson Review, Inc. *Words for the Wind* is reprinted by permission of HARPER'S BAZAAR, ENCOUNTER, and BOTTEGHE OSCURE. *Love's Progress* is reprinted by permission of the NEW REPUBLIC and BOTTEGHE OSCURE.

MURIEL RUKEYSER

Ajanta; Beast in View; Boy with His Hair Cut Short; Chapultepec Park; From the Duck-Pond to the Carousel; Then I Saw What the Calling Was; George Robinson: Blues; and FROM *The Cornfield* are from SELECTED

Acknowledgments

POEMS, copyright 1951 by Muriel Rukeyser. Reprinted by permission of the publisher, New Directions.

The Antagonists from *Ninth Elegy;* and *Children's Elegy* from *Eighth Elegy* are from ELEGIES, 1949, by Muriel Rukeyser. All rights reserved. Reprinted by permission of the publisher, New Directions.

Nuns in the Wind; A Charm for Cantinflas; Foghorn in Horror; and *The Return* are reprinted by permission of Muriel Rukeyser. *A Birth* and *Children, The Sandbar, That Summer* first appeared in POETRY. Reprinted by permission of Muriel Rukeyser.

JAMES SCHEVILL

The Will of Writing and *Perhaps a Prayer* are from TENSIONS (1947). *Lament for a Man Who Loved God* and *Confidential Data* are from THE AMERICAN FANTASIES (1951). *D-9; The Death of a Dove; A Song for Old Apis; Seurat; Fabre, the Bughunter; The Birth of Arachne, the Spider; Cheops; A Guilty Father to His Daughter; A Plea for Alias; Unnatural, Unusual and Unfair; The Coastguardsman in the Fog; The Old Pilot Tunnels under the English Channel; An Astonished Listener;* and *The Turtle* are from THE RIGHT TO GREET (1955). All these poems are reprinted by permission of the publisher, Bern Porter Books. *A Plea for Alias* is reprinted by permission also of the NEW REPUBLIC.

The Dancers with a Hop and *Drama of the Rose* are reprinted by permission of James Schevill.

DELMORE SCHWARTZ

Will You Perhaps; Do They Whisper; The Heavy Bear; For the One Who Would Take Man's Life in His Hands; Saint, Revolutionist; What Is to Be Given; and *In the Naked Bed, in Plato's Cave* are from IN DREAMS BEGIN RESPONSIBILITIES by Delmore Schwartz, copyright 1938 by New Directions.

Lincoln is from GENESIS by Delmore Schwartz, copyright 1943 by New Directions.

The Masters of the Heart Touched the Unknown; She Was the Girl within the Picture Frame; "One in a Thousand of Years of the Nights"; I Wish I Had Great Knowledge or Great Art; "There'll Be Others but Non So for Me"; She Lives with the Furies of Hope and Despair; Being Unused to Joyous Consciousness; The Morning Light for One with Too Much Luck; and *The Self Unsatisfied Runs Everywhere* are from VAUDEVILLE FOR A PRINCESS, copyright 1950 by New Directions.

The Fulfillment is reprinted by permission of the ART NEWS ANNUAL.

The First Morning of the Second World is reprinted by permission of the KENYON REVIEW.

WINFIELD TOWNLEY SCOTT

How Shall I Ever Come to Any Good?; Indian Summer—Buffalo Summer; and *Old Talk* are from WIND THE CLOCK (1941). *To L. B. S.; Baldness and the Swan; Green and Red and Darkness; To Marry Strangers;* and *The U.S. Sailor with the Japanese Skull* are from TO MARRY STRANGERS (1945). All are reprinted by permission of Winfield Townley Scott.

Gert Swasey and *Three American Women and a German Bayonet* are from MR. WHITTIER AND OTHER POEMS, copyright 1948 by Winfield Townley Scott. Reprinted by permission of The Macmillan Company.

Mrs. Severin and *Re-Run* are reprinted by permission of THE HOPKINS REVIEW. *Memento* is reprinted by permission of THE BELOIT POETRY JOURNAL. *Bermuda Suite, #5* and *Merrill's Brook* first appeared in POETRY. They are reprinted by permission of Winfield Townley Scott. *Exercise in Aesthetics* is reprinted by permission of the NEW REPUBLIC. *Codicil for Pvt. John Hogg's Will* is reprinted by permission of THE VIRGINIA QUARTERLY REVIEW. *"The Hour Is Late"* is reprinted by permission of the ATLANTIC MONTHLY.

Unsexed by the Cold Sea originally appeared in DISCOVERY NO. 5, published by Pocket Books, Inc. Reprinted by permission of Winfield Townley Scott.

KARL SHAPIRO

Adam and Eve; Love for a Hand; and *The Tingling Back* are from POEMS 1940–1953, copyright 1951, 1952, 1953 by Karl Shapiro. *Drug Store; Haircut; Mongolian Idiot; October 1;* and *Waitress* are from PERSON, PLACE AND THING, copyright 1941, 1942, by Karl Shapiro. *The Southerner* and *Recapitulations I, II, V and XIII* are from TRIAL OF A POET, copyright 1946, 1947 by Karl Shapiro. *V-Letter* is from V-LETTER AND OTHER POEMS, copyright 1943 by Karl Shapiro. *Love for a Hand; The Southerner;* and *V-Letter* originally appeared in THE NEW YORKER. All Mr. Shapiro's poems appearing in this anthology are reprinted by permission of Random House, Inc.

ROBERT PENN WARREN

Eidolon; Revelation; Pursuit; Original Sin: A Short Story; Variation: Ode to Fear; Mexico Is a Foreign Country; and *Bearded Oaks* are from

Acknowledgments

SELECTED POEMS 1923–1943 by Robert Penn Warren, copyright 1944 by Harcourt, Brace and Company, Inc.

To a Little Girl, One Year Old, in Ruined Fortress, is reprinted by permission of the PARTISAN REVIEW. Copyright 1955 by PARTISAN REVIEW.

RICHARD WILBUR

Cicadas; In a Bird Sanctuary; Lightness; The Beautiful Changes; and *Winter Spring* are from THE BEAUTIFUL CHANGES, copyright 1947 by Richard Wilbur. Reprinted by permission of Harcourt, Brace and Company, Inc.

Driftwood; In the Elegy Season; Juggler; Years-End; A Simile for Her Smile; Ceremony; Castles and Distances; Marché aux Oiseaux; A World without Objects Is a Sensible Emptiness; and *Lament* are from CEREMONY, copyright 1948, 1949, 1950 by Richard Wilbur. Reprinted by permission of Harcourt, Brace and Company, Inc.

All These Birds (1955), *A Black November Turkey* (1953), and *Exeunt* (1952; originally *Exodus*) copyrighted in the respective years shown by The New Yorker Magazine, Inc. *Beasts* is reprinted from THE HUDSON REVIEW, VI-1, Spring, 1953; copyright 1953 by The Hudson Review, Inc. *Beasts* and *Love Calls Us to the Things of This World* are reprinted by permission of BOTTEGHE OSCURE. All these poems are from THINGS OF THIS WORLD, © 1956 by Richard Wilbur. Reprinted by permission of Harcourt, Brace and Company, Inc.

Preface

This book aims to represent the middle generation of American poets, not those like Frost, Cummings, Stevens, W. C. Williams, Jeffers, MacLeish, and Ransom, whose reputations are by now quite firmly fixed, nor those like Hecht, Merwin, and Moss, who are still on the way. All fifteen of these poets are still actively producing poetry (which is being published not only in volumes of their verse but also in literary magazines), and all have been known for several years. Among the poets who must surely be included in any such list the oldest is Richard Eberhart (1904) and the youngest Richard Wilbur (1921). Their birth dates have set the age limits of the poets to be selected.

Each poet has been allotted about twenty pages, share and share alike, on the hypothesis that college courses in the study of modern poetry for the most part benefit more from a sizable representation from several poets than from a smattering from fifty or a hundred. I feel that these twenty pages provide adequate room for representing each poet's work and that the omission of very long poems does not impose upon the reader a distorted introduction to the work of any one of these poets. One who would otherwise have been included has had to be left out because his publisher refuses reprint rights to paperbound anthologies.

In selecting the poems I have tried to include fairly recent work so that a reader of this collection might have an idea of what these poets have been doing in the early fifties as well as of what they were doing in the forties and (most of them) in the thirties. I have excluded translations and prose poems.

The notes are intended only to give aid with facts not readily come by but of some importance to understanding the poems. Take, for example, "The Savages" by Josephine Miles. Every American college student who is likely to read this anthology can be expected to know who President Jackson and Henry David Thoreau were. Pastor Smiley and Professor Roy Harvey Pearce, in the poem, are rather typical than individual; the Pastor and Professor are more important than the Smiley and Pearce. Miss Benedict, however, is Ruth Benedict, an anthropologist whose book "Patterns of Culture" contains the ideas referred to in the stanza attributed to her, and I doubt that most students have read her book; yet, unless they know something of it, at least as much information as a note provides, I think they would have unnecessary trouble understanding the statement, "The partial era of enlightenment in which we live brings Dionysus to the mesa and the cottonwood grove."

Poets frequently use the names of persons and places from their quite personal experience. Usually in successful poems the poet will make as clear as the poem demands who or what the proper name stands for; it will become a part of the essential, not accidental, meaning of the poem. So I have not thought it important to indicate that, for instance, Pvt. John Hogg was the grandfather of W. T. Scott.

The most difficult lines to draw are explanations of learned references. Most poets are great and curious readers; what they have learned becomes a part of their available experience but frequently exceeds what a student, or any other "common reader," might be expected to know. Always my criterion has been, in deciding whether to explain some learned reference (and, if so, how fully to explain it): To what extent does the poem depend upon understanding this reference? Hugo in Jersey (in Schwartz's "The Masters of the Heart Touched the Unknown") seemed to me to merit the brief note that the poet spent the last years of his life in that island off the west coast of France, since he "like a sunset shone." And the very title of Jarrell's "Seele im Raum" is not only literary in reference but German in language; the poet himself provides a note explaining it.

Except where the author is credited, I am responsible for the notes. I owe debts of gratitude for assistance in preparing them to Johann Hannesson, Arthur Knodel, and Brother S. Robert, F.S.C.

An anthologist of current poetry seeks both Excellence and Sales; these do not always combine well, and they are very hard to be sure of ahead of time. Therefore, in making his actual choices he blends what he has at hand, his own Taste and the poet's Reputation (both of which he knows to be fallible), and thanks God when the two are identical. When they are not identical, he blends and blends and blends.

G. P. E.

Ithaca, New York
February, 1956

CONTENTS

Contents

Contents

Contents

WINFIELD TOWNLEY SCOTT

DELMORE SCHWARTZ

ELIZABETH BISHOP

A Miracle for Breakfast

At six o'clock we were waiting for coffee,
waiting for coffee and the charitable crumb
that was going to be served from a certain balcony,
— like kings of old, or like a miracle.
It was still dark. One foot of the sun
steadied itself on a long ripple in the river.

The first ferry of the day had just crossed the river.
It was so cold we hoped that the coffee
would be very hot, seeing that the sun
was not going to warm us; and that the crumb
would be a loaf each, buttered, by a miracle.
At seven a man stepped out on the balcony.

He stood for a minute alone on the balcony
looking over our heads toward the river.
A servant handed him the makings of a miracle,
consisting of one lone cup of coffee
and one roll, which he proceeded to crumb,
his head, so to speak, in the clouds — along with the sun.

Was the man crazy? What under the sun
was he trying to do, up there on his balcony!
Each man received one rather hard crumb,
which some flicked scornfully into the river,
and, in a cup, one drop of the coffee.
Some of us stood around, waiting for the miracle.

I can tell what I saw next; it was not a miracle.
A beautiful villa stood in the sun
and from its doors came the smell of hot coffee.
In front, a baroque white plaster balcony

added by birds, who nest along the river,
— I saw it with one eye close to the crumb —

and galleries and marble chambers. My crumb
my mansion, made for me by a miracle,
through ages, by insects, birds, and the river
working the stone. Every day, in the sun,
at breakfast time I sit on my balcony
with my feet up, and drink gallons of coffee.

We licked up the crumb and swallowed the coffee.
A window across the river caught the sun
as if the miracle were working, on the wrong balcony.

The Unbeliever

He sleeps on the top of a mast. BUNYAN

He sleeps on the top of a mast
with his eyes fast closed.
The sails fall away below him
like the sheets of his bed,
leaving out in the air of the night the sleeper's head.

Asleep he was transported there,
asleep he curled
in a gilded ball on the mast's top,
or climbed inside
a gilded bird, or blindly seated himself astride.

'I am founded on marble pillars,'
said a cloud. 'I never move.
See the pillars there in the sea?'
Secure in introspection
he peers at the watery pillars of his reflection.

A gull had wings under his
and remarked that the air

was 'like marble.' He said: 'Up here
I tower through the sky
for the marble wings on my tower-top fly.'

But he sleeps on the top of his mast
with his eyes closed tight.
The gull inquired into his dream,
which was, 'I must not fall.
The spangled sea below wants me to fall.
It is hard as diamonds; it wants to destroy us all.'

Cirque d'Hiver

Across the floor flits the mechanical toy,
fit for a king of several centuries back.
A little circus horse with real white hair.
His eyes are glossy black.
He bears a little dancer on his back.

She stands upon her toes and turns and turns.
A slanting spray of artificial roses
is stitched across her skirt and tinsel bodice.
Above her head she poses
another spray of artificial roses.

His mane and tail are straight from Chirico.
He has a formal, melancholy soul.
He feels her pink toes dangle toward his back
along the little pole
that pierces both her body and her soul

and goes through his, and reappears below,
under his belly, as a big tin key.
He canters three steps, then he makes a bow,
canters again, bows on one knee,
canters, then clicks and stops, and looks at me.

The dancer, by this time, has turned her back.
He is the more intelligent by far.
Facing each other rather desperately —
his eye is like a star —
we stare and say, 'Well, we have come this far.'

Roosters

At four o'clock
in the gun-metal blue dark
we hear the first crow of the first cock

just below
the gun-metal blue window
and immediately there is an echo

off in the distance,
then one from the back-yard fence,
then one, with horrible insistence,

grates like a wet match
from the broccoli patch,
flares, and all over town begins to catch.

Cries galore
come from the water-closet door,
from the dropping-plastered henhouse floor,

where in the blue blur
their rustling wives admire,
the roosters brace their cruel feet and glare

with stupid eyes
while from their beaks there rise
the uncontrolled, traditional cries.

Deep from protruding chests
in green-gold medals dressed,
planned to command and terrorize the rest,

the many wives
who lead hens' lives
of being courted and despised;

deep from raw throats
a senseless order floats
all over town. A rooster gloats

over our beds
from rusty iron sheds
and fences made from old bedsteads,

over our churches
where the tin rooster perches,
over our little wooden northern houses,

making sallies
from all the muddy alleys,
marking out maps like Rand McNally's:

glass headed pins,
oil-golds and copper greens,
anthracite blues, alizarins,

each one an active
displacement in perspective;
each screaming, 'This is where I live!'

Each screaming
'Get up! Stop dreaming!'
Roosters, what are you projecting?

You, whom the Greeks elected
to shoot at on a post, who struggled
when sacrificed, you whom they labeled

"Very combative . . ."
what right have you to give
commands and tell us how to live,

cry "Here!" and "Here!"
and wake us here where are
unwanted love, conceit and war?

The crown of red
set on your little head
is charged with all your fighting blood.

Yes, that excrescence
makes a most virile presence,
plus all that vulgar beauty of iridescence.

Now in mid-air
by twos they fight each other.
Down comes a first flame-feather,

and one is flying,
with raging heroism defying
even the sensation of dying.

And one has fallen,
but still above the town
his torn-out, bloodied feathers drift down;

and what he sung
no matter. He is flung
on the gray ash-heap, lies in dung

with his dead wives
with open, bloody eyes,
while those metallic feathers oxidize.

St. Peter's sin
was worse than that of Magdalen
whose sin was of the flesh alone;

of spirit, Peter's,
falling, beneath the flares,
among the 'servants and officers.'

Old holy sculpture
could set it all together
in one small scene, past and future:

Christ stands amazed,
Peter, two fingers raised
to surprised lips, both as if dazed.

But in between
a little cock is seen
carved on a dim column in the travertine,

explained by *gallus canit;*
flet Petrus underneath it.
There is inescapable hope, the pivot;

yes, and there Peter's tears
run down our chanticleer's
sides and gem his spurs.

Tear-encrusted thick
as a medieval relic
he waits. Poor Peter, heart-sick,

still cannot guess
those cock-a-doodles yet might bless,
his dreadful rooster come to mean forgiveness,

a new weathervane
on basilica and barn,
and that outside the Lateran

there would always be
a bronze cock on a porphyry
pillar so the people and the Pope might see

7

that even the Prince
of the Apostles long since
had been forgiven, and to convince

all the assembly
that "Deny deny deny,"
is not all the roosters cry.

In the morning
a low light is floating
in the backyard, and gilding

from underneath
the broccoli, leaf by leaf;
how could the night have come to grief?

gilding the tiny
floating swallow's belly
and lines of pink cloud in the sky,

the day's preamble
like wandering lines in marble.
The cocks are now almost inaudible.

The sun climbs in,
following "to see the end,"
faithful as enemy, or friend.

The Fish

I caught a tremendous fish
and held him beside the boat
half out of water, with my hook
fast in a corner of his mouth.
He didn't fight.
He hadn't fought at all.

He hung a grunting weight,
battered and venerable
and homely. Here and there
his brown skin hung in strips
like ancient wall-paper,
and its pattern of darker brown
was like wall-paper:
shapes like full-blown roses
stained and lost through age.
He was speckled with barnacles,
fine rosettes of lime,
and infested
with tiny white sea-lice,
and underneath two or three
rags of green weed hung down.
While his gills were breathing in
the terrible oxygen
— the frightening gills,
fresh and crisp with blood,
that can cut so badly —
I thought of the coarse white flesh
packed in like feathers,
the big bones and the little bones,
the dramatic reds and blacks
of his shiny entrails,
and the pink swim-bladder
like a big peony.
I looked into his eyes
which were far larger than mine
but shallower, and yellowed,
the irises backed and packed
with tarnished tinfoil
seen through the lenses
of old scratched isinglass.
They shifted a little, but not
to return my stare.
— It was more like the tipping
of an object toward the light.
I admired his sullen face,
the mechanism of his jaw,

and then I saw
that from his lower lip
— if you could call it a lip —
grim, wet, and weapon-like,
hung five old pieces of fish-line,
or four and a wire leader
with the swivel still attached,
with all their five big hooks
grown firmly in his mouth.
A green line, frayed at the end
where he broke it, two heavier lines,
and a fine black thread
still crimped from the strain and snap
when it broke and he got away.
Like medals with their ribbons
frayed and wavering,
a five-haired beard of wisdom
trailing from his aching jaw.
I stared and stared
and victory filled up
the little rented boat,
from the pool of bilge
where oil had spread a rainbow
around the rusted engine
to the bailer rusted orange,
the sun-cracked thwarts,
the oarlocks on their strings,
the gunnels — until everything
was rainbow, rainbow, rainbow!
And I let the fish go.

Late Air

From a magician's midnight sleeve
        the radio-singers
distribute all their love-songs
over the dew-wet lawns.

        And like a fortune-teller's
their marrow-piercing guesses are whatever you believe.

But on the Navy-Yard aerial I find
        better witnesses
for love on summer nights.
Five remote red lights
        keep their nests there; Phoenixes
burning quietly, where the dew cannot climb.

A Cold Spring

For Jane Dewey. Maryland
Nothing is so beautiful as spring. HOPKINS

A cold spring:
the violet was flawed on the lawn.
For two weeks or more the trees hesitated;
the little leaves waited,
carefully indicating their characteristics.
Finally a grave green dust
settled over your big and aimless hills.
One day, in a chill white blast of sunshine,
on the side of one a calf was born.
The mother stopped lowing
and took a long time eating the after-birth,
a wretched flag,
but the calf got up promptly
and seemed inclined to feel gay.

The next day
was much warmer.
Greenish-white dogwood infiltrated the wood,
each petal burned, apparently, by a cigarette-butt,
and the blurred redbud stood
beside it, motionless, but almost more
like movement than any placeable color.
Four deer practised leaping over your fences.

The infant oak-leaves swung through the sober oak,
Song-sparrows were wound up for the summer,
and in the maple the complementary cardinal
cracked a whip, and the sleeper awoke,
stretching miles of green limbs from the south.
In his cap the lilacs whitened,
then one day they fell like snow.

Now, in the evening,
a new moon comes.
The hills grow softer. Tufts of long grass show
where each cow-flop lies.
The bull-frogs are sounding,
slack strings plucked by heavy thumbs.
Beneath the light, against your white front door,
the smallest moths, like Chinese fans,
flatten themselves, silver and silver-gilt
over pale yellow, orange, or gray.
Now, from the thick grass, the fireflies begin to rise:
up, then down, then up again:
lit on the ascending flight,
drifting simultaneously to the same height,
— exactly like the bubbles in champagne.
— Later on they rise much higher.
And your shadowy pastures will be able to offer
these particular glowing tributes
every evening now throughout the summer.

Over 2000 Illustrations and a

Complete Concordance

Thus should have been our travels:
serious, engravable.
The Seven Wonders of the World are tired
and a touch familiar, but the other scenes,
innumerable, though equally sad and still,

are foreign. Often the squatting Arab,
or group of Arabs, plotting, probably,
against our Christian Empire,
while one apart, with outstretched arm and hand
points to the Tomb, the Pit, the Sepulcher.
The branches of the date-palms look like files.
The cobbled courtyard, where the Well is dry,
is like a diagram, the brickwork conduits
are vast and obvious, the human figure
far gone in history or theology,
gone with its camel or its faithful horse.
Always the silence, the gesture, the specks of birds
suspended on invisible threads above the Site,
or the smoke rising solemnly, pulled by threads.
Granted a page alone or a page made up
of several scenes arranged in cattycornered rectangles
or circles set on stippled gray,
granted a grim lunette,
caught in the toils of an initial letter,
when dwelt upon, they all resolve themselves.
The eye drops, weighted, through the lines
the burin made, the lines that move apart
like ripples above sand,
dispersing storms, God's spreading fingerprint,
and painfully, finally, that ignite
in watery prismatic white-and-blue.

Entering the Narrows at St. Johns
the touching bleat of goats reached to the ship.
We glimpsed them, reddish, leaping up the cliffs
among the fog-soaked weeds and butter-and-eggs.
And at St. Peter's the wind blew and the sun shone madly.
Rapidly, purposefully, the Collegians marched in lines,
crisscrossing the great square with black, like ants.
In Mexico the dead man lay
in a blue arcade; the dead volcanoes
glistened like Easter lilies.
The juke-box went on playing "Ay, Jalisco!"
And at Volubilis there were beautiful poppies
splitting the mosaics; the fat old guide made eyes.

In Dingle harbor a golden length of evening
the rotting hulks held up their dripping plush.
The Englishwoman poured tea, informing us
that the Duchess was going to have a baby.
And in the brothels of Marrakesh
the little pockmarked prostitutes
balanced their tea-trays on their heads
and did their belly-dances; flung themselves
naked and giggling against our knees,
asking for cigarettes. It was somewhere near there
I saw what frightened me most of all:
A holy grave, not looking particularly holy,
one of a group under a keyhole-arched stone baldaquin
open to every wind from the pink desert.
An open, gritty, marble trough, carved solid
with exhortation, yellowed
as scattered cattle-teeth;
half-filled with dust, not even the dust
of the poor prophet paynim who once lay there.
In a smart burnoose Khadour looked on amused.

Everything only connected by "and," and "and."
Open the book. (The gilt rubs off the edges
of the pages and pollinates the fingertips.)
Open the heavy book. Why couldn't we have seen
this old Nativity while we were at it?
— the dark ajar, the rocks breaking with light,
and undisturbed, unbreathing flame,
colorless, sparkless, freely fed on straw,
and, lulled within, a family with pets,
— and looked and looked our infant sight away.

View of the Capitol

from the Library of Congress

Moving from left to left, the light
is heavy on the Dome, and coarse.

One small lunette turns it aside
and blankly stares off to the side
like a big white old wall-eyed horse.

On the east steps the Air Force Band
in uniforms of Air Force blue
is playing hard and loud, but — queer —
the music doesn't quite come through.

It comes in snatches, dim then keen,
then mute, and yet there is no breeze.
The giant trees stand in between.
I think the trees must intervene,

catching the music in their leaves
like gold-dust, till each big leaf sags.
Unceasingly the little flags
feed their limp stripes into the air,
and the band's efforts vanish there.

Great shades, edge over,
give the music room.
The gathered brasses want to go
boom — boom.

The Prodigal

The brown enormous odor he lived by
was too close, with its breathing and thick hair,
for him to judge. The floor was rotten; the sty
was plastered halfway up with glass-smooth dung.
Light-lashed, self-righteous, above moving snouts,
the pigs' eyes followed him, a cheerful stare —
even to the sow that always ate her young —
till, sickening, he leaned to scratch her head.
But sometimes mornings after drinking bouts

15

(he hid the pints behind a two-by-four),
the sunrise glazed the barnyard mud with red;
the burning puddles seemed to reassure.
And then he thought he almost might endure
his exile yet another year or more.

But evenings the first star came to warn.
The farmer whom he worked for came at dark
to shut the cows and horses in the barn
beneath their overhanging clouds of hay,
with pitchforks, faint forked lightnings, catching light,
safe and companionable as in the Ark.
The pigs stuck out their little feet and snored.
The lantern — like the sun, going away —
laid on the mud a pacing aureole.
Carrying a bucket along a slimy board,
he felt the bats' uncertain staggering flight,
his shuddering insights, beyond his control,
touching him. But it took him a long time
finally to make his mind up to go home.

Arrival at Santos

Here is a coast; here is a harbor;
here, after a meager diet of horizon, is some scenery:
impractically shaped and — who knows? — self-pitying, mountains,
sad and harsh beneath their frivolous greenery,

with a little church on top of one. And some warehouses,
some of them painted a feeble pink, or blue,
and some tall, uncertain palms. Oh, tourist,
is this how this country is going to answer you

and your immodest demands for a different world,
and a better life, and complete comprehension
of both at last, and immediately,
after eighteen days of suspension?

Finish your breakfast. The tender is coming,
a strange and ancient craft, flying a strange and brilliant rag.
So that's the flag. I never saw it before.
I somehow never thought of there *being* a flag,

but of course there was, all along. And coins, I presume,
and paper money; they remain to be seen.
And gingerly now we climb down the ladder backward,
myself and a fellow passenger named Miss Breen,

descending into the midst of twenty-six freighters
waiting to be loaded with green coffee beans.
Please, boy, do be more careful with that boat hook!
Watch out! Oh! It has caught Miss Breen's

skirt! There! Miss Breen is about seventy,
a retired police lieutenant, and six feet tall,
with beautiful bright blue eyes and a kind expression.
Her home, when she is at home, is in Glens Fall

s, New York. There. We are settled.
The customs officials will speak English, we hope,
and leave us our Scotch and cigarettes.
Ports are necessities, like postage stamps, or soap,

but they seldom seem to care what impression they make,
or, like this, only attempt, since it does not matter,
the unassertive colors of soap, or postage stamps —
wasting away like the former, slipping the way the latter

do when we mail the letters we wrote on the boat,
either because the glue here is very inferior
or because of the heat. We leave Santos at once;
we are driving to the interior.

At the Fishhouses

Although it is a cold evening,
down by one of the fishhouses

an old man sits netting,
his net, in the gloaming almost invisible
a dark purple-brown,
and his shuttle worn and polished.
The air smells so strong of codfish
it makes one's nose run and one's eyes water.
The five fishhouses have steeply peaked roofs
and narrow, cleated gangplanks slant up
to storerooms in the gables
for the wheelbarrows to be pushed up and down on.
All is silver: the heavy surface of the sea,
swelling slowly as if considering spilling over,
is opaque, but the silver of the benches,
the lobster pots, and masts, scattered
among the wild jagged rocks,
is of an apparent translucence
like the small old buildings with an emerald moss
growing on their shoreward walls.
The big fish tubs are completely lined
with layers of beautiful herring scales
and the wheelbarrows are similarly plastered
with creamy iridescent coats of mail,
with small iridescent flies crawling on them.
Up on the little slope behind the houses,
set in the sparse bright sprinkle of grass,
is an ancient wooden capstan,
cracked, with two long bleached handles
and some melancholy stains, like dried blood,
where the ironwork has rusted.

The old man accepts a Lucky Strike.
He was a friend of my grandfather.
We talk of the decline in the population
and of codfish and herring
while he waits for a herring boat to come in.
There are sequins on his vest and on his thumb.
He has scraped the scales, the principal beauty,
from unnumbered fish with that black old knife,
the blade of which is almost worn away.

Down at the water's edge, at the place
where they haul up the boats, up the long ramp
descending into the water, thin silver
tree trunks are laid horizontally
across the gray stones, down and down
at intervals of four or five feet.

Cold dark deep and absolutely clear,
element bearable to no mortal,
to fish and to seals . . . One seal particularly
I have seen here evening after evening.
He was curious about me. He was interested in music;
like me a believer in total immersion,
so I used to sing him Baptist hymns.
I also sang "A Mighty Fortress Is Our God."
He stood up in the water and regarded me
steadily, moving his head a little.
Then he would disappear, then suddenly emerge
almost in the same spot, with a sort of shrug
as if it were against his better judgment.
Cold dark deep and absolutely clear,
the clear gray icy water . . . Back, behind us,
the dignified tall firs begin.
Bluish, associating with their shadows,
a million Christmas trees stand
waiting for Christmas. The water seems suspended
above the rounded gray and blue-gray stones.
I have seen it over and over, the same sea, the same,
slightly, indifferently swinging above the stones,
icily free above the stones,
above the stones and then the world.
If you should dip your hand in,
your wrist would ache immediately,
your bones would begin to ache and your hand would burn
as if the water were a transmutation of fire
that feeds on stones and burns with a dark gray flame.
If you tasted it, it would first taste bitter,
then briny, then surely burn your tongue.
It is like what we imagine knowledge to be:

dark, salt, clear, moving, utterly free,
drawn from the cold hard mouth
of the world, derived from the rocky breasts
forever, flowing and drawn, and since
our knowledge is historical, flowing, and flown.

RICHARD EBERHART

This Fevers Me

This fevers me, this sun on green,
On grass glowing, this young spring.
The secret hallowing is come,
Regenerate sudden incarnation,
Mystery made visible
In growth, yet subtly veiled in all,
Ununderstandable in grass,
In flowers, and in the human heart,
This lyric mortal loveliness,
The earth breathing, and the sun.
The young lambs sport, none udderless.
Rabbits dash beneath the brush.
Crocuses have come; wind flowers
Tremble against quick April.
Violets put on the night's blue,
Primroses wear the pale dawn,
The gold daffodils have stolen
From the sun. New grass leaps up;
Gorse yellows, starred with day;
The willow is a graceful dancer
Poised; the poplar poises too.
The apple takes the seafoam's light,
And the evergreen tree is densely bright.
April, April, when will he
Be gaunt, be old, who is so young?
This fevers me, this sun on green,
On grass glowing, this young spring.

For a Lamb

I saw on the slant hill a putrid lamb,
Propped with daisies. The sleep looked deep,

The face nudged in the green pillow
But the guts were out for crows to eat.

Where's the lamb? whose tender plaint
Said all for the mute breezes.
Say he's in the wind somewhere,
Say, there's a lamb in the daisies.

In a Hard Intellectual Light

In a hard intellectual light
I will kill all delight,
And I will build a citadel
Too beautiful to tell

O too austere to tell
And far too beautiful to see,
Whose evident distance
I will call the best of me.

And this light of intellect
Will shine on all my desires,
It will my flesh protect
And flare my bold constant fires,

For the hard intellectual light
Will lay the flesh with nails.
And it will keep the world bright
And closed the body's soft jails.

And from this fair edifice
I shall see, as my eyes blaze,
The moral grandeur of man
Animating all his days.

And peace will marry purpose,
And purity married to grace
Will make the human absolute
As sweet as the human face.

Until my hard vision blears,
And Poverty and Death return
In organ music like the years,
Making the spirit leap, and burn

For the hard intellectual light
That kills all delight
And brings the solemn, inward pain
Of truth into the heart again.

Two Loves

That her serene influence should spread
An afternoon of soft autumnal light
Is to my heart not unaccountable
For she was young, and is not dead.
And still her cheek is red and white.

But that this stealthy still insistent power
Pervades my mind and will not slumber me
Is delicate woe and glory hard to bear;
Her life lives in a ghost-wrought hour,
From whose chill spirit I am not free.

The one was willow to an ardent touch
And she was mood that had a right to die.
But she, the other, the passion of my mind
Long-living still, does overmuch
Come from the dead, and from the sky.

When Golden Flies
upon My Carcass Come

When golden flies upon my carcass come,
Those pretty monsters, shining globules

Like tautened oily suns, and congregate
Fixing their several gems upon one core
That shines a blossom then of burning gold,
'Tis as the sun's burning glass and diadem
They work, at the first chance of rotten flesh,
And, senseless little messengers of time,
Some beauty keep even at the guts of things,
Which is a fox caught, and I watch the flies.

If I Could Only Live at the Pitch That Is near Madness

If I could only live at the pitch that is near madness
When everything is as it was in my childhood
Violent, vivid, and of infinite possibility:
That the sun and the moon broke over my head.

Then I cast time out of the trees and fields,
Then I stood immaculate in the Ego;
Then I eyed the world with all delight,
Reality was the perfection of my sight.

And time has big handles on the hands,
Fields and trees a way of being themselves.
I saw battalions of the race of mankind
Standing stolid, demanding a moral answer.

I gave the moral answer and I died
And into a realm of complexity came
Where nothing is possible but necessity
And the truth wailing there like a red babe.

Rumination

When I can hold a stone within my hand
And feel time make it sand and soil, and see

The roots of living things grow in this land,
Pushing between my fingers flower and tree,
Then I shall be as wise as death,
For death has done this and he will
Do this to me, and blow his breath
To fire my clay, when I am still.

Cover Me Over

Cover me over, clover;
Cover me over, grass.
The mellow day is over
And there is night to pass.

Green arms about my head,
Green fingers on my hands.
Earth has no quieter bed
In all her quiet lands.

A Meditation

Now you are holding my skull in your hand.
I am not anybody. I am dead.
God has taken my life away. You are holding
My skull in your hand, the wind is blowing
(Blowing, the ineffable structure of the wind)
The wind is blowing through my skull like a horn
And you are thinking of the world's unearthly music
And of the beauty beyond the earth and seas,
You think the tune will tell you of the truth,
You are thinking: thinking, are you? — are you
Thinking? I am dead. I am dead and in your hand.

Now what does it matter whether I lived or died
Or when I lived or when I died or what I tried

To do of all the things there are to do in the world,
You might be musing upon a finch, or a melon,
You might be not you but somebody else, some other,
Some utter muser, maybe, in some other land
With some other kind of brains or bones, or both,
Some lack of bile to make these peregrinations;
You might be a man who never found me at all,
That miraculous fellow, that idiotic genius
Who never had to think of the wind in my skull at all.

There, you see I am so helpless in your hands.
I cannot get back, cannot reach or yearn back,
Nor summon love enough, nor the intellectual care —
Being dead, you talk as if I had spirit at all —
To come back to you and tell you who I am.
You do me too much honor with your grave words
And quizzical head bent down, trace of a lovable smile,
Too much too much honor for one so windless,
And witless, wizened long past wandering and pondering.
Go back to your strict duties of the earth, man,
Make love to your girl long nights, and long summer days.

But there, you hold me, a philosopher! If philosophical,
You had better put me back in the earth,
Hold nothing at all! Hold your own hand, man!
Now you can feel the dainty wind playing through it
Weaving among your fingers what you want to know.
There is the place to love and make your contemplations
For you can still make your fingers fly and go.
Of all symbols the cunning mind devises
None can be so strict, so purely right
As the hand that makes the fingers fashion the love
Contending in immaterial mastery.

But something touches you, deeply, beyond all comment,
Something so tender, wise, human; you are only human
And grief makes you as a little child that weeps
For you do not know why you are in the world
Nor how you got here, in any real sense, nor how long
Before some ruthless shock will end you forever,

That peculiar you you must cherish, the uniqueness,
The kind not like the skull that is in your hand
But that is fixed in its intricate nicety, —
As who can imagine, seeing a fine bull in pasture
That that magnificent creature will lie down and die?

God has taken my life away. I am dead,
I am not anybody. I am no oracle. You be
An oracle, if you can. You be full of imagination.
You see beyond me, which is seeing beyond yourself,
Yours is the purely human burden and the prophecy.
These things can only be talked of by men.
Man is the talking machine; or the arcane marionette
Who like a god thinks himself to be immune
From the terrible void and absolute darkness
The unthinkable loss and final destitution
Upon which he builds (O! yes!) his mighty hierarchies.

But if I had the power to seem to be,
Or could even wish to be powerful, and say
'I am Lord of Life. I am Eternal Life' —
I could not say it, the contradiction is too great.
This goes too far, and lacks a certain humor.
You build a fiction of what I am, or could be,
And amidst the limits of your mentality and words
Revolve, with all your feelings stumbling blocks
And your keenest thoughts barbs of fiery wire.
O dear sweet little timeful poor creature
Tell this skull what it cares not to say

Life blows like the wind away

You have run the weirs of the emotions,
Even as I did; but they are not through with you yet.
There will be many complicated messages,
Memory will make of your heart a veritable mill,
The need for action jerk your legs, ambition
Choke you, rage consume you almost to inanition,
Conquest will thrill you, and defeat annul you.
And you will not have enough, but lust of life

Drive you on to the cold, very brink of the grave
With man's old captive, cyclic wish to know
What it is all about, meaning and moral dimension.

What is it all about, you are asking me now
For it is less of me than of yourself you are thinking,
Surely more of yourself, flesh-bound as you are —
You would withdraw in horror at my secret,
You would not want to know, your long-lashed eyes aglare,
Of the cold absolute blankness and fate of death,
Of the depths of being beyond all words to say,
Of your profound or of the world's destiny,
Of the mind of God, rising like a mighty fire
Pure and calm beyond all mortal instances
Magnificent, eternal, Everlasting, sweet and mild.

No, I rise a little, I come to life a little.
If I could only make you see the simple truth,
So simple it is so hard to say, hard to believe,
That you are to be man, that is, to be human,
You are imperfect, will never know perfection,
You must strive, but the goal will recede forever,
That you must do what the great poets and the sages say,
Obeying scripture even in the rotten times,
That you must, also, not think nor feel too much
(For the Greeks knew what they were talking about),
And that, as you have lived, so must you die

And blow like the wind away

Now you walk back among the flowers of the world.
You have put me down and I am myself again.
Now you return, return from your solemn meditation
Among the strange shadows, the strange veils of longing
And through the cathartic action of beautiful contemplation
Seek among your fellow creatures whatever is good in life,
Purified by this; for, as sin purifies lust,
As war purges society, as death rarefies life,

So the contemplation of death is valuable
Restorative of the soul to new even reaches
Easing a little the burden of our suffering

Before we blow like the wind away

And blow like the wind away

Imagining How It Would Be to Be Dead

Imagining how it would be to be dead,
Until my tender filaments
From mere threads air have become
And this is all my consciousness
(While like a world of rock and stone
My body cumbersome and big
Breathes out a vivid atmosphere
Which is the touchless breach of the air)
I lost my head, and could not hold
Either my hands together or my heart
But was so sentient a being
I seemed to break time apart
And thus became all things air can touch
Or could touch could it touch all things,
And this was an embrace most dear,
Final, complete, a flying without wings.
From being bound to one poor skull,
And that surrounded by one earth,
And the earth in one universe forced,
And that chained to some larger gear,
I was the air, I was the air,
And then I pressed on eye and cheek
The sightless hinges of eternity
That make the whole world creak.

New Hampshire, February

Nature had made them hide in crevices,
Two wasps so cold they looked like bark.
Why I do not know, but I took them
And I put them
In a metal pan, both day and dark.

Like God touching his finger to Adam
I felt, and thought of Michelangelo,
For whenever I breathed on them,
The slightest breath,
They leaped, and preened as if to go.

My breath controlled them always quite.
More sensitive than electric sparks
They came into life
Or they withdrew to ice,
While I watched, suspending remarks.

Then one in a blind career got out,
And fell to the kitchen floor. I
Crushed him with my cold ski boot,
By accident. The other
Had not the wit to try or die.

And so the other is still my pet.
The moral of this is plain.
But I will shirk it.
You will not like it. And
God does not live to explain.

Go to the Shine That's on a Tree

Go to the shine that's on a tree
When dawn has laved with liquid light

With luminous light the nighted tree
And take that glory without fright.

Go to the song that's in a bird
When he has seen the glistening tree,
That glorious tree the bird has heard
Give praise for its felicity.

Then go to the earth and touch it keen,
Be tree and bird, be wide aware
Be wild aware of light unseen,
And unheard song along the air.

What If Remembrance?

When I am lying under
A roof of green grass
That trembles when the thunder
And the white rain pass

And all my meaning gone
In the rhythmic turn of earth,
Senseless under the lawn
Even when grass takes birth

What if remembrance should come
Into the earth of my brain
And all my being plumb
Again
Pain?

Reality! Reality! What Is It?

Christ, I have walked around your erection,
The Cross, that begot, upon a sky of prayer

A billion men, devoted in humility
And I have denied You, a yea-sayer

Yet in pride and ignorance in sin
Too heady, too extreme, too willing
The breadth of the worlds I have travelled in
Should give me insight into all religions; who, milling

In the grips of poverty, or of sexuality,
In sophistication, or in imagination
Have sought all men as my division
And considered the first truth tragedy

Christ, though I should die tonight in hells
Of torture of struggle yet unknown to me
I sense the perfect and queer impetus of my blood
The sole guide upon this helpless flood

Of the light of the life I asked never for
And the triumph of glory I have known
The holiness of death I sheer affirm
And the harsh beatitudes of cruelty

O stars, glitterers, mere salt
Or chemic stuff students sometimes tell
Though great beyond measurement, and ants so small
There are human beings in the world still

Whose passion, rich as the superb pearl
Of holy love they fling in the mire of the real
Burns at the white heat of realization
Of the destruction it is to feel;

And whose cleft natures destroy themselves
Caught in the flaw of their self's largess,
Plungers of the earth's infinitudes
Who most because they deny, cry Yes

O Christ of Easter, impossible Man, Lord, and God
I, cold geographer, map Your clear estate

As one sentient, yet a prisoner, clashing Thy
Cymbal in the gliding sound of my dying,

Christ of Christ, what are you, beast or God,
Must I deny that sweat upon that cross?
Must I affirm what is not whatever I am,
Christ, Christ! reality! reality! what is it?

The Horse Chestnut Tree

Boys in sporadic but tenacious droves
Come with sticks, as certainly as Autumn,
To assault the great horse chestnut tree.

There is a law governs their lawlessness.
Desire is in them for a shining amulet
And the best are those that are highest up.

They will not pick them easily from the ground.
With shrill arms they fling to the higher branches,
To hurry the work of nature for their pleasure.

I have seen them trooping down the street
Their pockets stuffed with chestnuts shucked, unshucked.
It is only evening keeps them from their wish.

Sometimes I run out in a kind of rage
To chase the boys away: I catch an arm,
Maybe, and laugh to think of being the lawgiver.

I was once such a young sprout myself
And fingered in my pocket the prize and trophy.
But still I moralize upon the day

And see that we, outlaws on God's property,
Fling out imagination beyond the skies,
Wishing a tangible good from the unknown.

And likewise death will drive us from the scene
With the great flowering world unbroken yet,
Which we held in idea, a little handful.

Seals, Terns, Time

The seals at play off Western Isle
In the loose flowing of the summer tide
And burden of our strange estate —

Resting on the oar and lolling on the sea,
I saw their curious images,
Hypnotic, sympathetic eyes

As the deep elapses of the soul.
O ancient blood, O blurred kind forms
That rise and peer from elemental water:

I loll upon the oar, I think upon the day,
Drawn by strong, by the animal soft bonds
Back to a dim pre-history;

While off the point of Jagged Light
In hundreds, gracefully, the fork-tailed terns
Draw swift esprits across the sky.

Their aspirations dip in mine,
The quick order of their changing spirit,
More freedom than the eye can see.

Resting lightly on the oarlocks,
Pondering, and balanced on the sea,
A gauze and spindrift of the world,

I am in compulsion hid and thwarted,
Pulled back in the mammal water,
Enticed to the release of the sky.

Forms of the Human

I wanted to be more human
For I felt I thought too much
And for all the thinking I did —
More rabbits in the same hutch.

And how to be more human, I said?
I will tell you the way, I said.
I know how to do it, I said.
But what I said was not what I did.

I took an old garden hoe
And dug the earth, and planted there,
Not forgetting the compost too,
Three small beans that one might grow.

Three grew tall, but one was wild
So I cut off the other two,
And now I have a wild bean flower
The sweetest that ever grew.

The Human Being Is a
Lonely Creature

It is borne in upon me that pain
Is essential. The bones refuse to act.
Recalcitrancy is life's fine flower.
The human being is a lonely creature.

Fear is of the essence. You do not fear?
I say you lie. Fear is the truth of time.
If it is not now, it will come hereafter.
Death is waiting for the human creature.

Praise to harmony and love.
They are best, all else is false.
Yet even in love and harmony
The human being is a lonely creature.

The old sloughed off, the new new-born,
What fate and what high hazards join
As life tries out the soul's enterprise.
Time is waiting for the human creature.

Life is daring all our human stature.
Death looks, and waits for each bright eye.
Love and harmony are our best nurture.
The human being is a lonely creature.

Idols of Imagination

I put the idols by. I left the place;
I journeyed where the eagles are
To sail upon necessity
Under a lucid star.

Far out upon the sea
Where talon meets the fin
I was perplexed again
As pure thinkers are.

What natural act can teach
Up to the soul's reach,
Though killer and killed are one,
What but idols of imagination?

Grant me then no lucid star
And freedom give me now
To cast the dual nature out,
And net a sinewy idolatry.

Cold Fall

The coldness that falls upon the hours
As the years go by.
      It was the tremolo in a voice said this.
      It was when the voice and music became one.

      Quietly from the whole heartbreak of the world
      Was distilled a single consciousness:
The coldness that falls upon the hours
As the years go by.

Sestina

I die, no matter what I do I die.
Is this the sum of what man has to do?
There is no use to fly to be at ease.
Man flies, but knows not what he does.
It is in war you want to be in peace.
In Heaven, in Heaven I want to be in Hell.

The mortal span to find out Heaven and Hell!
No matter what I have to do I die,
The gods comply to cancel you to peace.
Before this then what is it man should do?
And after, does it matter what he does?
Will Christ-like Christ then put him at his ease?

Will will will him his own, a fabled ease?
Will, some say, is the whole road to Hell.
But man is bound to Hell whatever he does.
No matter what he does he has to die.
It is the dying that you have to do
Defies the hyaline luster of the peace.

Despair has not the end in view of peace
Nor has desire the purposes of ease,
But action, while you live, is what's to do.
Thought is three crossed roads that lead to Hell,
Your thought is fatal and will make you die,
For thinking kills as much as action does.

It is not what he thinks, nor what he does
Nor what cold mystery of the Prince of Peace
Avails—no matter what I do I die,
May nothing, nothing put me at my ease
Except the reality of Heaven and Hell.
No one told me what I ought to do.

The scriptures told you what you ought to do.
They are unreasonable truth, and what man does
Believe when most he believes in Heaven and Hell.
That passes understanding, that is peace.
But sky-fallen man will not be put at ease.
I die, no matter what I do I die.

No matter what I do I have no peace.
No matter what man does he has no ease.
Heaven and Hell are changeless when I die.

The Day-Bed

I

It is green, it is made of willow.
I am baffled: I cannot talk about it.
An obsession of twenty-seven years.
I am brutalized to look at it.

The very form of love. Of time
The essence, which is memory.

The flash of light, and a long sleep.
This is the bed of day, and night.

No, but soft, but untold love
Arises. The very heart of love!
So long ago that suffering form
Slowly grew to death through pain,

Here on this very furniture.
It seems impossible. Time lies.
I do not see her lying there,
Great eyes, great gray-black hair.

I do not see that agonizing stare
That's deep through all my nights and days,
Substratum of the flying years;
The great pain without a cure.

II

Reality is a passing thing.
The Day-Bed lives, remains, reminds
Of the eternity of change
To this same, writing finger.

The emblem remains, bounteous gift,
The strange, pure gift of memory,
A blooded drench, a flushed presentiment;
And throngs and throngs of images.

Day-Bed of Life-in-Death,
That while my eyes shall change and see,
I look upon this furniture,
The not estranging imagery.

But summon up the love, and see
The very form and flesh of love
As it is with all mankind,
The loves long lost, the loves most near.

Who cursed the blood within the veins
Apparelling day with source of night
Shall dream upon a lovely dream
Though the deep heart choke, and fight.

III

It is green, it is made of willow.
Lithe winds of Spring wave over it.
It is a new time and a new day,
New flesh here springs in harmony.

Laughs and tumbles and is gay.
Is gay! Is lithe as winds of Spring
And bends to nature as a willow
Triumphing in its green, cool stay.

Two lovers here electing unity
Flaunt eclectic idols in the day,
Consuming the great world of sense,
And laughing in its careless sway.

They sway. They laugh. And leaping
Loosen the mind from iron prisons,
Celebrating speeds of instancy
In vernal cells of intimacy.

Green and willowy marriage time!
Time of the beliefless flesh!
Time of the chargers of the ruddy blood,
Joy that is swift and free, pure joy.

IV

Other years and other foils
Requite the ancient mysteries,
Persuading of some subtle balance
Between the losing and the winning battles,

Here on this very furniture,
Day-Bed of Life-in-Death!

A child plays in boisterous industry,
Truth off the old bones of mating.

Embroiled in fate he does not know,
Smiling mischievous and saintly,
Evidently impossible to quell,
The very future in his active eye,

The willow Day-Bed of past time
That taught death in the substratum
Couches now the bliss of man,
A bright shape, a green new dream.

RANDALL JARRELL

A Girl in a Library

An object among dreams, you sit here with your shoes off
And curl your legs up under you; your eyes
Close for a moment, your face moves toward sleep . . .
You are very human.
                        But my mind, gone out in tenderness,
Shrinks from its object with a thoughtful sigh.
This is a waist the spirit breaks its arm on.
The gods themselves, against you, struggle in vain.
This broad low strong-boned brow; these heavy eyes;
These calves, grown muscular with certainties;
This nose, three medium-sized pink strawberries
— But I exaggerate. In a little you will leave:
I'll hear, half squeal, half shriek, your laugh of greeting —
Then, *decrescendo*, bars of that strange speech
In which each sound sets out to seek each other,
Murders its own father, marries its own mother,
And ends as one grand transcendental vowel.

(Yet for all I know, the Egyptian Helen spoke so.)
As I look, the world contracts around you:
I see Brünnhilde had brown braids and glasses
She used for studying; Salome straight brown bangs,
A calf's brown eyes, and sturdy light-brown limbs
Dusted with cinnamon, an apple-dumpling's . . .
Many a beast has gnawn a leg off and got free,
Many a dolphin curved up from Necessity —
The trap has closed about you, and you sleep.
If someone questioned you, *What doest thou here?*
You'd knit your brows like an orangoutang
(But not so sadly; not so thoughtfully)
And answer with a pure heart, guilelessly:
I'm studying. . . .
                        If only you were not!

42

Assignments,
        recipes,
              the *Official Rulebook*
Of Basketball — ah, let them go; you needn't mind.
The soul has no assignments, neither cooks
Nor referees: it wastes its time.
                    It wastes its time.
Here in this enclave there are centuries
For you to waste: the short and narrow stream
Of Life meanders into a thousand valleys
Of all that was, or might have been, or is to be.
The books, just leafed through, whisper endlessly . . .
Yet it is hard. One sees in your blurred eyes
The "uneasy half-soul" Kipling saw in dogs'.
One sees it, in the glass, in one's own eyes.
In rooms alone, in galleries, in libraries,
In tears, in searchings of the heart, in staggering joys
We memorize once more our old creation,
Humanity: with what yawns the unwilling
Flesh puts on its spirit, O my sister!

So many dreams! And not one troubles
Your sleep of life? no self stares shadowily
From these worn hexahedrons, beckoning
With false smiles, tears? . . .
                  Meanwhile Tatyana
Larina (gray eyes nickel with the moonlight
That falls through the willows onto Lensky's tomb;
Now young and shy, now old and cold and sure)
Asks, smiling: "But what is she dreaming of, fat thing?"
I answer: She's not fat. She isn't dreaming.
She purrs or laps or runs, all in her sleep;
Believes, awake, that she is beautiful;
She never dreams.
            Those sunrise-colored clouds
Around man's head — that inconceivable enchantment
From which, at sunset, we come back to life
To find our graves dug, families dead, selves dying:
Of all this, Tanya, she is innocent.
For nineteen years she's faced reality:

They look alike already.

                             They say, man wouldn't be
The best thing in this world — and isn't he? —
If he were not too good for it. But she
— She's good enough for it.

                       And yet sometimes
Her sturdy form, in its pink strapless formal,
Is as if bathed in moonlight — modulated
Into a form of joy, a Lydian mode;
This Wooden Mean's a kind, furred animal
That speaks, in the Wild of things, delighting riddles
To the soul that listens, trusting . . .

                           Poor senseless Life:
When, in the last light sleep of dawn, the messenger
Comes with his message, you will not awake.
He'll give his feathery whistle, shake you hard,
You'll look with wide eyes at the dewy yard
And dream, with calm slow factuality:
"Today's Commencement. My bachelor's degree
In Home Ec., my doctorate of philosophy
In Phys. Ed.

         [Tanya, they won't even *scan*]
Are waiting for me. . . ."

                     Oh, Tatyana,
The Angel comes: better to squawk like a chicken
Than to say with truth, "But I'm a *good* girl,"
And Meet his Challenge with a last firm strange
Uncomprehending smile; and — then, then! — see
The blind date that has stood you up: your life.
(For all this, if it isn't, perhaps, life,
Has yet, at least, a language of its own
Different from the books'; worse than the books'.)
And yet, the ways we miss our lives are life.
Yet . . . yet . . .

             to have one's life add up to *yet!*

You sigh a shuddering sigh. Tatyana murmurs,
"Don't cry, little peasant"; leaves us with a swift
"Good-bye, good-bye . . . Ah, don't think ill of me . . ."
Your eyes open: you sit here thoughtlessly.

I love you — and yet — and yet — I love you.

Don't cry, little peasant. Sit and dream.
One comes, a finger's width beneath your skin,
To the braided maidens singing as they spin;
There sound the shepherd's pipe, the watchman's rattle
Across the short dark distance of the years.
I am a thought of yours: and yet, you do not think . . .
The firelight of a long, blind, dreaming story
Lingers upon your lips; and I have seen
Firm, fixed forever in your closing eyes,
The Corn King beckoning to his Spring Queen.

Seele im Raum

It sat between my husband and my children.
A place was set for it — a plate of greens.
It had been there: I had seen it
But not somehow — but this was like a dream —
Not seen it so that I knew I saw it.
It was as if I could not know I saw it
Because I had never once in all my life
Not seen it. It was an eland.
An eland! *That* is why the children
Would ask my husband, for a joke, at Christmas:
"Father, is it Donner?" He would say, "No, Blitzen."
It had been there always. Now we put silver
At its place at meals, fed it the same food
We ourselves ate, and said nothing. Many times
When it breathed heavily (when it had tried
A long useless time to speak) and reached to me
So that I touched it — of a different size
And order of being, like the live hard side
Of a horse's neck when you pat the horse —
And looked with its great melting tearless eyes
Fringed with a few coarse wire-like lashes
Into my eyes, and whispered to me

So that my eyes turned backward in their sockets
And they said nothing —
                    many times
I have known, when they said nothing,
That it did not exist. If they had heard
They *could* not have been silent. And yet they heard;
Heard many times what I have spoken
When it could no longer speak, but only breathe —
When I could no longer speak, but only breathe.

And, after some years, the others came
And took it from me — it was ill, they told me —
And cured it, they wrote me: my whole city
Sent me cards like lilac-branches, mourning
As I had mourned —
                    and I was standing
By a grave in flowers, by dyed rolls of turf,
And a canvas marquee the last brown of earth.

It is over.
It is over so long that I begin to think
That it did not exist, that I have never —
And my son says, one morning, from the paper:
"An eland. Look, an eland!"
                        — It was so.

Today, in a German dictionary, I saw *elend*
And the heart in my breast turned over, it was —

It was a word one translates *wretched*.

It is as if someone remembered saying:
"This is an antimacassar that I grew from seed,"
And this were true.
                And, truly,
One could not wish for anything more strange —
For anything more. And yet it wasn't *interesting* . . .
       — It was worse than impossible, it was a joke.

And yet when it was, I *was* —
Even to think that I once thought
That I could see it is to feel the sweat
Like needles at my hair-roots, I am blind

— It was not even a joke, not even a joke.

Yet how can I believe it? Or believe that I
Owned it, a husband, children? Is my voice the voice
Of that skin of being — of what owns, is owned
In honor or dishonor, that is borne and bears —
Or of that raw thing, the being inside it
That has neither a wife, a husband, nor a child
But goes at last as naked from this world
As it was born into it —

And the eland comes and grazes on its grave.

          This is senseless?
Shall I make sense or shall I tell the truth?
Choose either — I cannot do both.

I tell myself that. And yet it is not so,
And what I say afterwards will not be so:
To be at all is to be wrong.
          Being is being old
And saying, almost comfortably, across a table
From —
      from what I don't know —
              in a voice
Rich with a kind of longing satisfaction:
"To own an eland! That's what I call life!"

The Black Swan

When the swans turned my sister into a swan
   I would go to the lake, at night, from milking:
The sun would look out through the reeds like a swan,

A swan's red beak; and the beak would open
And inside there was darkness, the stars and the moon.

Out on the lake a girl would laugh.
   "Sister, here is your porridge, sister,"
I would call; and the reeds would whisper,
   "Go to sleep, go to sleep, little swan."
My legs were all hard and webbed, and the silky

Hairs of my wings sank away like stars
   In the ripples that ran in and out of the reeds:
I heard through the lap and hiss of water
   Someone's "Sister . . . sister," far away on the shore,
And then as I opened my beak to answer

I heard my harsh laugh go out to the shore
   And saw — saw at last, swimming up from the green
Low mounds of the lake, the white stone swans:
   The white, named swans . . . "It is all a dream,"
I whispered, and reached from the down of the pallet

To the lap and hiss of the floor.
   And "Sleep, little sister," the swans all sang
From the moon and stars and frogs of the floor.
   But the swan my sister called, "Sleep at last, little sister,"
And stroked all night, with a black wing, my wings.

The Orient Express

One looks from the train
Almost as one looked as a child. In the sunlight
What I see still seems to me plain,
I am safe; but at evening
As the lands darken, a questioning
Precariousness comes over everything.

Once after a day of rain
I lay longing to be cold; and after a while

I was cold again, and hunched shivering
Under the quilt's many colors, gray
With the dull ending of the winter day.
Outside me there were a few shapes
Of chairs and tables, things from a primer;
Outside the window
There were the chairs and tables of the world. . . .
I saw that the world
That had seemed to me the plain
Gray mask of all that was strange
Behind it — of all that *was* — was all.

But it is beyond belief.
One thinks, "Behind everything
An unforced joy, an unwilling
Sadness (a willing sadness, a forced joy)
Moves changelessly"; one looks from the train
And there is something, the same thing
Behind everything: all these little villages,
A passing woman, a field of grain,
The man who says good-bye to his wife —
A path through a wood full of lives, and the train
Passing, after all unchangeable
And not now ever to stop, like a heart —

It is like any other work of art.
It is and never can be changed.
Behind everything there is always
The unknown unwanted life.

The Märchen

(Grimm's Tales)

Listening, listening; it is never still.
This is the forest: long ago the lives
Edged armed into its tides (the axes were its stone
Lashed with the skins of dwellers to its boughs);

We felled our islands there, at last, with iron.
The sunlight fell to them, according to our wish,
And we believed, till nightfall, in that wish;
And we believed, till nightfall, in our lives.

The bird is silent; but its cold breast stirs
Raggedly, and the gloom the moonlight bars
Is blurred with the fluff its long death strewed
In the crumpled fern; and far off something falls.
If the firs forget their breath, if the leaf that perishes
Holds, a bud, to spring; sleeps, fallen, under snow —
It is never still. The darkness quakes with blood;
From its pulse the dark eyes of the hunter glow
Green as their forest, fading images
Of the dream in the firelight: shudder of the coals
In their short Hell, vined skeleton
Of the charcoal-burner dozing in the snow.
Hänsel, to map the hard way, cast his bones
Up clouds to Paradise; His sparrows ate
And he plunged home, past peat and measures, to his kin
Furred in the sooty darkness of the cave
Where the old gods nodded. How the devil's beard
Coiled round the dreaming Hänsel, till his limbs
Grew gnarled as a fakir's on the spindling Cross
The missions rowed from Asia: eternal corpse
Of the Scapegoat, gay with His blood's watered beads,
Red wax in the new snow (strange to His warmed stare);
The wooden mother and the choir of saints, His stars;
And God and His barons, always, iron behind.
Gorged Hänsel felt His blood burn thin as air
In a belly swollen with the airy kine;
How many ages boiled Christ's bark for soup!
Giddy with emptiness, a second wife
Scolding the great-eyed children of a ghost,
He sends them, in his tale, not out to death
(Godfather Death, the reaping messenger),
Nor to the devil cringing in the gloom,
Shifting his barred hooves with a crunch like snow —
But to a king: the blind untroubled Might
Renting a destiny to men on terms —

Come, mend me and wed half of me, my son!
Behind, the headsman fondles his gnawn block.
So men have won a kingdom — there are kings;
Are giants, warlocks, the unburied dead
Invulnerable to any power — the Necessity
Men spring from, die under: the unbroken wood.

Noon, the gold sun of hens and aldermen
Inked black as India, on the green ground,
Our patterns, homely, mercenary, magnified —
Bewitching as the water of Friar Bacon's glass.
(*Our* farmer fooled the devil with a turnip,
Our tailor won a queen with seven flies;
Mouser and mousie and a tub of fat
Kept house together — and a louse, a louse
Brewed small beer in an eggshell with a flea.)
But at evening the poor light, far-off, fantastic —
Sun of misers and of mermen, the last foolish gold
Of soldiers wandering through the country with a crutch —
Scattered its leagues of shadows on the plots
Where life, horned sooty lantern patched with eyes,
Hides more than it illumines, dreams the hordes
Of imps and angels, all of its own hue.
In the great world everything is just the same
Or just the opposite, we found (we never went).
The tinkers, peddlers brought their pinch of salt:
In our mouths the mill of the unresting sea
Ground till their very sores were thirsty.
Quaking below like quicksand, there is fire —
The dowser's twig dips not to water but to Hell;
And the Father, uncomfortable overseer,
Shakes from the rain-clouds Heaven's branding bolt.
Beyond, the Alps ring, avalanche on avalanche,
And the lost palmers freeze to bliss, a smile
Baring their poor teeth, blackened as the skulls
Of sanctuaries — splinters of the Cross, the Ark, the Tree
Jut from a saint's set jawbone, to put out
With one bought vision many a purging fire.
As the circles spread, the stone hopes like a child.
The weak look to the helpless for their aid —

The beasts who, ruled by their god, Death,
Bury the son with their enchanted thanks
For the act outside their possibility:
The victim spared, the labors sweated through, for love
Neither for mate nor litter, but for — anything.
When had it mattered whom we helped? It always paid.
When the dead man's heart broke they found written there
(He could not write): *The wish has made it so.*
Or so he wished. The platter appliquéd
With meals for parents, scraps for children, gristle
For Towser, a poor dog; the walnut jetting wine;
The broom that, fretting for a master, swept a world;
The spear that, weeping for a master, killed a child;
And gold to bury, from the deepest mines —
These neither to wisdom nor to virtue, but to Grace,
The son remembered in the will of God —
These were wishes. The glass in which I saw
Somewhere else, someone else: the field upon which sprawled
Dead, and the ruler of the dead, my twin —
Were wishes? Hänsel, by the eternal sea,
Said to the flounder for his first wish, *Let me wish
And let my wish be granted;* it was granted.
Granted, granted. . . . Poor Hänsel, once too powerless
To shelter your own children from the cold
Or quiet their bellies with the thinnest gruel,
It was not power that you lacked, but wishes.
Had you not learned — have we not learned, from tales
Neither of beasts nor kingdoms nor their Lord,
But of our own hearts, the realm of death —
Neither to rule nor die? to change, to change!

The Sleeping Beauty:

Variation of the Prince

After the thorns I came to the first page.
He lay there gray in his fur of dust:
As I bent to open an eye, I sneezed.

But the ball looked by me, blue
As the sky it stared into . . .
And the sentry's cuirass is red with rust.

Children play inside: the dirty hand
Of the little mother, an inch from the child
That has worn out, burst, and blown away,
Uncurling to it — does not uncurl.
The bloom on the nap of their world
Is set with thousands of dawns of dew.

But at last, at the center of all the webs
Of the realm established in your blood,
I find you; and — look! — the drop of blood
Is there still, under the dust of your finger:
I force it, slowly, down from your finger
And it falls and rolls away, as it should.

And I bend to touch (just under the dust
That was roses once) the steady lips
Parted between a breath and a breath
In love, for the kiss of the hunter, Death.
Then I stretch myself beside you, lay
Between us, there in the dust, His sword.

When the world ends — it will never end —
The dust at last will fall from your eyes
In judgment, and I shall whisper:
"For hundreds of thousands of years I have slept
Beside you, here in the last long world
That you had found; that I have kept."

When they come for us — no one will ever come —
I shall stir from my long light sleep,
I shall whisper, "Wait, wait! . . . She is asleep."
I shall whisper, gazing, up to the gaze of the hunter,
Death, and close with the tips of the dust of my hand
The lids of the steady —
               Look, He is fast asleep!

A Utopian Journey

"In a minute the doctor will find out what is wrong
And cure me," the patients think as they wait.
They are as patient as their name, and look childishly
And religiously at the circumstances of their hope,
The nurse, the diplomas, the old magazines.

And their childishness is natural; here in this office
The natural perplexities of their existence,
The demands they can neither satisfy nor understand,
Are reduced to the child's, "I hurt," the bare
Intention of any beast: to go on being.

And they go in to the doctor at last
And go out to the hospitals, sanatoria, or graves
He prescribes — look into the masked unnoticing
Faces of their saviors, smell the sick
Sweet smell of nothing, leave, send back their checks;

But what was it? What am I?
The convalescent stitched up with black thread,
His pains withering, his uneasy head
Quieted with enemas and orange-juice, the inconclusive
Evasive silence — remembers, silently, a sweet,

Evasive, and conclusive speech . . . Goes back to his living,
Day and Night ask, *Child, have you learned anything?*
He answers, *Nothing* — walled in these live ends,
In these blind blossoming alleys of the maze
That lead, through a thousand leaves, to the beginning

Or that lead at last into — dark, leaved — a door.

90 North

At home, in my flannel gown, like a bear to its floe,
I clambered to bed; up the globe's impossible sides
I sailed all night — till at last, with my black beard,
My furs and my dogs, I stood at the northern pole.

There in the childish night my companions lay frozen,
The stiff furs knocked at my starveling throat,
And I gave my great sigh: the flakes came huddling,
Were they really my end? In the darkness I turned to my rest.

— Here, the flag snaps in the glare and silence
Of the unbroken ice. I stand here,
The dogs bark, my beard is black, and I stare
At the North Pole . . .
                              And now what? Why, go back.

Turn as I please, my step is to the south.
The world — my world spins on this final point
Of cold and wretchedness: all lines, all winds
End in this whirlpool I at last discover.

And it is meaningless. In the child's bed
After the night's voyage, in that warm world
Where people work and suffer for the end
That crowns the pain — in that Cloud-Cuckoo-Land

I reached my North and it had meaning.
Here at the actual pole of my existence,
Where all that I have done is meaningless,
Where I die or live by accident alone —

Where, living or dying, I am still alone;
Here where North, the night, the berg of death
Crowd to me out of the ignorant darkness,
I see at last that all the knowledge

I wrung from the darkness — that the darkness flung me —
Is worthless as ignorance: nothing comes from nothing,
The darkness from the darkness. Pain comes from the darkness
And we call it wisdom. It is pain.

Loss

Bird of the spray, the tree of bones:
The tendrils shower you with dew, the smells
Of petals patter to the holes of bone —
The yellow nostrils feathered with a bar
That stripes, like blood, your ragged wings;
But the harsh, stopped sounds, the iron of your life,
Rust in the rains of autumn; and the drifts
Entomb, at last, the small nest where a skull
Flimsier than an egg, a drumstick like a straw
Lie like the crushed works of a watch: your child. . . .
When the roofs rise to you, and last year's limb
Holds a cone to your bill, and you hang hammering,
Does the down pulse still, an aching ball,
In your sleek, beaked, uncertain skull?

The Death of the Ball Turret Gunner

From my mother's sleep I fell into the State,
And I hunched in its belly till my wet fur froze.
Six miles from earth, loosed from its dream of life,
I woke to black flak and the nightmare fighters.
When I died they washed me out of the turret with a hose.

Losses

It was not dying: everybody died.
It was not dying: we had died before
In the routine crashes — and our fields

Called up the papers, wrote home to our folks,
And the rates rose, all because of us.
We died on the wrong page of the almanac,
Scattered on mountains fifty miles away;
Diving on haystacks, fighting with a friend,
We blazed up on the lines we never saw.
We died like aunts or pets or foreigners.
(When we left high school nothing else had died
For us to figure we had died like.)

In our new planes, with our new crews, we bombed
The ranges by the desert or the shore,
Fired at towed targets, waited for our scores —
And turned into replacements and woke up
One morning, over England, operational.
It wasn't different: but if we died
It was not an accident but a mistake
(But an easy one for anyone to make).
We read our mail and counted up our missions —
In bombers named for girls, we burned
The cities we had learned about in school —
Till our lives wore out; our bodies lay among
The people we had killed and never seen.
When we lasted long enough they gave us medals;
When we died they said, "Our casualties were low."

They said, "Here are the maps"; we burned the cities.

It was not dying — no, not ever dying;
But the night I died I dreamed that I was dead,
And the cities said to me: "Why are you dying?
We are satisfied, if you are; but why did I die?"

A Lullaby

For wars his life and half a world away
The soldier sells his family and days.

He learns to fight for freedom and the State;
He sleeps with seven men within six feet.

He picks up matches and he cleans out plates;
Is lied to like a child, cursed like a beast.
They crop his head, his dog tags ring like sheep
As his stiff limbs shift wearily to sleep.

Recalled in dreams or letters, else forgot,
His life is smothered like a grave, with dirt;
And his dull torment mottles like a fly's
The lying amber of the histories.

2nd Air Force

Far off, above the plain the summer dries,
The great loops of the hangars sway like hills.
Buses and weariness and loss, the nodding soldiers
Are wire, the bare frame building, and a pass
To what was hers; her head hides his square patch
And she thinks heavily: My son is grown.
She sees a world: sand roads, tar-paper barracks,
The bubbling asphalt of the runways, sage,
The dunes rising to the interminable ranges,
The dim flights moving over clouds like clouds.
The armorers in their patched faded green,
Sweat-stiffened, banded with brass cartridges,
Walk to the line; their Fortresses, all tail,
Stand wrong and flimsy on their skinny legs,
And the crews climb to them clumsily as bears.
The head withdraws into its hatch (a boy's),
The engines rise to their blind laboring roar,
And the green, made beasts run home to air.
Now in each aspect death is pure.
(At twilight they wink over men like stars

And hour by hour, through the night, some see
The great lights floating in — from Mars, from Mars.)
How emptily the watchers see them gone.

They go, there is silence; the woman and her son
Stand in the forest of the shadows, and the light
Washes them like water. In the long-sunken city
Of evening, the sunlight stills like sleep
The faint wonder of the drowned; in the evening,
In the last dreaming light, so fresh, so old,
The soldiers pass like beasts, unquestioning,
And the watcher for an instant understands
What there is then no need to understand;
But she wakes from her knowledge, and her stare,
A shadow now, moves emptily among
The shadows learning in their shadowy fields
The empty missions.
                    Remembering,
She hears the bomber calling, *Little Friend!*
To the fighter hanging in the hostile sky,
And sees the ragged flame eat, rib by rib,
Along the metal of the wing into her heart:
The lives stream out, blossom, and float steadily
To the flames of the earth, the flames
That burn like stars above the lands of men.

She saves from the twilight that takes everything
A squadron shipping, in its last parade —
Its dogs run by it, barking at the band —
A gunner walking to his barracks, half-asleep,
Starting at something, stumbling (above, invisible,
The crews in the steady winter of the sky
Tremble in their wired fur); and feels for them
The love of life for life. The hopeful cells
Heavy with someone else's death, cold carriers
Of someone else's victory, grope past their lives
Into her own bewilderment: The years meant *this?*

But for them the bombers answer everything.

A Ward in the States

The ward is barred with moonlight,
    The owl hoots from the snowy park.
The wind of the rimed, bare branches
    Slips coldly into the dark

Warmed ward where the muttering soldiers
    Toss, dreaming that they still sigh
For home, for home; that the islands
    Are stretched interminably

Past their lives — past their one wish, murmured
    In the endless, breathless calm
By the grumbling surf, by the branches
    That creak from the splintered palm.

In bed at home, in the moonlight,
    Ah, one lies warm
With fever, the old sweat darkens
    Under the upflung arm

The tangled head; and the parted
    Lips chatter their old sigh,
A breath of mist in the moonlight
    That beams from the wintry sky.

The Metamorphoses

Where I spat in the harbor the oranges were bobbing
All salted and sodden, with eyes in their rinds;
The sky was all black where the coffee was burning,
And the rust of the freighters had reddened the tide.

But soon all the chimneys were burning with contracts,
The tankers rode low in the oil-black bay,
The wharves were a maze of the crated bombers,
And they gave me a job and I worked all day.

And the orders are filled; but I float in the harbor,
All tarry and swollen, with gills in my sides,
The sky is all black where the carrier's burning,
And the blood of the transports is red on the tide.

ROBERT LOWELL

Colloquy in Black Rock

Here the jack-hammer jabs into the ocean;
My heart, you race and stagger and demand
More blood-gangs for your nigger-brass percussions,
Till I, the stunned machine of your devotion,
Clanging upon this cymbal of a hand,
Am rattled screw and footloose. All discussions

End in the mud-flat detritus of death.
My heart, beat faster, faster. In Black Mud
Hungarian workmen give their blood
For the martyre Stephen, who was stoned to death.

Black Mud, a name to conjure with: O mud
For watermelons gutted to the crust,
Mud for the mole-tide harbor, mud for mouse,
Mud for the armored Diesel fishing tubs that thud
A year and a day to wind and tide; the dust
Is on this skipping heart that shakes my house,

House of our Savior who was hanged till death.
My heart, beat faster, faster. In Black Mud
Stephen the martyre was broken down to blood:
Our ransom is the rubble of his death.

Christ walks on the black water. In Black Mud
Darts the kingfisher. On Corpus Christi, heart,
Over the drum-beat of St. Stephen's choir
I hear him, *Stupor Mundi,* and the mud
Flies from his hunching wings and beak — my heart,
The blue kingfisher dives on you in fire.

The Quaker Graveyard in Nantucket

(For Warren Winslow, Dead at Sea)

Let man have dominion over the fishes of the sea and the
fowls of the air and the beasts and the whole earth, and
every creeping creature that moveth upon the earth.

I

A brackish reach of shoal off Madaket, —
The sea was still breaking violently and night
Had steamed into our North Atlantic Fleet,
When the drowned sailor clutched the drag-net. Light
Flashed from his matted head and marble feet,
He grappled at the net
With the coiled, hurdling muscles of his thighs:
The corpse was bloodless, a botch of reds and whites,
Its open, staring eyes
Were lustreless dead-lights
Or cabin-windows on a stranded hulk
Heavy with sand. We weight the body, close
Its eyes and heave it seaward whence it came,
Where the heel-headed dogfish barks its nose
On Ahab's void and forehead; and the name
Is blocked in yellow chalk.
Sailors, who pitch this portent at the sea
Where dreadnaughts shall confess
Its hell-bent deity,
When you are powerless
To sand-bag this Atlantic bulwark, faced
By the earth-shaker, green, unwearied, chaste
In his steel scales: ask for no Orphean lute
To pluck life back. The guns of the steeled fleet
Recoil and then repeat
The hoarse salute.

II

Whenever winds are moving and their breath
Heaves at the roped-in bulwarks of this pier,

The terns and sea-gulls tremble at your death
In these home waters. Sailor, can you hear
The Pequod's sea wings, beating landward, fall
Headlong and break on our Atlantic wall
Off 'Sconset, where the yawing S-boats splash
The bellbuoy, with ballooning spinnakers,
As the entangled, screeching mainsheet clears
The blocks: off Madaket, where lubbers lash
The heavy surf and throw their long lead squids
For blue-fish? Sea-gulls blink their heavy lids
Seaward. The winds' wings beat upon the stones,
Cousin, and scream for you and the caws rush
At the sea's throat and wring it in the slush
Of this old Quaker graveyard where the bones
Cry out in the long night for the hurt beast
Bobbing by Ahab's whaleboats in the East.

III

All you recovered from Poseidon died
With you, my cousin, and the harrowed brine
Is fruitless on the blue beard of the god,
Stretching beyond us to the castles in Spain,
Nantucket's westward haven. To Cape Cod
Guns, cradled on the tide,
Blast the eelgrass about a waterclock
Of bilge and backwash, roil the salt and sand
Lashing earth's scaffold, rock
Our warships in the hand
Of the great God, where time's contrition blues
Whatever it was these Quaker sailors lost
In the mad scramble of their lives. They died
When time was open-eyed,
Wooden and childish; only bones abide
There, in the nowhere, where their boats were tossed
Sky-high, where mariners had fabled news
Of IS, the whited monster. What it cost
Them is their secret. In the sperm-whale's slick
I see the Quakers drown and hear their cry:
"If God himself had not been on our side,

If God himself had not been on our side,
When the Atlantic rose against us, why,
Then it had swallowed us up quick."

IV

This is the end of the whaleroad and the whale
Who spewed Nantucket bones on the thrashed swell
And stirred the troubled waters to whirlpools
To send the Pequod packing off to hell:
This is the end of them, three-quarters fools,
Snatching at straws to sail
Seaward and seaward on the turntail whale,
Spouting out blood and water as it rolls,
Sick as a dog to these Atlantic shoals:
Clamavimus, O depths. Let the sea-gulls wail

For water, for the deep where the high tide
Mutters to its hurt self, mutters and ebbs.
Waves wallow in their wash, go out and out,
Leave only the death-rattle of the crabs,
The beach increasing, its enormous snout
Sucking the ocean's side.
This is the end of running on the waves;
We are poured out like water. Who will dance
The mast-lashed master of Leviathans
Up from this field of Quakers in their unstoned graves?

V

When the whale's viscera go and the roll
Of its corruption overruns this world
Beyond tree-swept Nantucket and Wood's Hole
And Martha's Vineyard, Sailor, will your sword
Whistle and fall and sink into the fat?
In the great ash-pit of Jehoshaphat
The bones cry for the blood of the white whale,
The fat flukes arch and whack about its ears,
The death-lance churns into the sanctuary, tears
The gun-blue swingle, heaving like a flail,

And hacks the coiling life out: it works and drags
And rips the sperm-whale's midriff into rags,
Gobbets of blubber spill to wind and weather,
Sailor, and gulls go round the stoven timbers
Where the morning stars sing out together
And thunder shakes the white surf and dismembers
The red flag hammered in the mast-head. Hide,
Our steel, Jonas Messias, in Thy side.

VI

OUR LADY OF WALSINGHAM

There once the penitents took off their shoes
And then walked barefoot the remaining mile;
And the small trees, a stream and hedgerows file
Slowly along the munching English lane,
Like cows to the old shrine, until you lose
Track of your dragging pain.
The stream flows down under the druid tree,
Shiloah's whirlpools gurgle and make glad
The castle of God. Sailor, you were glad
And whistled Sion by that stream. But see:

Our Lady, too small for her canopy,
Sits near the altar. There's no comeliness
At all or charm in that expressionless
Face with its heavy eyelids. As before,
This face, for centuries a memory,
Non est species, neque decor,
Expressionless, expresses God: it goes
Past castled Sion. She knows what God knows,
Not Calvary's Cross nor crib at Bethlehem
Now, and the world shall come to Walsingham.

VII

The empty winds are creaking and the oak
Splatters and splatters on the cenotaph,
The boughs are trembling and a gaff

Bobs on the untimely stroke
Of the greased wash exploding on a shoal-bell
In the old mouth of the Atlantic. It's well;
Atlantic, you are fouled with the blue sailors,
Sea-monsters, upward angel, downward fish:
Unmarried and corroding, spare of flesh
Mart once of supercilious, wing'd clippers,
Atlantic, where your bell-trap guts its spoil
You could cut the brackish winds with a knife
Here in Nantucket, and cast up the time
When the Lord God formed man from the sea's slime
And breathed into his face the breath of life,
And blue-lung'd combers lumbered to the kill.
The Lord survives the rainbow of His will.

Children of Light

Our fathers wrung their bread from stocks and stones
And fenced their gardens with the Redman's bones;
Embarking from the Nether Land of Holland,
Pilgrims unhouseled by Geneva's night,
They planted here the Serpent's seeds of light;
And here the pivoting searchlights probe to shock
The riotous glass houses built on rock,
And candles gutter by an empty altar,
And light is where the landless blood of Cain
Is burning, burning the unburied grain.

The Drunken Fisherman

Wallowing in this bloody sty,
I cast for fish that pleased my eye
(Truly Jehovah's bow suspends
No pots of gold to weight its ends);

Only the blood-mouthed rainbow trout
Rose to my bait. They flopped about
My canvas creel until the moth
Corrupted its unstable cloth.

A calendar to tell the day;
A handkerchief to wave away
The gnats; a couch unstuffed with storm
Pouching a bottle in one arm;
A whiskey bottle full of worms;
And bedroom slacks: are these fit terms
To mete the worm whose molten rage
Boils in the belly of old age?

Once fishing was a rabbit's foot —
O wind blow cold, O wind blow hot,
Let suns stay in or suns step out:
Life danced a jig on the sperm-whale's spout —
The fisher's fluent and obscene
Catches kept his conscience clean.
Children, the raging memory drools
Over the glory of past pools.

Now the hot river, ebbing, hauls
Its bloody waters into holes;
A grain of sand inside my shoe
Mimics the moon that might undo
Man and Creation too; remorse
Stinking, has puddled up its source;
Here tantrums thrash to a whale's rage.
This is the pot-hole of old age.

Is there no way to cast my hook
Out of this dynamited brook?
The Fisher's sons must cast about
When shallow waters peter out.
I will catch Christ with a greased worm,
And when the Prince of Darkness stalks
My bloodstream to its Stygian term . . .
On water the Man-Fisher walks.

Between the Porch and the Altar

MOTHER AND SON

Meeting his mother makes him lose ten years,
Or is it twenty? Time, no doubt, has ears
That listen to the swallowed serpent, wound
Into its bowels, but he thinks no sound
Is possible before her, he thinks the past
Is settled. It is honest to hold fast
Merely to what one sees with one's own eyes
When the red velvet curves and haunches rise
To blot him from the pretty driftwood fire's
Façade of welcome. Then the son retires
Into the sack and selfhood of the boy
Who clawed through fallen houses of his Troy,
Homely and human only when the flames
Crackle in recollection. Nothing shames
Him more than this uncoiling, counterfeit
Body presented as an idol. It
Is something in a circus, big as life,
The painted dragon, a mother and a wife
With flat glass eyes pushed at him on a stick;
The human mover crawls to make them click.
The forehead of her father's portrait peels
With rosy dryness, and the schoolboy kneels
To ask the benediction of the hand,
Lifted as though to motion him to stand,
Dangling its watch-chain on the Holy Book —
A little golden snake that mouths a hook.

II

ADAM AND EVE

The Farmer sizzles on his shaft all day.
He is content and centuries away
From white-hot Concord, and he stands on guard.

Or is he melting down like sculptured lard?
His hand is crisp and steady on the plough.
I quarrelled with you, but am happy now
To while away my life for your unrest
Of terror. Never to have lived is best;
Man tasted Eve with death. I taste my wife
And children while I hold your hands. I knife
Their names into this elm. What is exempt?
I eye the statue with an awed contempt
And see the puritanical façade
Of the white church that Irish exiles made
For Patrick — that Colonial from Rome
Had magicked the charmed serpents from their home,
As though he were the Piper. Will his breath
Scorch the red dragon of my nerves to death?
By sundown we are on a shore. You walk
A little way before me and I talk,
Half to myself and half aloud. They lied,
My cold-eyed seedy fathers when they died,
Or rather threw their lives away, to fix
Sterile, forbidding nameplates on the bricks
Above a kettle. Jesus rest their souls!
You cry for help. Your market-basket rolls
With all its baking apples in the lake.
You watch the whorish slither of a snake
That chokes a duckling. When we try to kiss,
Our eyes are slits and cringing, and we hiss;
Scales glitter on our bodies as we fall.
The Farmer melts upon his pedestal.

III

KATHERINE'S DREAM

It must have been a Friday. I could hear
The top-floor typist's thunder and the beer
That you had brought in cases hurt my head;
I'd sent the pillows flying from my bed,
I hugged my knees together and I gasped.
The dangling telephone receiver rasped

Like someone in a dream who cannot stop
For breath or logic till his victim drop
To darkness and the sheets. I must have slept,
But still could hear my father who had kept
Your guilty presents but cut off my hair.
He whispers that he really doesn't care
If I am your kept woman all my life,
Or ruin your two children and your wife;
But my dishonor makes him drink. Of course
I'll tell the court the truth for his divorce.
I walk through snow into St. Patrick's yard.
Black nuns with glasses smile and stand on guard
Before a bulkhead in a bank of snow,
Whose charred doors open, as good people go
Inside by twos to the confessor. One
Must have a friend to enter there, but none
Is friendless in this crowd, and the nuns smile.
I stand aside and marvel; for a while
The winter sun is pleasant and it warms
My heart with love for others, but the swarms
Of penitents have dwindled. I begin
To cry and ask God's pardon of our sin.
Where are you? You were with me and are gone.
All the forgiven couples hurry on
To dinner and their nights, and none will stop.
I run about in circles till I drop
Against a padlocked bulkhead in a yard
Where faces redden and the snow is hard.

IV

AT THE ALTAR

I sit at a gold table with my girl
Whose eyelids burn with brandy. What a whirl
Of Easter eggs is colored by the lights,
As the Norwegian dancer's crystalled tights
Flash with her naked leg's high-booted skate,
Like Northern Lights upon my watching plate.
The twinkling steel above me is a star;

71

I am a fallen Christmas tree. Our car
Races through seven red-lights — then the road
Is unpatrolled and empty, and a load
Of ply-wood with a tail-light makes us slow.
I turn and whisper in her ear. You know
I want to leave my mother and my wife,
You wouldn't have me tied to them for life . . .
Time runs, the windshield runs with stars. The past
Is cities from a train, until at last
Its escalating and black-windowed blocks
Recoil against a Gothic church. The clocks
Are tolling. I am dying. The shocked stones
Are falling like a ton of bricks and bones
That snap and splinter and descend in glass
Before a priest who mumbles through his Mass
And sprinkles holy water; and the Day
Breaks with its lightning on the man of clay,
Dies amara valde. Here the Lord
Is Lucifer in harness: hand on sword,
He watches me for Mother, and will turn
The bier and baby-carriage where I burn.

After the Surprising Conversions

September twenty-second, Sir: today
I answer. In the latter part of May,
Hard on our Lord's Ascension, it began
To be more sensible. A gentleman
Of more than common understanding, strict
In morals, pious in behavior, kicked
Against our goad. A man of some renown,
An useful, honored person in the town,
He came of melancholy parents; prone
To secret spells, for years they kept alone —
His uncle, I believe, was killed of it:
Good people, but of too much or little wit.
I preached one Sabbath on a text from Kings;
He showed concernment for his soul. Some things

In his experience were hopeful. He
Would sit and watch the wind knocking a tree
And praise this countryside our Lord has made.
Once when a poor man's heifer died, he laid
A shilling on the doorsill; though a thirst
For loving shook him like a snake, he durst
Not entertain much hope of his estate
In heaven. Once we saw him sitting late
Behind his attic window by a light
That guttered on his Bible; through that night
He meditated terror, and he seemed
Beyond advice or reason, for he dreamed
That he was called to trumpet Judgment Day
To Concord. In the latter part of May
He cut his throat. And though the coroner
Judged him delirious, soon a noisome stir
Palsied our village. At Jehovah's nod
Satan seemed more let loose amongst us: God
Abandoned us to Satan, and he pressed
Us hard, until we thought we could not rest
Till we had done with life. Content was gone.
All the good work was quashed. We were undone.
The breath of God had carried out a planned
And sensible withdrawal from this land;
The multitude, once unconcerned with doubt,
Once neither callous, curious nor devout,
Jumped at broad noon, as though some peddler groaned
At it in its familiar twang: "My friend,
Cut your own throat. Cut your own throat. Now! Now!"
September twenty-second, Sir, the bough
Cracks with the unpicked apples, and at dawn
The small-mouth bass breaks water, gorged with spawn.

Where the Rainbow Ends

I saw the sky descending, black and white,
Not blue, on Boston where the winters wore
The skulls to jack-o'-lanterns on the slates,

And Hunger's skin-and-bone retrievers tore
The chickadee and shrike. The thorn tree waits
Its victim and tonight
The worms will eat the deadwood to the foot
Of Ararat: the scythers, Time and Death,
Helmed locusts, move upon the tree of breath;
The wild ingrafted olive and the root

Are withered, and a winter drifts to where
The pepperpot, ironic rainbow, spans
Charles River and its scales of scorched-earth miles,
I saw my city in the Scales, the pans
Of judgment rising and descending. Piles
Of dead leaves char the air —
And I am a red arrow on this graph
Of Revelations. Every dove is sold
The Chapel's sharp-shinned eagle shifts its hold
On Serpent-Time, the rainbow's epitaph.

In Boston serpents whistle at the cold.
The victim climbs the altar steps and sings:
"Hosannah to the lion, lamb, and beast
Who fans the furnace-face of IS with wings:
I breathe the ether of my marriage feast."
At the high altar, gold
And a fair cloth. I kneel and the wings beat
My cheek. What can the dove of Jesus give
You now but wisdom, exile? Stand and live,
The dove has brought an olive branch to eat.

Noli Me Tangere

We park and stare. A full sky of the stars
Wheels from the pumpkin setting of the moon
And sparks the windows of the yellow farm
Where the red-flanneled madmen look through bars
At windmills thrashing snowflakes by an arm

Of the Atlantic. Soon
The undertaker who collects antiques
Will let his motor idle at the door
And set his pine-box on the parlor floor.
Our homicidal sheriff howled for weeks;

We kiss. The State had reasons: on the whole,
It acted out of kindness when it locked
Its servant in this place and had him watched
Until an ordered darkness left his soul
A *tabula rasa;* when the Angel knocked
The sheriff laid his notched
Revolver on the table for the guest.
Night draws us closer in its bearskin wrap
And our loved sightless smother feels the tap
Of the blind stars descending to the west
To lay the Devil in the pit our hands
Are draining like a windmill. Who'll atone
For the unsearchable quicksilver heart
Where spiders stare their eyes out at their own
Spitting and knotted likeness? We must start:
Our aunt, his mother, stands
Singing *O Rock of Ages,* as the light
Wanderers show a man with a white cane
Who comes to take the coffin in his wain,
The thirsty Dipper on the arc of night.

Death from Cancer

This Easter, Arthur Winslow, less than dead,
Your people set you up in Phillips' House
To settle off your wrestling with the crab —
The claws drop flesh upon your yachting blouse
Until longshoreman Charon come and stab
Through your adjusted bed
And crush the crab. On Boston Basin, shells
Hit water by the Union Boat Club wharf:

You ponder why the coxes' squeakings dwarf
The *resurrexit dominus* of all the bells.

Grandfather Winslow, look, the swanboats coast
That island in the Public Gardens, where
The bread-stuffed ducks are brooding, where with tub
And strainer the mid-Sunday Irish scare
The sun-struck shallows for the dusky chub
This Easter, and the ghost
Of risen Jesus walks the waves to run
Arthur upon a trumpeting black swan
Beyond Charles River to the Acheron
Where the wide waters and their voyager are one.

Falling Asleep over the Aeneid

The sun is blue and scarlet on my page,
And *yuck-a, yuck-a, yuck-a, yuck-a,* rage
The yellowhammers mating. Yellow fire
Blankets the captives dancing on their pyre,
And the scorched lictor screams and drops his rod.
Trojans are singing to their drunken God,
Ares. Their helmets catch on fire. Their files
Clank by the body of my comrade — miles
Of filings! Now the scythe-wheeled chariot rolls
Before their lances long as vaulting poles,
And I stand up and heil the thousand men,
Who carry Pallas to the bird-priest. Then
The bird-priest groans, and as his birds foretold,
I greet the body, lip to lip. I hold
The sword that Dido used. It tries to speak,
A bird with Dido's sworded breast. Its beak
Clangs and ejaculates the Punic word
I hear the bird-priest chirping like a bird.
I groan a little. "Who am I, and why?"
It asks, a boy's face, though its arrow-eye
Is working from its socket. "Brother, try,

O Child of Aphrodite, try to die:
To die is life." His harlots hang his bed
With feathers of his long-tailed birds. His head
Is yawning like a person. The plumes blow;
The beard and eyebrows ruffle. Face of snow,
You are the flower that country girls have caught,
A wild bee-pillaged honey-suckle brought
To the returning bridegroom — the design
Has not yet left it, and the petals shine;
The earth, its mother, has, at last, no help:
It is itself. The broken-winded yelp
Of my Phoenician hounds, that fills the brush
With snapping twigs and flying, cannot flush
The ghost of Pallas. But I take his pall,
Stiff with its gold and purple, and recall
How Dido hugged it to her, while she toiled,
Laughing — her golden threads, a serpent coiled
In cypress. Now I lay it like a sheet;
It clinks and settles down upon his feet,
The careless yellow hair that seemed to burn
Beforehand. Left foot, right foot — as they turn,
More pyres are rising: armored horses, bronze,
And gagged Italians, who must file by ones
Across the bitter river, when my thumb
Tightens into their wind-pipes. The beaks drum;
Their headman's cow-horned death's-head bites its tongue,
And stiffens, as it eyes the hero slung
Inside his feathered hammock on the crossed
Staves of the eagles that we winged. Our cost
Is nothing to the lovers, whoring Mars
And Venus, father's lover. Now his car's
Plumage is ready, and my marshals fetch
His squire, Acoetes, white with age, to hitch
Aethon, the hero's charger, and its ears
Prick, and it steps and steps, and stately tears
Lather its teeth; and then the harlots bring
The hero's charms and baton — but the King,
Vain-glorious Turnus, carried off the rest.
"I was myself, but Ares thought it best
The way it happened." At the end of time,

He sets his spear, as my descendants climb
The knees of Father Time, his beard of scalps,
His scythe, the arc of steel that crowns the Alps.
The elephants of Carthage hold those snows,
Turms of Numidian horse unsling their bows,
The flaming turkey-feathered arrows swarm
Beyond the Alps. "Pallas," I raise my arm
And shout, "Brother, eternal health. Farewell
Forever." Church is over, and its bell
Frightens the yellowhammers, as I wake
And watch the whitecaps wrinkle up the lake.
Mother's great-aunt, who died when I was eight,
Stands by our parlor sabre. "Boy, it's late.
Vergil must keep the Sabbath." Eighty years!
It all comes back. My Uncle Charles appears.
Blue-capped and bird-like. Phillips Brooks and Grant
Are frowning at his coffin, and my aunt,
Hearing his colored volunteers parade
Through Concord, laughs, and tells her English maid
To clip his yellow nostril hairs, and fold
His colors on him. . . . It is I, I hold
His sword to keep from falling, for the dust
On the stuffed birds is breathless, for the bust
Of young Augustus weighs on Vergil's shelf:
It scowls into my glasses at itself.

Mother Marie Therese

Drowned in 1912

Old sisters at our Maris Stella House
Remember how the Mother's strangled grouse
And snow-shoe rabbits matched the royal glint
Of Pio Nono's vestments in the print
That used to face us, while our aching ring
Of stationary rockers saw her bring
Our cake. Often, when sunset hurt the rocks
Off Carthage, and surprised us knitting socks
For victims of the Franco-Prussian War,

Our scandal'd set her frowning at the floor;
And vespers struck like lightning through the gloom
And oaken ennui of her sitting room.
It strikes us now, but cannot re-inspire;
False, false and false, I mutter to my fire.
The good old times, ah yes! But good, that all's
Forgotten like our Province's cabals;
And Jesus, smiling earthward, finds it good;
For we were friends of Cato, not of God.
This sixtieth Christmas, I'm content to pray
For what life's shrinkage leaves from day to day;
And it's a sorrow to recall our young
Raptures for Mother, when her trophies hung,
Fresh in their blood and color, to convince
Even Probationers that Heaven's Prince,
Befriending, whispered: "Is it then so hard?
Tarry a little while, O disregard
Time's wings and armor, when it flutters down
Papal tiaras and the Bourbon crown;
For quickly, priest and prince will stand, their shields
Before each other's faces, in the fields,
Where, as I promised, virtue will compel
Michael and all his angels to repel
Satan's advances, till his forces lie
Beside the Lamb in blissful fealty."
Our Indian summer! Then, our skies could lift,
God willing; but an Indian brought the gift.
"A sword," said Father Turbot, "not a saint";
Yet He who made the Virgin without taint,
Chastised our Mother to the Rule's restraint.
Was it not fated that the sweat of Christ
Would wash the worldly serpent? Christ enticed
Her heart that fluttered, while she whipped her hounds
Into the quicksands of her manor grounds
A lordly child, her habit fleur-de-lys'd
There she dismounted, sick; with little heed,
Surrendered. Like Proserpina, who fell
Six months a year from earth to flower in hell;
She half-renounced by Candle, Book and Bell
Her flowers and fowling pieces for the Church.

She never spared the child and spoiled the birch;
And how she'd chide her novices, and pluck
Them by the ears for gabbling in Canuck,
While she was reading Rabelais from her chaise,
Or parroting the *Action Française*.
Her letter from the soi-disant French King,
And the less treasured golden wedding ring
Of her shy Bridegroom, yellow; and the regal
Damascus shot-guns, pegged upon her eagle
Emblems from Hohenzollern standards, rust.
Our world is passing; even she, whose trust
Was in its princes, fed the gluttonous gulls,
That whiten our Atlantic, when like skulls
They drift for sewage with the emerald tide.
Perpetual novenas cannot tide
Us past that drowning. After Mother died,
"An émigrée in this world and the next,"
Said Father Turbot, playing with his text.
Where is he? Surely, he is one of those,
Whom Christ and Satan spew! But no one knows
What's happened to that porpoise-bellied priest.
He lodged with us on Louis Neuvième's Feast,
And celebrated her memorial mass.
His bald spot tapestried by colored glass,
Our angels, Prussian blue and flaking red,
He squeaked and stuttered: "N-n-nothing is so d-dead
As a dead s-s-sister." Off Saint Denis' Head,
Our Mother, drowned on an excursion, sleeps.
Her billy goat, or its descendant, keeps
Watch on a headland, and I hear it bawl
Into this sixty-knot Atlantic squall,
"Mamamma's Baby," past Queen Mary's Neck,
The ledge at Carthage — almost to Quebec,
Where Monsieur de Montcalm, on Abraham's
Bosom, asleep, perceives our world that shams
His New World, lost — however it atones
For Wolfe, the Englishman, and Huron bones
And priests'. O Mother, here our snuffling crones
And cretins feared you, but I owe you flowers:
The dead, the sea's dead, has her sorrows, hours

On end to lie tossing to the east, cold,
Without bed-fellows, washed and bored and old,
Bilged by her thoughts, and worked on by the worms,
Until her fossil convent come to terms
With the Atlantic. Mother, there is room
Beyond our harbor. Past its wooden Boom
Now weak and waterlogged, that Frontenac
Once diagrammed, she welters on her back.
The bell-buoy, whom she called the Cardinal,
Dances upon her. If she hears at all,
She only hears it tolling to this shore,
Where our frost-bitten sisters know the roar
Of water, inching, always on the move
For virgins, when they wish the times were love,
And their hysterical hosannahs rouse
The loveless harems of the buck ruffed grouse,
Who drums, untroubled now, beside the sea —
As if he found our stern virginity
Contra naturam. We are ruinous;
God's Providence through time has mastered us:
Now all the bells are tongueless, now we freeze,
A later Advent, pruner of warped trees,
Whistles about our nunnery slabs, and yells,
And water oozes from us into wells;
A new year swells and stirs. Our narrow Bay
Freezes itself and us. We cannot say
Christ even sees us, when the ice floes toss
His statue, made by Hurons, on the cross,
That Father Turbot sank on Mother's mound —
A whirligig! Mother, we must give ground,
Little by little; but it does no good.
Tonight, while I am piling on more driftwood,
And stooping with the poker, you are here,
Telling your beads; and breathing in my ear,
You watch your orphan swording at her fears.
I feel you twitch my shoulder. No one hears
Us mock the sisters, as we used to, years
And years behind us, when we heard the spheres
Whirring *venite;* and we held our ears.
My mother's hollow sockets fill with tears.

JOSEPHINE MILES

Herald

Delivers papers to the doors of sleep
Tosses up news upon the shores of sleep
In the day's damp, in the street's swamp wades deep
And is himself the boy drowned, drowned with sleep.

Crosses to the corner with the lamp
Already dark, even asleep the lamp,
Treads in the wet grass, wares, leaps as in swamp
The gutters dark with darkening of the lamp.

Hears only the thud and thud against the doors
Of the news falling asleep against the doors,
The slip and drip of mist on the two shores,
Sees without light or sight the coasts of doors.

Sees at a door a light, Herald, Sir?
Wakes to the whistle and light, Herald, Sir?
To the latch lifted and the face's blur
Wakes; wakes coin, day, greeting, Herald, Sir.

Lark

Lark hit us in the face with his rising sound.
We were unstruck by wind before and raced
Train, and saw all signs with one eye only,
And were shelled against sky
And all that we went by.

Now lark said something in the field and we heard it,
And it mounted and rode upon our ears as we sped.

And we heard windshield rattle and canvas creak thereafter,
And pondered every line
Of hill and sign.

Lineman Calling

Sat on a telephone pole talking to his girl,
Member of the number seven crew,
Addressed his wit at trees he looked into.

That's another, said to his girl,
Loud, so apartment windows high as he
Took eyes and looked to see.

That's what they all say, said to his girl,
Ignoring morning as it stood below him
And was too short to know him.

Nothing, nothing suddenly said to his girl,
The world and windows listening heard instead
The noon whistles breaking over him, what they said.

Driver Saying

Lady hold your horses, sit down in your seat,
Wrap your feet around the leg of the chair,
Even in my heart I can feel your heart beat.

We move, however, on schedule of need
Of the general public, see, standing on the corner there,
Holding hats, lifting canes, cutting down our speed.

Lady calm down, we'll be stopping and starting
On your nerves and my brakes ten corners more,
There'll be plenty feet to watch climbing up and departing.

There is also a good signboard at the Filmart
To look at and keep your mind on when we pass there.
Lady, even in second I can hear your heart.

Enlightenment

I wish we could take a statistic with more grace, beloved,
I wish it would circle out in our minds to the very brim,
And we could be illumined by data one by one, as by candles,
As by the cheerful faces of cherubim.

But see we respond only to archangelic doctrine,
Look up and glow at the actual pronouncement of grace,
Swallow at once all the high powered radiance,
And let the commandments shine upon the face.

This is a tremendous lot of revelation we gather,
Beloved, and beam at it in the proper spirit.
Nevertheless I wish we had one or two facts to go by,
And a less arclighted kingdom to inherit.

For Futures

When the lights come on at five o'clock on street corners
That is Evolution by the bureau of power,
That is a fine mechanic dealing in futures:
For the sky is wide and warm upon that hour,

But like the eyes that burned once at sea bottom,
Widening in the gloom, prepared for light,
The ornamental standards, the glazed globes softly
Perceive far off how probable is night.

Government Injunction

Restraining Harlem Cosmetic Co.

They say La Jac Brite Pink Skin Bleach avails not,
They say its Orange Beauty Glow does not glow,
Nor the face grow five shades lighter nor the heart
Five shades lighter. They say no.

They deny good luck, love, power, romance, and inspiration
From La Jac Brite ointment and incense of all kinds,
And condemn in writing skin brightening and whitening
And whitening of minds.

There is upon the federal trade commission a burden of glory
So to defend the fact, so to impel
The plucking of hope from the hand, honor from the complexion,
Sprite from the spell.

Appointment in Doctor's Office

The lady put off her fur, it was so warm in the outer office,
She was pale but not because she was frightened. She was afraid.
She looked at the framed pictures, particularly one of mountains
                                                    with sunlight,
Then she got out her glasses and read Harper's Bazaar
In which was a striking tea set of cream and jade.
She smoothed her gloves because she was afraid.

The lady would not look at the little boy waiting in the outer office,
Because he kept his hands together and did not smile.
She would not look at the one who held him
Reminding him at intervals not to cry.

85

And yet thereafter she did reassuringly smile
For what was evidently a long while.

The lady sat with her little broken bone and thought about Hawaii,
Now and again stopping and taking breath.
Every chair was filled with the smoke of waiting,
The pages turning in intense parlor atmosphere,
Till when at the long long long overdue beckon she took breath
The lady was sick unto death.

Moonrise in City Park

Here you have sky high one wall
And one at its shoulder to the sixth floor,
Here you have the two story house with the colonial door;
And says the sign, Beauty Culture,
Beauty Culture, says the sign.

Here you have the stack of dentist offices,
Here shoulder high the Philharmonic wall:
The nice culture of the mouth and music. Over all
The sign glows beauty,
Beauty, glows the sign.

Here rises from the blank and black the moon,
The blond beauty at the colonial door,
The bright blond face ascending from the sixth floor,
With the sign suggesting culture,
Culture, suggesting the sign.

From this park bench look up and say divine,
To the dark levels speak and say divine,
To the moon whisper also and say divine,
And the sign will join you, saying Beauty
Culture, saying the sign.

Preliminary to Classroom Lecture

My quiet kin, must I affront you
With a telling tongue?
Will not a mission or request content you
To move as you belong
The fields of doubt among?

The voice to burden down a tale upon you
Were indolent with din.
Would better ask and have the answer from you.
And would you then begin
Querying too, querying, my quiet kin?

Polo Match. Sunday, 2 P.M.

Polo has that gravy look game,
Tough brushed out and thus adaptable,
Rare, but thick and springy,
Thought up as a grist well chewed by a gold tooth.

The soppers of that gravy save all Sunday for it
And picnic at its bounds; they sit on Sunday papers
And pay no fee but the warning distant gasp
Of the multitude so good for a good pony.

Polo picks up an area of turf and takes it
Right down the lines, it biasses the natural green,
It goals the very day, with evidence
Of practice flavoring that efficiency.

Riders have the watchers licking chops,
Not only in the pleased way of relatives and friends,
But in the ready gust of the professional eaters
Taking the taste up deftly from a distance.

Gravy, gravy of the haunch and flexion
Sliding and righting, at a chewable degree
Soaks down the Sunday aft in a feast for the breadwinners,
The bread winners winning it all up deep to saturation.

Housewife

Occasional mornings when an early fog
Not yet dispersed stands in every yard
And drips and undiscloses, she is severely
Put to the task of herself.

Usually here we have view window dawns,
The whole East Bay at least some spaces into the room,
Puffing the curtains, and then she is out
In the submetropolitan stir.

But when the fog at the glass pauses and closes
She is put to ponder
A life-line, how it chooses to run obscurely
In her hand, before her.

Opal

The steamfitter had no notion of buying an opal,
But a stone comes sudden in its meaning often.

He looked for a new watch, that part of his life, there was none,
He had to furnish his own time sense.

But this opal. Fire of time that burned in the antique reaches,
Roman omen, power of the sooth.

How comes so much actual straight evil into an opal?
Fix on a streak of bad luck, it goes out.

How comes so much red, then green, into an opal?
There aren't those colors in a glass of milk.

His wife didn't want the jewel but he bought it
And took that burden on, which fate forbore.

The Thoroughgoing

He killed and kept.
He doused the capital city in kerosene,
He chopped the maples up for firewood
And then it was the city they kept warm.
All winter warmed preserved and kept
For him.

He told the city fathers: die, and they
Died with unwillingness and shock and met again
Next weekday morning for the usual course
Of minor and perhaps a major bill.
All morning voted and vetoed the village ways and means
For him.

He had his uncle understand the old was dead,
Laid down the old man's bay in earth for a leaner muscle,
And grayly from the grave came home to find
The glitter of watch chain crossed his uncle's dinner.
Saved for him. The heirloom worn aloft and soft and now and still
Saved for him.

The Sympathizers

To this man, to his boned shoulders
Came the descent of pain.
All kinds

Cruel, blind, dear, horrid, hallowed,
Rained, again, again.

To this small white blind boned face
Wherever it was
Descended
The blows of pain, it took as it were blinded,
As it were made for this.

We were there. We uneasy
Did not know if it were.
Knew neither
The reason nor the man nor whether
To share, or to beware.

What Followed

In all happiness and peace of mind
The man spoke a villainy, he was sore at it
And would have it back but it was gone already,
Ducked in the pool of the past and there no diver,
It was done for and he with it, he said.

But the very villainy got up of itself,
It was so light it ran, and he after it,
Asking everybody as he ran where it went to,
All had seen it and spoke of it to him,
They knew him by it.

When one summer eve in another county
He met up with the villainy at a band concert,
Asked how it did, said here am I
My whole life and place of life changed by chasing you,
He found he held its leash, it was his seeing eye
Purchased and instructed.

Harvest Moon

Long as I was able, in the town of my birth,
I listened to the old men tell Indian stories,
And learned to patter them, while every fall
Came quicker in the year, and every Indian
Lay dustier dust.

It was astonishing that the Santa Fe railway
Both came and went, both travelled and returned,
Under a noon dust or an evening star,
And never stayed. I heard its journey
Both sides my sleep.

Now with the new airfield at Pylon's Corners,
I tremble to think what next will enter my mind.
Some semblance of an eternal Siberian winter
Blowing over the steppes of imagination
To blast an Indian story.

Bombay

If I woke in Bombay it would be possible
The rooftops would confuse me, and the dying men,
Accustomed as I am to the skyline of the living
And the jerrybuildings of tomorrow's life.

But it is not possible that when in confusion
I fled in the street, frantic for familiar sight,
I should not see in some face there
Your look as Indian as dense with life.

Statute

The way I would look at the world, the houses
Take up half, the horizon
Moves straight across the view.
And the base half is houses, the roof lines of houses
Marking off the blue.

By what aerial license would it be possible
To promote any other line?
The piteous valley vista, or the terrible
Subordination
Seen by plane?

I would legislate against the Icarian downfall
As against the ascent of F6,
And take care
That the great legal skies of human vision
Observe their human shore.

Kind

When I think of my kindness which is tentative and quiet
And of yours which is intense and free,
I am in elaboration of knowledge impatient
Of even the patientest immobility.

I think of my kind, which is the human fortune
To live in the world and make war among its friends,
And of my version, which is to be moderately peaceful,
And of your version; and must make amends

By my slow word to your wish which is mobile,
Active and moving in its generous sphere.
This is the natural and the supernatural
Of humankind of which I grow aware.

The Halt

The halt looks into the eyes of the halt and looks away.
No response there that he can see
To receive amply or repay.

But the halt will lead the blind; indeed
Note how the generous stick gestures to precede
The blind, blundering in his black, black, black need.

Pride

My pride should effect your escape,
It carries every key.
Its own trusty, and a good chiseling trusty,
It can at its own price set everybody free.

And that is pride's advantage, that though it keep
Jailed itself at an interminable wall,
It recognizes the graces of the free
And can dispense freedom from its cell.

The Day the Winds

The day the winds went underground I gasped for breath,
Did you not? — oxygen gone from the chest wall,
Nostrils pinched in the scant weather, strictest
Sort of equilibrium at street corners.

It was a pity. Who could walk in the hills now
Or run for a train? The water in a storm
Ran down the sides of buildings and the bark of trees
Straight down, like tears.

In the first days it was not so desperate;
I remember, though short of breath,
Thinking with relief in the dense quiet,
Fall will be quiet.

But more and more as the streets clogged with traffic
And the smog of the city's production lay on its eyes,
One could notice persons burrowing, hearts hammering,
Toward the risks of the wind.

Idea of Joy

The idea of joy, abruptly,
Like the idea of day,
Came and clothed the body of the lady
In an array

As of field or fire
And she withheld
Any comment on this procedure
Until it was revealed

That garmented in this glory
And clothed in this joy
She was at a loss for words completely
And knew not how to say.

So that I write for her
With secretarial speed
What she would have faithfully
Conceived and said,

That it was not joy which dressed her
So sudden as the day,
So bright as the fire,
But the idea of joy.

Meeting

One there lived on the east side of the city
One who wished to meet
One who lived on the west side of the city,
A thousand miles away.

A thousand years went by.

Then the one who lived on the east side of the city
Set out on the main street
And met the one who lived on the west side of the city
Coming that way.

A thousand years.

Miraculous life! that in its brief and mortal
Progress achieved this union of intents,
Inevitability sprung from the improbable,
Volition moving in the paths of chance.

Education

I would sit in the windows ledge
At Los Angeles High School
To watch the pecking sparrows
To hear the bickering girls
Their warm and lively life.

The sun that shone thereon
Would draw to warmest life
The coldest bone and silent
To ruffle in its dust
Bicker its edge of sun.

Now what shall I say of the cat
That sprang the pecking sparrows
What of the aunt that ate
The slightest bickering girls
What of the heart

Once warmed by delicate rays
Now sheltering all that sun
Till it would bless and blaze
A thousand windows in
A universe of schools?

Riddle

You are a riddle I would not unravel,
You are the riddle my life comprehends.
And who abstracts the marvel
Abstracts the story to its sorriest ends.

But not your riddle. It is patent,
Never more than it says, and since that is
Impossible, it is the marvel
Nobody, as I am nobody, believes.

The Plastic Glass

A saint I heard of saw the world
Suspended in a golden globe; so I saw
Shattuck Avenue and the Safeway Stores
In Herndon's globe of friendly credit.

And where the car moved on, there the whole trash
Flats of Berkeley floated in suspense
Gold to the Gate and bellied to the redwood
Cottages.

And I would ask the saint at what expense
This incorporeal vision falls to the lay mind,
And search the breast
For revelations of unquietude.

But in this dear and christian world the blessing
Falls not from above; the grace
Goldens from everyman, his singular credit
In the beatitude of place.

Son

Men have their alien sons and love them,
The dear fist clenched in theirs,
The foreign taste fed at their table,
The wayward walking in their name,
They love their handsome son.

But they hate the foreign, though an open
Five-fingered hand like theirs,
The gall taste deep as another nation,
The ugly accent in an alien name,
Hate all but him, dear father, and dear son.

Sale

Went into a shoestore to buy a pair of shoes,
There was a shoe salesman humming the blues
Under his breath; over his breath
Floated a peppermint lifesaver, a little wreath.

I said please I need a triple-A,
And without stopping humming or swallowing his lifesaver away
He gave one glance from toe to toe
And plucked from the mezzanine the very shoe.

Skill of the blessed, that at their command
Blue and breathless comes to hand
To send, from whatever preoccupation, feet
Implacably shod into the perfect street.

Belief

Mother said to call her if the H bomb exploded
And I said I would, and it about did
When Louis my brother robbed a service station
And lay cursing on the oily cement in handcuffs.

But by that time it was too late to tell Mother,
She was too sick to worry the life out of her
Over *why why*. Causation is sequence
And everything is one thing after another.

Besides, my other brother, Eddie, had got to be President,
And you can't ask too much of one family.
The chances were as good for a good future
As bad for a bad one.

Therefore it was surprising that, as we kept the newspapers
                              from Mother,
She died feeling responsible for a disaster unverified,
Murmuring, in her sleep as it seemed, the ancient slogan
Noblesse oblige.

Reason

Said, Pull her up a bit will you, Mac, I want to unload there.
Said, Pull her up my rear end, first come first serve.
Said, Give her the gun, bud, he needs a taste of his own bumper.
Then the usher came out and got into the act:

Said, Pull her up, pull her up a bit, we need this space, sir.
Said, For God's sake, is this still a free country or what?
Said, You go back and take care of Gary Cooper's horse
And leave me handle my own car.

Saw them unloading the lame old lady,
Ducked out under the wheel and gave her an elbow,
Said, All you needed to do was just explain;
Reason, Reason is my middle name.

Monkey

God, a man at Yale, adopted a monkey
In order to raise him up in his own image,
But only in some respects could the monk identify,
Could learn manners, but not the word of God.

Ah, always it was so, meditated the monkey dazzled and befuddled,
Out of my tree I fell in the forest of Eden,
Or if I mannerly ate, it was the wrong apple,
Or if I climbed I died.

And this is all, I guess, a semantical series
Of my ascent and fall.
His tree is not my tree; His word, my word;
His Yale, my Yale.

The Savages

As we rowed from our ships and set foot on the shore
In the still coves,
We met our images.

99

Our brazen images emerged from the mirrors of the wood
Like yelling shadows,
So we searched our souls,

And in that hell and pit of everyman
Placed the location of their ruddy shapes.
We must be cruel to ourselves.

Then through the underbrush we cut our hopes
Forest after forest to within
The inner hush where Mississippi flows

And were in ambush at the very source,
Scalped to the cortex. Yet bought them off.
It was an act of love to seek their salvation.

President Jackson asked,
What good man would prefer a forested country ranged with
    savages
To our extensive republic studded with cities
With all the improvements art can devise or industry execute?

Pastor Smiley inquired,
What good man would allow his sins or his neighbors'
To put on human dress and run in the wilds
To leap out on innocent occasions?

Miss Benedict proposed,
The partial era of enlightenment in which we live
Brings Dionysus to the mesa and the cottonwood grove,
And floats Apollo to the barrows of the civic group
To ratify entreaties and to harp on hope.

Professor Roy Harvey Pearce quoted,
These savages are outlandish Tartars and Cain's children
Though someone reported once, "They do not withhold assent
From the truth set forth in a credible manner."
Is it possible?

Henry David Thoreau,
The most popular highbrow overseas reading-material

For the armed forces, because while they work and wait
They see before them in the green shade
His ruddy image, said, as his last word when he died, *Indians.*

Reading today this manual of wisdom,
In the still coves
We meet our images

And, in ambush at the very source,
Would buy them off. It is an act of love
To seek their salvation.

One party to the purchase
Receipts the purchase price and hands us back
His token of negotiation which redeems:
We cannibals must help these Christians.

Mercury

Then have mercy upon me.
Let one who has no care,
Sees not me there,
Likes not if he sees
And would not had he care,
Have mercy upon me.

He is my black mercury
Against the world's glass
By which all figures come and pass
Fair as they are in their own loving sight.
He is the black night
That brings myself to the face of the glass.

In my indelibility
Have mercy upon me,
Quick neutral who does me forget.

Stand not
Fast at the sheer glass of my life
To make my life myself.

Confessed

My gracious friend, whose arts are all refining
Into the arts of conscience, pity me.
I cannot bring a blame to such explaining
I cannot peel a problem to such planning
Of conscience sacred in its sympathy.

Where will your care remove you after luncheon?
To home and shadow of a curtain keeping
A stripe of dark over your silver sleeping,
A permanent color in adapted pattern
To say, I err; to tell you, pity me.

HOWARD NEMEROV

The Frozen City

1.   Visionary and not believed
Is no longer the position
Nor the prerogative of
Saints, mystics, and the holy poor.
Rather on reefers and coke
I expound to the multitude
Traumatic aggrandizements
Of my person in triplicate
At least; for this receiving
The indifference of belief
From those who love the miracle
And let the doctrine go.

I enter upon my song and dance:

2.   I saw by moonlight New York
Which was called in my dream
The Island of God, and achieved
In the paralysis of distance
A splendid fixity, as though
The parable of a town.
Cold space parted me from
The marvelous towers
Towards which I strained.
With every appearance of
Solidity the city yet
Possessed the radiant dead
Purity of ice, glass, reflecting
Clearly the multitudinous stars.
Under the constellation of
A sword, Blake and Augustine
Swam the middle air

Extending their perpetually
Protecting benediction
Over the silver port.
All bridges were down, and ships
Sharply broke up in the frozen rivers.
My eyes, from the abysmal
Heaven of the dream's stance,
Detected no commerce or action,
And the snow lay undisturbed
By wheel or step and flashed
With sidereal brilliance the
Respeculation of Heaven.

This was, as the dream understood,
The artifice of eternity
Produced by efficient suffering
And the total wish for death.
How the committees had worked,
Organizations of ladies begged
The people to refrain from eating:
The assault on Heaven's justice
(Scorning mercy) had been conducted
By many the most eminent
Citizens and public men;
The rape of God's attention
Employed the methods commended
By the superior saints, with only
A hint of economic condescension
And the irony of the best people.

Descending and moving closer
I saw the sad patience of
The people awaiting death
(They crossed their bony legs,
Their eyes stared, hostile and
Bright as broken glass). The dream said:
You must know that the period
Of partial damage is complete:
Nothing now will defray the costly

Agonies of the sempiternal.
Understand that these are dying
Into grace by an act of the will;
And if some still stare at the harbor
And mutter of nipples or ten per cent
This ghostly quality of lust retains
No understanding of itself: for as
All words are prayer, all words
Are meaningless, by the last fiat
Of the last secular council.

This was true. Moving, I saw
The murderer staring at his knife,
Unable to understand, and a banker
Regarding a dollar bill with fixed
Incomprehension. Queerest of all,
Children rolled skulls in the street,
The sound of their light laughter
Contrasting strangely with their
Gangrenous flesh and the
Convulsive motions of their limbs.
Parents looked on from doorways
And were alert with approval
For the quickest among the children:
But more than once I saw envy in
Their shining eyes.
                              Some, while
I watched, died (their heads
Rolled off, this signifying
An abdication of the will)
But the cold preserved them in
Their charnel integrity.
As from a distance, down
Halls of column and arch, I heard
Meanwhile many voices singing:

Tuba mirum spargens sonum
Per sepulcra regionum,
Coget omnes ante thronum.

Looking skyward then, I heard
The mighty guardians reply
To the city's qualified despair.
Tears spun from their eyes
Like suns, and wheeled glittering
Out to space, new planets of
Compassionate experiment:

William
Blake. Jerusalem, desiring the vine
Blindly we have built the machine:
For the eye altered alters all.

Saint
Augus-
tine. Quomodo ardebam, deus meus,
Revolare a terrenis ad te,
Et nesciebam quid ageres mecum.

Then in my dream the blind
Mercy of the Lamb was loosed
Upon the moral world: the sun
Burned Heaven from the town,
Flowers grew with monstrous
Innocent speed. The dead arose,
And began with spastic hands
To gather money from the streets:
As though ravaged by intolerable
Heat of life, people ran to the cool
Marble vaults of bank and tomb
And threw themselves upon the cold
Gold or earth, it seemed for
Sovereign unredeeming solace.

I found myself leaving the city
And fading from my own dream.
From a distance the scene
Showed no unusual activity.
My last sight was of Blake
And Augustine, in whose glacial
Eyes, frozen by their last tears,
City and dream were locked together.

3.   Waking, close to midnight and
By irony in the same city,
I listened to the usual noises:
The argument of two women, the drunk
Singing in the back yard, and
Various metal, rubber, wooden
Sounds that spoke of the normal.

The healthy man, waking at
Midnight, turns over to sleep
Again. What sound began and
Ended at once his dream, in time
Immeasurable by clocks or
Time for meals, was his only
Warning from the metaphysical,
Suspected not even by his sleep.

A Chromium-Plated Hat: Inlaid
with Scenes from Siegfried

Choreography by the
New York Times *Book Review*

Greatness. Warmth, and human insight. Music.
But greatness. The greatness of Socrates
And Dante and Alexander Woollcott, and the
True charm of Horatio Alger, Jr. Also,
The greatness of eighteen-year-old girls,
The warmth of retired corporation lawyers,
The impossibility of having enough books
About truth. The important thing is
The relation of truth to our time to Kitty Foyle.

In addition, music. It is good to have music,
But not at the expense of greatness:
Better to be truly great and unmusical.
If you are merely musical you are probably

Not one of the great authors. The place
Of the glorious few is in that case
Not for you, but for Thomas B. Costain,
Who is welcome here almost any time.

To sum up, the truth of the matter is,
Quoting William Lyon Phelps, "There is
No masterpiece like *Lohengrin*, that
Masterpiece," and it may be better anyhow
To have human warmth than greatness:
Like Grandpa, who sat by the fire all
Winter long, in a buffalo rug with fleas.

A Poem of Margery Kempe

I creature being mad
They locked me in my room,
Where, bound upon the bed
With smiling Satan there,
I would have broke my side
And given the heart to God.
Men said it was pride
Brought me to that despair.

> *Alas! that ever I did sin,*
> *It is full merry in heaven.*

The priest so angered me
That I would not confess.
I suffered his reproof
Scornfully, for my God
(I said) has mercy enough.
His kingdom I see
And Lucifer His rod
In my wretchedness.

> *Alas! that ever I did sin,*
> *It is full merry in heaven.*

When I recovered reason
I would have lived chaste,
And mocking my husband's right
I for a little season
Kept me for the sweet Christ,
Who said to me, "Dear Bride,
Rather the good man's lust
Than this dry pride."

> *Alas! that ever I did sin,*
> *It is full merry in heaven.*

But I, except in bed,
Wore hair-cloth next the skin,
And nursed more than my child
That grudge against my side.
Now, spirit and flesh assoil'd,
Against the wild world
I lace my pride in,
Crying out odd and even,

> *Alas! that ever I did sin,*
> *It is full merry in heaven.*

Sonnet at Easter

You splice together two broomsticks, then reef
A tie (a Christmas present) at the throat.
A hat must rattle on the knob, a coat
Keep warm the chest (for he has little beef).
You set this person up disguised as you
And let him flap. He hangs lonely as grief.
His wraithless hull, no blood and no belief,
Your children don't despise but your crows do.

He is a habit now, perennial,
One of your pieties. You plant him deep,
And though you have no earthly use for him

You dress him in your father's coat, and call
Good Evening sometimes when the light is dim,
Seeing he stands for you in upright sleep.

The Lives of Gulls and Children

Around the headland, at the end
Where they had not been before,
Paced by the white and the grey gull
With loud shrieking, and by the neat
Black-hooded tern, they found the place of death.
When they looked back along their way they saw
The footprints lonely and loud on the sand.

Few bones at first their feet kicked up,
Then more, a flat thicket of bone
And tangled cartilage, dry white and clean,
Tasting of salt when the children licked them.
Further on were feathers, then flesh
Strung on the bone ragged and rotting,
With still red tendons curled. Twice they saw
The whole delicate skeletons with the hard
Hornlike feet peacefully displayed, and there
A loud few flies buzzed on the torn meat
And dishevelled feathers; a sick and wrong
Smell mingled with the heat of the salt wind.

Silence strangely was twisted there
By the voices of the children, by
The outcries of the living gulls aloft
Swinging over the wash and rush of the sea
Between the heat of the sand and the blind sun of noon.

They saw there a great gull dying,
Huddled in the sun and shuddering out
Now and again a heavy wing in cold
Effortful motion; he stared at them
Out of a steady and majestic eye

Like a sun part baffled in cloud,
So rheumed over with the morning of death.

They would have reached out hands to him
To comfort him in that human kind
They just were learning — how anything alive,
They thought, hated loneliness most; but he,
A grim great-uncle with a cane, struck out,
Sullen and weakly fierce, with hooked beak and a claw.
He would have flown, but had not strength to rise,
Could not even, ridiculous, waddle away.

The children watched him for a moment more,
But at a distance, and did not see him die;
For he, making his death, would out-endure
What interest they had, who, being humankind,
Had homes to go to, and a bed this side of death.

But they knew the Atlantic kind he was,
And for this moment saw him swaying
In the grey dark above the cold sea miles,
Wingtips ticking the spray of the slow waves,
Leaning on the unhavening air the dangerous
Sustaining of his own breastbone; they knew
The indifference of time dragging him down.
And when after silence they turned away,
"No one has ever been here before,"
They cried, "no one, no one, no one."
Their mournful word went out, no one,
Along the shore, now that they turned for home
Bearing the lonely pride of those who die,
And paced by the sweet shrieking of the quick.

The Ecstasies of Dialectic

Her laughter was infectious; so, some found,
Her love. Several young men reasonably
Regret inciting her to gratitude
And learning of her ardent facility.

She has gone, back it may be to the world,
To ply her silken exercise elsewhere.
Now is occasion for the medication
(As possible) of ills not all of the heart,

And certain hints, conveyed in sermon or
By private word, are reasoning the weight
Of pleasures, pains. Thus her capable joys
Are debased by her ignominious communications.

"The flesh, the rouged cheekbones of Babylon,
The unclean loins, the thief of legal delight,
O ye generations!" "The spider that eats up
Her mate!" "The test-tube of iniquity!"

Despite the wisdom of Christian Epicures
Many of the affected more regret
Her going than her legacy. They huddle
At street corners, before drugstores, and moon

Over the hour of pestilent delight,
The yellow taste good times will always have.
"The proof of the apple is in the worm," they say,
And hug their new knowledge of life and death.

The Winter Lightning

For Paul

Over the snow at night,
And while the snow still fell,
A sky torn to the bone
Shattered the ghostly world with light;
As though this were the moon's hell,
A world hard as a stone,
    Cold, and blue-white.

As if the storming sea
Should sunder to its floor,
And all things hidden there
Gleam in the moment silently,
So does the meadow at the door
To split and sudden air
      Show stone and tree.

From the drowned world of dark
The sleeping innocence
Surrenders all its seeming;
Under the high, charged carbon arc
Light of the world, a guilty sense
Stiffens the secret dreaming
      Animal park.

So in the camera's glare
The fortunate and famed,
For all their crooked smiles,
Reveal through their regarded stare
How all that's publicly acclaimed
One brutal flash reviles
      For cold despair.

So is the murderer caught
When his lost victim rises
Glaring through dream and light
With icy eyes. That which was thought
In secret, and after wore disguises,
Silts up the drowning sight
      Mind inwrought.

So may the poem dispart
The mirror from the light
Where none can see a seam;
The poet, from his wintry heart
And in the lightning second's sight,
Illuminate this dream
      With a cold art.

The Pond

At the long meadow's end, where the road runs
High on a bank, making a kind of wall,
The rains of last October slowly built
Us up this pond some hundred yards across
And deep maybe to the height of a man's thigh
At the deepest place. It was surprising how
Slowly the water gained across the land
All autumn, no one noticing, until
We had the pond where none had been before
To any memory — most surprising in
This country where we think of contours as
Fixed on a map and named and permanent,
Where even if a stream runs dry in summer
You have the stream-bed still to go by and
The chartered name — Red Branch, and Henry's Creek,
And Anthony's Race — for reassurance, though
The reason of those names be sunken with
The men who named them so, in the natural past
Before our history began to be
Written in book or map; our history,
Or the settled story that we give the world
Out of the mouths of crones and poachers
Remembering or making up our kinship
In the overgrown swamplands of the mind;
And precious little reassurance, if
You think of it, but enough about that.
Here was, at any rate, surprisingly,
This piece of water covering the ground:
Clear blue, and pale, and crisping up to black
Squalls when the north wind moved across its face;
The question whether it would go or stay
Never came up, and no one gave it a name —
Only the water-birds on their way south
Accepted it, and rested there at night,
Coming at dusk down the meadow on wide wings
And splashing up on beating wings at dawn.

By Christmastime the pond was frozen solid
Under a foot of snow, level and white
Across the meadow so you couldn't say
Except from memory where the water was
And where the land; and maybe no adult
Would have remembered, but the children did
And brought their skates, and someone's father patched
Together a plough from plank and two-by-four
That half-a-dozen kids could lean against
And clear the snow down to the glittering ice.
They skated all the darkening afternoons
Until the sun burnt level on the ice,
And built their fires all along the shore
To warm their hands and feet, and skated nights
Under the full moon or the dark; the ice
Mirrored the moon's light, or the fire's, cold.
There was a tragedy, if that is what
One calls it, the newspapers called it that:
"Pond Claims First Victim" (it still had no name),
As though a monster underneath the ice
Had been in wait to capture the little boy
Skating in darkness all alone, away
From the firelight — the others heard his cry
But he was gone before they found the place — ,
Or else as though, a tribe of savages,
We sanctified our sports with sacrifice.
At any rate, the skating didn't stop
Despite the funeral and motherly gloom
And editorials; what happened was
The pond took the boy's name of Christopher,
And this was voted properly in meeting
For a memorial and would be so
On the next map, when the next map was drawn:
Christopher Pond: if the pond should still be there.

The winter set its teeth; near Eastertide
Before the pond was free of ice all night;
And by that time the birds were coming back
Leisurely, staying a day or so before

They rose and vanished in the northward sky;
Their lonely cries across the open water
Played on the cold, sweet virginal of spring
A chaste, beginning tune carried along
With a wind out of the east. Killdeer and plover
Came and were gone; grackle, starling and flicker
Settled to stay; and the sparrowhawk would stand
In the height of noon, a stillness on beating wings,
While close over the water swallows would trace
A music nearly visible in air,
Snapping at newborn flies. Slowly the pond
Warmed into life: cocoon and bud and egg,
All winter's seed and shroud, unfolded being
In the pond named for Christopher, who drowned.
By day the birds, and then the frogs at night,
Kept up a music there, part requiem,
Part hunting-song; among the growing reeds
The water boatman worked his oar, the strider
Walked between air and water, dragonfly
Climbed to be born, and dazzled on clear wings.
Then day by day, in the heat of June, the green
World raised itself to natural arrogance,
And the air sang with summer soon to come.

In sullen August, under the massy heat
Of the sun towering in the height, I sat
At the pond's edge, the indeterminate
Soft border of what no longer was a pond
But a swamp, a marsh, with here and there a stretch
Of open water, even that half spread
With lily pads and the rich flesh of lilies.
And elsewhere life was choking on itself
As though, in spite of all the feeding there,
Death could not keep the pace and had to let
Life curb itself: pondweed and pickerel-weed
And bladderwort, eel-grass and delicate
Sundew and milfoil, peopled thick the city
Of themselves; and dragonfly and damselfly
By hundreds darted among the clustering leaves,
Striders by hundreds skated among the stalks

Of pitcher-plant and catkin; breathless the air
Under the intense quiet whining of
All things striving to breathe; the gift of life
Turning its inward heat upon itself.
So, Christopher, I thought, this is the end
Of dedication, and of the small death
We sought to make a name and sacrifice.
The long year has turned away, and the pond
Is drying up, while its remaining life
Grasps at its own throat: the proud lilies wilt,
The milfoil withers, catkins crack and fall,
The dragonfly glitters over it all;
All that your body and your given name
Could do in accidental consecrations
Against nature, returns to nature now,
And so, Christopher, goodbye.

                          But with these thoughts
There came a dragonfly and settled down
On a stem before my eyes, and made me think
How in nature too there is a history,
And that this winged animal of light,
Before it could delight the eye, had been
In a small way a dragon of the deep,
A killer and meat-eater on the floor
Beneath the April surface of the pond;
And that it rose and cast its kind in May
As though putting away costume and mask
In the bitter play, and taking a lighter part.
And thinking so, I saw with a new eye
How nothing given us to keep is lost
Till we are lost, and immortality
Is ours until we have no use for it
And live anonymous in nature's name
Though named in human memory and art.
Not consolation, Christopher, though rain
Fill up the pond again and keep your name
Bright as the glittering water in the spring;
Not consolation, but our acquiescence.
And I made this song for a memorial
Of yourself, boy, and the dragonfly together.

The Salt Garden

I

A good house, and ground whereon
With an amateur's toil
Both lawn and garden have been won
From a difficult, shallow soil
That, now inland, was once the shore
And once, maybe, the ocean floor.
Much patience, and some sweat,
Have made the garden green,
And even green the lawn.
Turnip and bean and violet
In a decent order set,
Grow, flourish and are gone;
Even the ruins of stalk and shell,
The vine when it goes brown,
Look civil and die well.
Sometimes in the late afternoon
I sit out with my wife,
Watching the work that we have done
Bend in the salt wind,
And think that here our life
Might be a long and happy one;
Though restless over the sand
The ocean's wrinkled green
Maneuvers in its sleep,
And I despise what I had planned,
Every work of the hand
For what can man keep?

II

Restless, rising at dawn,
I saw the great gull come from the mist
To stand upon the lawn.
And there he shook his savage wing

To quiet, and stood like a high priest
Bird-masked, mantled in grey.
Before his fierce austerity
My thought bowed down, imagining
The wild sea lanes he wandered by
And the wild waters where he slept
Still as a candle in the crypt.
Noble, and not courteous,
He stared upon my green concerns,
Then, like a merchant prince
Come to some poor province,
Who, looking all about, discerns
No spice, no treasure house,
Nothing that can be made
Delightful to his haughty trade,
And so spreads out his sail,
Leaving to savage men
Their miserable regimen;
So did he rise, making a gale
About him by his wings,
And fought his huge freight into air
And vanished seaward with a cry —
A strange tongue but the tone clear.
He faded from my troubled eye
There where the ghostly sun
Came from the mist.
                    When he was gone
I turned back to the house
And thought of wife, of child,
And of my garden and my lawn
Serene in the wet dawn;
And thought that image of the wild
Wave where it beats the air
Had come, brutal, mysterious,
To teach the tenant gardener,
Green fellow of this paradise,
Where his salt dream lies.

The Goose Fish

On the long shore, lit by the moon
To show them properly alone,
Two lovers suddenly embraced
So that their shadows were as one.
The ordinary night was graced
For them by the swift tide of blood
That silently they took at flood,
And for a little time they prized
      Themselves emparadised.

Then, as if shaken by stage-fright
Beneath the hard moon's bony light,
They stood together on the sand
Embarrassed in each other's sight
But still conspiring hand in hand,
Until they saw, there underfoot,
As though the world had found them out,
The goose fish turning up, though dead,
      His hugely grinning head.

There in the china light he lay,
Most ancient and corrupt and grey.
They hesitated at his smile,
Wondering what it seemed to say
To lovers who a little while
Before had thought to understand,
By violence upon the sand,
The only way that could be known
      To make a world their own.

It was a wide and moony grin
Together peaceful and obscene;
They knew not what he would express,
So finished a comedian
He might mean failure or success,
But took it for an emblem of

Their sudden, new and guilty love
To be observed by, when they kissed,
    That rigid optimist.

So he became their patriarch,
Dreadfully mild in the half-dark.
His throat that the sand seemed to choke,
His picket teeth, these left their mark
But never did explain the joke
That so amused him, lying there
While the moon went down to disappear
Along the still and tilted track
    That bears the zodiac.

Young Woman

Naked before the glass she said,
"I see my body as no man has,
Nor any shall unless I wed
And naked in a stranger's house
Stand timid beside his bed.
There is no pity in the flesh."

"Or else I shall grow old," she said,
"Alone, and change my likeliness
For a vile, slack shape, a head
Shriveled with thinking wickedness
Against the day I must be dead
And eaten by my crabbed wish."

"One or the other way," she said,
"How shall I know the difference,
When wrinkles come, to spinster or bride?
Whether to marry or burn is bless-
ed best, O stranger to my bed,
There is no pity in the flesh."

The Snow Globe

A long time ago, when I was a child,
They left my light on while I went to sleep,
As though they would have wanted me beguiled
By brightness if at all; dark was too deep.

And they left me one toy, a village white
With the fresh snow and silently in glass
Frozen forever. But if you shook it,
The snow would rise up in the rounded space

And from the limits of the universe
Snow itself down again. O world of white,
First home of dreams! Now that I have my dead,
I want so cold an emblem to rehearse
How many of them have gone from the world's light,
As I have gone, too, from my snowy bed.

HYAM PLUTZIK

An Equation

For instance: $y - xa + mx^2(a^2 + 1) = 0$

Coil upon coil, the grave serpent holds
Its implacable strict pose, under a light
Like marble. The artist's damnation, the rat of time,
Cannot gnaw this form, nor event touch it with age.
Before it was, it existed, creating the mind
Which created it, out of itself. It will dissolve
Into itself, though in another language.
Its changes are not in change, nor its times in time.

And the coiled serpent quivering under a light
Crueler than marble, unwinds slowly, altering
Deliberate the great convolutions, a dancer,
A mime on the brilliant stage. The sudden movement,
Swifter than creases of lightning, renews a statue:
There by its skin a snake rears beaten in copper.

It will not acknowledge the incense on your altars,
Nor hear at night in your room the weeping. . . .

The Begetting of Cain

Longing at twilight the lovesick Adam saw
The belly of Eve upon the golden straw
Of Paradise, under the limb of the Tree.
He thought that none was near, but there were three
Who were upon the mortal grass that dusk,
Under the wispy cloud, breathing the musk
Of the young world. Creature of pointed ear,

Of the cleft hoof and the tight-mouthed sneer,
The other passed, wound round within his thought.
And Adam in his mounting passion caught
The white shoulders of that woman there. . . .
All were engulfed — these two, the birds of the air,
The burrowers of the earth, by the quenchless mind
Roaming insatiate on that lowland, blind
In its lonely hunger, lusting to make all things
One with itself. Brief as the flutter of wings
Was his mastery, though ranging through world and void
To the dusk-star shining. But all, all were destroyed:
The two on the odorous earth in the garden there;
The beasts, the birds in the nest, the fireflies in the air.

On the Photograph of a Man
I Never Saw

My grandfather's beard
Was blacker than God's
Just after the tablets
Were broken in half.

My grandfather's eyes
Were sterner than Moses'
Just after the worship
Of the calf.

O ghost! ghost!
You foresaw the days
Of the fallen Law
In the strange place.

Where ten together
Lament David,
Is the glance softened?
Bowed the face?

He Inspects His Armory

Phoebus, the car
And the galloping horses
Are dead, dead,
And in their stead
Inanimate forces
And a minor star.

    Cynthia too,
    Whom Edmund and John
    So quaintly adored,
    Ignored, ignored,
    Wrinkled and wan,
    A hag in the blue.

        And Zephyrus eke,
        Vulcan or Thor,
        Are all together
        Weather, weather,
        And nothing more.
        Useless as Greek.

           Remains the least
           Of the living for art —
           Loneliest, latest,
           The greatest, greatest,
           The occult heart
           Of the talking beast.

Divisibility

The limitary nature of a wall
Is partial only, to keep out dogs and insects,
Contain the furniture, exclude the rain.

But space flies through it like a mad commuter.
Rooms are thus always strange, as if you entered
Another by error in the same hotel,

And saw incredulous no known landmarks,
The bed moved, new luggage on the floor,
And a window staring at you from the wrong corner.

And desire goes through a wall as wild geese
Pass and cry over reedy waters. Memory
Knows no walls. They are elementary limits.

Only a fool would cut the sea with a knife,
Or say to a wind: Exceed this line at your peril.

Mr. Pollington Remembers a Poet

Weather bothered him, and the delicate muscular,
Neural and cortical events within him:
Fancies of the pressure of the air
Within his nostrils, the blood in the arteries.

He built his gauges out of an incantation
Of scraps and boards, a nail, a snip of string,
And then — at evening perhaps — by means of a mirror,
With glances over his shoulder for possible ghosts,

He read the remoter records of the machine
Of his own self, its shifting digestive balance
With minerals, oxygen and the protein complex,
The wavelengths of sound, light, and stellar synthesis.

The data became memories; they too were marked
On the crooked dials of his instruments —
While always, turning within, he sought a constant
Of pure numbers glowing like phosphorus.

He will be forgotten like his friends the Greeks,
Whose notation, too, was inept, and who had no mechanics
For their curious dreams. I still remember him
As he talked to himself stumbling across the yard.

Argumentum ad Hominem

Who has seen the pageant
Of the falling leaf
Has won a grief
Prouder than joy:

    Has seen them fall,
    One and by one,
    The folk of the sun
    Kissing the earth,

        Will know, will know,
        What stuff is king
        Of everything,
        And its regent who.

Identity

To locate a person hidden in this room,
Who stands — in fact — before us, dispersed in a shape
Of primitive coinage, with arms, legs and a nose,
We need no deeper philosophy than subtraction,
Which takes from ten, the height of the room, his height
Of full six feet, leaving his selfhood suspended
(Where the brain beats, hoarding awareness and memory)
Some four feet from the ceiling, like a bird
Hovering in the wind, more like a bubble
Or unexpected balloon: a magician's secret
No greater in strangeness than a maid's way with a man.

My Sister

Now the swift rot of the flesh is over.
Now only the slow rot of the bones in the Northern damp.
Even the bones of that tiny foot that brought her doom.

Imagine a land where there is no rain as we know rain.
Not the quick dashing of water to the expectant face,
But the weary ooze of spent drops in the earth.

Imagine the little skeleton lying there —
In the terrible declination of the years —
On that solitary bed, in the crumbling shell of a world.

Amid the monsters with lipless teeth who lie there in wait —
The saurian multitudes who rest in that land —
And the men without eyes who forever glare at the sky.

And the ominous strangers ever entering.
Why are they angry? They keep their arms to themselves.
Comfort themselves in the cold. Whisper no word.

And the black dog has come, but he does not play.
And no one moves but the man who walks in the sky —
A strange man who comes to cut the grass.

Seventeen years. . . .

And already the fair flesh dispersed, the proud form broken.
Memory! Where are the ligaments to bind — the glowing cords —
As in this hand once touched, this hand that writes?

Seventeen years have passed and the way grows steeper.
The glaciers move from the north and the sun is dying.
And into the chasm of Time alone and tiny. . . .

The Man of War sits in the gleaming chair.
Struts through the halls. The Dispenser of Vengeance laughs,
Crying *victory! victory! victory! victory!*

Victory.

Exhortation to the Artists

(*Rabbi Elazer once became sick. Rabbi Jochanan came to visit him. . . .
Rabbi Elazer was weeping. "Why do you weep?" asked Rabbi Jochanan.
. . . "I weep," said Rabbi Elazer to him, "for the beauty which will
decay in the earth." "For that indeed," Rabbi Jochanan said, "you ought
to weep," and both wept.* THE TALMUD)

Two weeping for beauty perished, husband
And wife, lover and mistress, friend and friend,
    Shall mark the world's end.

As I was spinning a fable for this page,
There came ghosts weeping, two and two,
    In pity, dolor, or in rage.

Against the pillars of the heartless temple
Throw, whom knowledge blinded, your brute skill
    Though it is yourself you kill.

He crushes the sparrow fallen among the rocks;
The hunter is trapped with his quarry: the man and the fox —
    Even the little mouse on the hill.

For T. S. E. Only

You called me a name on such and such a day —
Do you remember? — you were speaking of Bleistein our brother,
The barbarian with the black cigar, and the pockets

Ringing with cash, and the eyes seeking Jerusalem,
Knowing they have been tricked. Come, brother Thomas,
We three must weep together for our exile.

I see the hunted look, the protestation,
The desperate seeking, the reticence and the brashness
Of the giver of laws to the worshippers of calves.
At times you speak as if the words were walls,
But your walls fell with mine to the torch of a Titus.
Come, let us weep together for our exile.

We two, no doubt, could accommodate ourselves:
We've both read Dante and we both dislike Chicago,
And both, you see, can be brutal — but you must bow down
To our brother Bleistein here, with the unaesthetic
Cigar and the somber look. Come, do so quickly,
For we must weep together for our exile.

O you may enwomb yourself in words or the Word
(The Word is a good refuge for people too proud
To swallow the milk of the mild Jesus' teaching),
Or a garden in Hampshire with a magic bird, or an old
Quotation from the Reverend Andrewes, yet someone or something
(Let us pause to weep together for our exile)

Will stick a needle in your balloon, Thomas.
Is it the shape that you saw upon the stair?
The four knights clanking toward the altar? the hidden
Card in the deck? the sinister man from Nippon?
The hordes on the eastern horizon? Come, brother Burbank,
And let us weep together for our exile.

In the time of sweet sighing you wept bitterly,
And now in the time of weeping you cannot weep.
Will you wait for the peace of the sailor with pearly bones?
Where is the refuge you thought you would find on the island
Where each man lives in his castle? O brother Thomas,
Come let us weep together for our exile.

You drew us first by your scorn, first by your wit;
Later for your own eloquent suffering.

We loved you first for the wicked things you wrote
Of those you acknowledged infinitely gentle.
Wit is the sin that you must expiate.
Bow down to them, and let us weep for our exile.

I see your words wrung out in pain, but never
The true compassion for creatures with you, that Dante
Knew in his nine hells. O eagle! master!
The eagle's ways of pride and scorn will not save
Though the voice cries loud in humility. Thomas, Thomas,
Come, let us pray together for our exile.

You, hypocrite lecteur! mon semblable! mon frère!

The Road

Imagine a road as straight as a wish,
Bright as a ribbon of purest salt,
Running endlessly over a marsh.

This is the road that Huey built
On a child's dream to Baton Rouge;
And that, in the distance, a terrible smudge.

Why do you shudder before you know
That these are some vultures croaking *ho*
For a fat pig killed by a hurtling car?

— A party of buzzards chomping sweet
On a gaudy mess of good hog's meat,
On the road, the road, the road that Huey built.

Enamored, they barely lift in the air
As the suave and sleek machine hums by,
To settle again. But the stricken eye

Must turn, must follow, follow the feast
To the final dot, afraid of the worst:
That this is beginning, middle and last.

Since the road that Huey built is as straight
As a knife, or a string for garroting,
Cruel and proud as a taloned foot,

You riders upon the cursed roads,
Route, or Via, or Autobahn,
That would match the thrust of the will of God —

What blood do you think is red in the sun?
Road and bogswamp are one and one.
Claw is knife or the tightened thong.

A crooked man built a crooked road
For the crooked toes of a wicked bird
And the black blood of a rooting beast
Over the empire of the frog.

Hail Huey, King of Kingfish, Builder of Roads,
Whose immortal stele stands on the Capitol.

Portrait

Notice with what careful nonchalance
He tries to be a Jew casually,
To ignore the monster, the mountain —
A few thousand years of history.

Of course he personally remembers nothing,
And the world has forgotten the older objections —
The new ones not being socially acceptable:
Hangdogs, hiding in the privies and alleys of the mind.

It is agreed
That he of all men has gained the right to his soul
(Though like the others he no longer believes in one).
He lives in his own house under his oak.
His smile is friendly; his hair is peacefully in place.
He stands by his car; he is shod in decently-grained leather;
His suit is carefully pressed; his cravat harmonious and expertly
                                                                    knotted;
His tiepin modest and wise as the eye of Sheba.

Whose father, it is whispered, stubbornly cried old clothes and
                                                                    bric-a-brac,
He of all men might yet be master of self, all self-possession,
Were it not (how gauche and incredible!) for the one ill-fitting
                                                                    garment —
The historical oversight in the antique wardrobe —
The shirt, the borrowed shirt,
The Greek shirt.

Notice how even when at ease he **is** somehow anxious,
Like a horse who whiffs smoke somewhere nearby faintly.
Notice with what nonchalance,
The magazine in his hand and the casual cigarette to his lips,
He wears a shirt by Nessus.

FROM *Horatio*

II. THE OSTLER

To the sound of the strange hooves on the midnight cobbles,
By the inn at Weser, Richard the ostler came running.
The lantern, held high, made caverns of his eyes
And his gaping mouth.

                    "Ha, have you heard the news?"

"Attend to my horse," I said. "What news, my friend?"

"From the court. Marry, but she was a bitch.
No, no, a ditch, in which merry Hamlet dabbled
When the mood caught him! I hear that he was lecherous
As my neighbor's seventy goats — but he's dead now,
And the King and Queen also."

                    "Of what do you speak?"

"You come from the north, yet have not heard the news?
The witless Hamlet who murdered his father last year
Has poisoned the good King Claudius and the Queen
With some hellebore he poured in their ears as they slept —
That he got from a ghost he waylaid on a stair —
But the staunch nephew of Norway, Fortinbras,
Tipped up this fiend with a happy thrust of his rapier
And rules now as our King, for which God be blessed."

The lantern shook in his hand.

                    "But consider," I said,
"I come from the court. I am Horatio
Who —"

                "A pleasant lie! I know you. You're a scholar
Going to study Pluto and Harris Tuttle
At Wittenberg I'll wager, with the other drunkards.
Horatio passed through our town this very week
(Though I did not see him) — a smooth and ample man,
The very mark of a courtier. Why, his sash
Was yellower than gold. He was the one
Who unmasked the wicked prince. He says that this Hamlet
Had him a bouncing doxy called Olivia
With whom he would play his game of double or nothing —
You know what I mean — we have a few such here
For your use, my master, and free of the pox I'll warrant —
If you have but a penny. Wait till I stable your horse
And I'll lead you to her. But tell me now, is it true
(If you came from the court, I mean) that when roaring mad
He would stick a straw in his nose and croak like a chicken
Wagging his head like this, or piss in the moat

From the upper windows, singing of Gog and Magog
(Two devils he played at dice with)? I have heard
He wore a pot for a hat and sometimes orated
To a fish or a dead man's bones or the empty air.
But tell me more of this madness."

                        I turned away
And took a few steps into the dark of the courtyard
And saw some stars, and retracing my footsteps went
Into the stable where the quiet-breathing horses
Buttressed the dark with a greater gloom — the lantern
Was dim in the corner.

                "You will learn soon," I began,
"All this you tell me is lies —" and paused, remembering
The friendly, beloved voice telling Horatio —
None other — to guard the hurt honor and name.

"Believe me," I cried, "I am Horatio,
Friend of the dear Prince Hamlet —"

                       "How dear, when he murdered
His own father?"

          I explained it patiently:
"That crime his uncle, later King Claudius,
Committed by pouring poison in his ear
As he slept —"

         "But that's how the cunning Hamlet killed
The King and Queen — by poison —"

                   "He did not kill them —"
(I was still civil, for truth was my sole mistress.)
"He stabbed the King —"

           ("Ha!")

                "— as the murderer
Of his father."

"Simpler and simpler," he said. "And the Queen?"

"She died of poison —"

"Poured in her ear by her son?"

"No! drunk by her and brewed by the King himself!"
I shook my head.

He closed in briskly:
"To kill his wife?"

"No, to poison Hamlet
If the tainted rapier did not work."

"What rapier?"

"The one," I said, mouthing it through my teeth,
"That young Laertes wielded in the duel
With Hamlet."

"What duel, and who was this Laertes?"

"Son of Polonius the Councillor!"

"I've got you there! His name was Rosencrantz."

"Rosencrantz —" I remarked, breathing heavily,
"Rosencrantz was a student friend of Hamlet's."

His eyes gleamed like a devil's as he whipped back:
"Ah, you are wrong, but that was Guildenstern! —
And tell me, how if Laertes wielded the rapier
Did Hamlet stab the King with it?"

"In fighting
They changed their weapons —"
136

"Was this Laertes mad
As the Lord Hamlet was? And tell me, pray,
Why should the King, as you say, will ill of Hamlet
To murder him?"

"Because the Prince discovered
That Claudius had killed the Old King Hamlet . . ."
Once more I paused, weighing again a retreat
From this unworthy foe and battlefield.
But a vow made at the sanctified hour of death
Is a stubborn metal — and I said quietly:
"Listen to me, I am Horatio,
Friend of the most gentle, honest prince
The world has seen, young Hamlet. Once at midnight
He met a ghost who called for him —"

"The ghost
He snatched the poison from upon the stairs?"

"The ghost of his father, who told him how this Claudius
Had poisoned him to get his throne and queen.
He asked revenge —"

"Then Hamlet killed the King?"

"No, not then, uncertain if this ghost
Were real or not and if he spoke the truth
(And baited by a subtler qualm or two).
But when the King grew pale during the play
And mumbled his repentance in his prayers,
He was assured that this was brother Cain —"

"For this he judged him guilty? My face is pale
From listening to you here. Am I a murderer?
And I say my prayers too. Soon you'll declare
That whore Olivia who sang foul songs
In the whole castle's ears was never ploughed,
And Hamlet not a madman but philosopher —
Like your Pluto and Harry Tuttle . . . And hold a moment!
Did not your Hamlet kill kind old Polonius?"

"By accident, he thought he was a rat."

"Get out, or I might think you one tonight.
And sleep alone. You'll have no wench from me."

III. FAUSTUS

"*Werden* and *Sein*, the old dichotomy! . . .
Here, let me pour this wretched German wine,
A bitter potion for one who's just returned
From sampling of the holy grapes of Italy . . ."

In the twelfth year after Prince Hamlet died,
Soon after I received from Fortinbras,
The king, title of lord and councillor,
With lands and goods commensurate to this honor,
Returning from an embassy to the Pope,
I paused in Wittenberg to dream a little,
And there I sat in the remembered chamber
Of the fierce-bearded Doctor I once had loved,
Who since — I shall not name him here — has taken
The old blasted path into damnation,
And with his blood, abjuring gentle Christ,
Matched his indenture with the Prince of Demons —
But when I knew him, wiser and more erudite
Than any of Europe's wise, whether at Paris,
Oxford or Bologna.

      "Ah, Lord Horatio,
How fortunate this meeting. Only lately
My thoughts, famished for a pithy bone, a clue,
Have been a-prowling through this old den, Europe,
With its kings, bishops, burghers and sweaty peasants,
Wars, alliances, strokes and counterstrokes
Of our political being: seeking a base
Within the flux, within the flow of things
That Heraclitus speaks of — or — if you will,
To grasp, in the mad events which history
In our own few years has heaped before our eyes,
The jewel, the precious philosophical stone,

The metal of meaning from the mountain of ore.
And here as I stand all sooty by my furnace,
With the stinking hills of slag to left and right,
You reach into their midst, and with your story
(Thought trivial before) of your friend Hamlet
Drag forth the one, the truly philosophical
Event in the mazy chronicle of our times.
Tell me, my old friend, what would you say
Is the highest *ergo* that we might draw from this tale?"

"That Hamlet was justified," I began, "and —"

                                        "Bah!
You speak like a sophomore, in petty terms —"

I grew warmer: "Justified — as a man,
A Christian, a noble, and —"

                        He swept me aside:
"The important point's that Claudius, the Queen,
Hamlet, Ophelia, you yourself, the ghost,
And your whole incredible catalogue of ghosts
Are no men and women here —"

                        "No men and women?"
I asked. "Prince Hamlet — there was a man —"

"My dear fellow, your Hamlet least of all!
For when a man who moved in history
Enters the universal, passing once
The abstract symbol before the haughty door
Of high philosophy, there's no return
Into the stupid hovel of bone and flesh.
Do not persist in trivial justifications
Chained to occasion — what this or that man did
On April-the-something — that's a world of quicksand.
The man you guard escapes you and stands on rock."

He paused and swallowed. "Ah, but this warms the stomach —
No, not this wine — a prime hog-swill from Saxony —

But your weighty story. And listen! The secret thoughts
That he told you of, our philosophical madman:
Those sentiments, the to-be-or-not-to-be,
Do you not see their drift? Just as I said:
It's *Sein* and *Werden,* the old dichotomy.
'To be' or 'to *become*' — do you get the meaning?
What is this Not-to-Be (the obverse of Being)
But only Becoming, a synonym for this life,
Fluid, changing, the thoughts of a child or a woman —
While Being's eternal, synonymous with Not-Being
In the vulgar sense, that is, with Death?
Therefore the two alternatives you saw
In 'to be or not to be' are not translatable
Into 'to live or die', but just the opposite:
'To die or live'! (Do let me write this down.
Yes, good, by God!) Or go one step beyond.
If Being and Becoming are the horns
Of our friend's dilemma — a lovely cuckoldry —
And, as I said, Becoming means this life,
Profuse in its vanity and brief as grass,
Then Being must imply some higher state.
Therefore the alternative lies not
As between Being — life — or Becoming — death —
But rather as between the higher life,
The philosophic, where man takes on eternity,
Is one with Idea; and the opposite:
This petty life of circumstance — dead kings,
Tedious councillors and lecherous queens
And ghosts in the cellarage. We know the choice
Lord Hamlet made."

         I glowed for a precious instant.

"But there's still," he smiled, "the skull —"

                "The skull!" I cried.

"Your jester's skull, your Yorick's. What a symbol —
(Since matter's but the husk of wit — or spirit —
As this whole world's an empty house of God) —

Symbol for earth, the bottom of the ladder
Where Being's far away, and all's Becoming!
From there we follow gravely, step by step;
See king and queen, servant and councillor,
Each at his rung of emergence into Being
(Though I'll not try to mark their order now),
Until we reach the loftiest pinnacle.

"And who," he eyed me, "stands there of our company?"

I offered brightly: "The lord Hamlet, of course?"

I swear he was about to blurt agreement,
Indeed, had opened his mouth to utter a yes,
When "No!" he cried, as a sudden perverse gleam
Brightened his eye. "No, not your lord Hamlet,
But rather —" he paused for effect — "the ghost!"

                                        "The ghost!"
(Would this man make a parrot out of me?)

"The ghost of his father . . . Ah, but this warms the stomach!"
He filled our cups and took a hurried gulp,
Resuming before the liquid was fairly swallowed:
"First, consider the circularity —
Yet straight as a plumbline up from earth to heaven:
From skull (as I said before, the type of earth),
To ghost (the type of spirit) — a perfect round.
So, if you add the skull and ghost together,
You have a man, the normal, imperfect hodgepodge
Of Being and Becoming. Withdraw the skull
And you've got pure spirit; or take away the ghost,
And earth remains."

                    He wagged an earnest finger
Into my face. "But move to our second point:
A ghost, by its very quality or nature,
Since it is least material of things,
Is fittest to stand on the topmost rung of our ladder.
Which brings us a third point, that a ghost's the limit

Toward which Hamlet, granted, like other men,
But more so as the central antagonist
Of this significant, tragical history,
Moves as toward a goal on his upward struggle
Toward reality and realization.
Ho! so we reach another, and neater, circle:
From ghost to ghost — the ghost who triggered the history
(The old Hamlet's), to that more important spectre
(Our friend's), who thus attains the full fruition
Referred to in his crucial words on Being.
The ghost of the father to the ghost of the son!
To — to — eureka!"

        A look of incredulity
Agitated his features. He rammed the quill-point
Into the bottle, and scraped a sputtering sentence
Across the page, meanwhile crying, "Ha!
But my good friend, this shadows the Holy Trini —
Wheel within wheel and orbit beyond orbit!"

As I looked at him, I frankly thought I saw
A cuttlefish waving a thousand arms.
How should I grasp it before it drained my blood?

But a welcome voice: "Your carriage waits, my lord!"

He wrung my hand: "You'll answer when I write,
As further questions arise? Thanks . . . thanks . . . thanks . . .
                        thanks . . ."

THEODORE ROETHKE

On the Road to Woodlawn

I miss the polished brass, the powerful black horses,
The drivers creaking the seats of the baroque hearses,
The high-piled floral offerings with sentimental verses,
The carriages reeking with varnish and stale perfume.

I miss the pallbearers momentously taking their places,
The undertaker's obsequious grimaces,
The craned necks, the mourners' anonymous faces,
— And the eyes, still vivid, looking up from a sunken room.

Root Cellar

Nothing would sleep in that cellar, dank as a ditch,
Bulbs broke out of boxes hunting for chinks in the dark,
Shoots dangled and drooped,
Lolling obscenely from mildewed crates,
Hung down long yellow evil necks, like tropical snakes.
And what a congress of stinks! —
Roots ripe as old bait,
Pulpy stems, rank, silo-rich,
Leaf-mould, manure, lime, piled against slippery planks.
Nothing would give up life:
Even the dirt kept breathing a small breath.

Moss-Gathering

To loosen with all ten fingers held wide and limber
And lift up a patch, dark-green, the kind for lining cemetery baskets,
Thick and cushiony, like an old-fashioned door-mat,

The crumbling small hollow sticks on the underside mixed with
    roots,
And wintergreen berries and leaves still stuck to the top, —
That was moss-gathering.
But something always went out of me when I dug loose those
    carpets
Of green, or plunged to my elbows in the spongy yellowish moss
    of the marshes:
And afterwards I always felt mean, jogging back over the logging
    road,
As if I had broken the natural order of things in that swampland;
Disturbed some rhythm, old and of vast importance,
By pulling off flesh from the living planet;
As if I had committed, against the whole scheme of life, a
    desecration.

Dolor

I have known the inexorable sadness of pencils,
Neat in their boxes, dolor of pad and paper-weight,
All the misery of manila folders and mucilage,
Desolation in immaculate public places,
Lonely reception room, lavatory, switchboard,
The unalterable pathos of basin and pitcher,
Ritual of multigraph, paper-clip, comma,
Endless duplication of lives and objects.
And I have seen dust from the walls of institutions,
Finer than flour, alive, more dangerous than silica,
Sift, almost invisible, through long afternoons of tedium,
Dropping a fine film on nails and delicate eyebrows,
Glazing the pale hair, the duplicate gray standard faces.

Give Way, Ye Gates

1

Believe me, knot of gristle, I bleed like a tree;
I dream of nothing but boards;
I could love a duck.

Such music in a skin!
A bird sings in the bush of your bones.
Tufty, the water's loose.
Bring me a finger. This dirt's lonesome for grass.
Are the rats dancing? The cats are.
And you, cat after great milk and vasty fishes,
A moon loosened from a stag's eye,
Twiced me nicely, —
In the green of my sleep,
In the green.

2

Mother of blue and the many changes of hay,
This tail hates a flat path.
I've let my nose out;
I could melt down a stone, —
How is it with the long birds?
May I look too, loved eye?
It's a wink beyond the world.
In the slow rain, who's afraid?
We're king and queen of the right ground.
I'll risk the winter for you.

You tree beginning to know,
You whisper of kidneys,
We'll swinge the instant! —
With jots and jogs and cinders on the floor:
The sea will be there, the great squashy shadows,
Biting themselves perhaps;
The shrillest frogs;
And the ghost of some great howl

Dead in a wall.
In the high-noon of thighs,
In the springtime of stones,
We'll stretch with the great stems.
We'll be at the business of what might be
Looking toward what we are.

3

You child with a beast's heart,
Make me a bird or a bear!
I've played with the fishes
Among the unwrinkling ferns
In the wake of a ship of wind;
But now the instant ages,
And my thought hunts another body.
I'm sad with the little owls.

4

Touch and arouse. Suck and sob. Curse and mourn.
It's a cold scrape in a low place.
The dead crow dries on a pole.
Shapes in the shade
Watch.

The mouth asks. The hand takes.
These wings are from the wrong nest.
Who stands in a hole
Never spills.

I hear the clap of an old wind.
The cold knows when to come.
What beats in me
I still bear.

The deep stream remembers:
Once I was a pond.
What slides away
Provides.

The Lost Son

1 THE FLIGHT

At Woodlawn I heard the dead cry:
I was lulled by the slamming of iron,
A slow drip over stones,
Toads brooding in wells.
All the leaves stuck out their tongues;
I shook the softening chalk of my bones,
Saying,
Snail, snail, glister me forward,
Bird, soft-sigh me home.
Worm, be with me.
This is my hard time.

Fished in an old wound,
The soft pond of repose;
Nothing nibbled my line,
Not even the minnows came.

Sat in an empty house
Watching shadows crawl,
Scratching.
There was one fly.

Voice, come out of the silence.
Say something.
Appear in the form of a spider
Or a moth beating the curtain.

Tell me:
Which is the way I take;
Out of what door do I go,
Where and to whom?

> Dark hollows said, lee to the wind,
> The moon said, back of an eel,
> The salt said, look by the sea,
> Your tears are not enough praise,

You will find no comfort here,
In the kingdom of bang and blab.

Running lightly over spongy ground,
Past the pasture of flat stones,
The three elms,
The sheep strewn on a field,
Over a rickety bridge
Toward the quick-water, wrinkling and rippling.

Hunting along the river,
Down among the rubbish, the bug-riddled foliage,
By the muddy pond-edge, by the bog-holes,
By the shrunken lake, hunting, in the heat of summer.

The shape of a rat?
    It's bigger than that.
    It's less than a leg
    And more than a nose,
    Just under the water
    It usually goes.

Is it soft like a mouse?
Can it wrinkle its nose?
Could it come in the house
On the tips of its toes?

    Take the skin of a cat
    And the back of an eel,
    Then roll them in grease, —
    That's the way it would feel.

    It's sleek as an otter
    With wide webby toes
    Just under the water
    It usually goes.

2   THE PIT

Where do the roots go?
    Look down under the leaves.

Who put the moss there?
   These stones have been here too long.
Who stunned the dirt into noise?
   Ask the mole, he knows.
I feel the slime of a wet nest.
   Beware Mother Mildew.
Nibble again, fish nerves.

3   THE GIBBER

At the wood's mouth,
By the cave's door,
I listened to something
I had heard before.

Dogs of the groin
Barked and howled,
The sun was against me,
The moon would not have me.

The weeds whined,
The snakes cried,
The cows and briars
Said to me: Die.

What a small song. What slow clouds. What dark water.
Hath the rain a father? All the caves are ice. Only the snow's here.
I'm cold. I'm cold all over. Rub me in father and mother.
Fear was my father, Father Fear.
His look drained the stones.

     What gliding shape
     Beckoning through halls,
     Stood poised on the stair,
     Fell dreamily down?

     From the mouths of jugs
     Perched on many shelves,
     I saw substance flowing
     That cold morning.

Like a slither of eels
That watery cheek
As my own tongue kissed
My lips awake.

Is this the storm's heart? The ground is unstilling itself.
My veins are running nowhere. Do the bones cast out their fire?
Is the seed leaving the old bed? These buds are live as birds.
Where, where are the tears of the world?
Let the kisses resound, flat like a butcher's palm;
Let the gestures freeze; our doom is already decided.
All the windows are burning! What's left of my life?
I want the old rage, the lash of primordial milk!
Good-by, good-by, old stones, the time-order is going,
I have married my hands to perpetual agitation,
I run, I run to the whistle of money.

Money money money
Water water water

How cool the grass is.
Has the bird left?
The stalk still sways.
Has the worm a shadow?
What do the clouds say?

These sweeps of light undo me.
Look, look, the ditch is running white!
I've more veins than a tree!
Kiss me, ashes, I'm falling through a dark swirl.

4   THE RETURN

The way to the boiler was dark,
Dark all the way,
Over slippery cinders
Through the long greenhouse.

The roses kept breathing in the dark.
They had many mouths to breathe with.

My knees made little winds underneath
Where the weeds slept.

There was always a single light
Swinging by the fire-pit,
Where the fireman pulled out roses,
The big roses, the big bloody clinkers.

> Once I stayed all night.
> The light in the morning came slowly over the white
> Snow.
> There were many kinds of cool
> Air.
> Then came steam.

> Pipe-knock.

Scurry of warm over small plants.
Ordnung! ordnung!
Papa is coming!

> A fine haze moved off the leaves;
> Frost melted on far panes;
> The rose, the chrysanthemum turned toward the light.
> Even the hushed forms, the bent yellowy weeds
> Moved in a slow up-sway.

5

It was beginning winter,
An in-between time,
The landscape still partly brown:
The bones of weeds kept swinging in the wind,
Above the blue snow.

It was beginning winter.
The light moved slowly over the frozen field,
Over the dry seed-crowns,
The beautiful surviving bones
Swinging in the wind.

Light traveled over the field;
Stayed.
The weeds stopped swinging.
The mind moved, not alone,
Through the clear air, in the silence.

    Was it light?
    Was it light within?
    Was it light within light?
    Stillness becoming alive,
    Yet still?

    A lively understandable spirit
    Once entertained you.
    It will come again.
    Be still.
    Wait.

Elegy for Jane

(My Student, Thrown by a Horse)

I remember the neckcurls, limp and damp as tendrils;
And her quick look, a sidelong pickerel smile;
And how, once startled into talk, the light syllables leaped for her,
And she balanced in the delight of her thought,
A wren, happy, tail into the wind,
Her song trembling the twigs and small branches.
The shade sang with her;
The leaves, their whispers turned to kissing;
And the mould sang in the bleached valleys under the rose.

Oh, when she was sad, she cast herself down into such a pure depth,
Even a father could not find her:
Scraping her cheek against straw;
Stirring the clearest water.

My sparrow, you are not here,
Waiting like a fern, making a spiny shadow.

The sides of wet stones cannot console me,
Nor the moss, wound with the last light.

If only I could nudge you from this sleep,
My maimed darling, my skittery pigeon.
Over this damp grave I speak the words of my love:
I, with no rights in this matter,
Neither father nor lover.

Four for Sir John Davies

I

THE DANCE

Is that dance slowing in the mind of man
That made him think the universe could hum?
The great wheel turns its axle when it can;
I need a place to sing, and dancing-room,
And I have made a promise to my ears
I'll sing and whistle romping with the bears.

For they are all my friends: I saw one slide
Down a steep hillside on a cake of ice, —
Or was that in a book? I think with pride:
A caged bear rarely does the same thing twice
In the same way: O watch his body sway! —
This animal remembering to be gay.

I tried to fling my shadow at the moon,
The while my blood leaped with a worldless song.
Though dancing needs a master, I had none
To teach my toes to listen to my tongue.
But what I learned there, dancing all alone,
Was not the joyless motion of a stone.

I take this cadence from a man named Yeats;
I take it, and I give it back again:

For other tunes and other wanton beats
Have tossed my heart and fiddled through my brain.
Yes, I was dancing-mad, and how
That came to be the bears and Yeats would know.

II

THE PARTNER

Between such animal and human heat
I find myself perplexed. What is desire? —
The impulse to make someone else complete?
That woman would set sodden straw on fire.
Was I the servant of a sovereign wish,
Or ladle rattling in an empty dish?

We played a measure with commingled feet:
The lively dead had taught us to be fond.
Who can embrace the body of his fate?
Light altered light along the living ground.
She kissed me close, and then did something else.
My marrow beat as wildly as my pulse.

I'd say it to my horse: we live beyond
Our outer skin. Who's whistling up my sleeve?
I see a heron prancing in his pond;
I know a dance the elephants believe.
The living all assemble! What's the cue? —
Do what the clumsy partner wants to do!

Things loll and loiter. Who condones the lost?
This joy outleaps the dog. Who cares? Who cares?
I gave her kisses back, and woke a ghost.
O what lewd music crept into our ears!
The body and the soul know how to play
In that dark world where gods have lost their way.

III

THE WRAITH

Incomprehensible gaiety and dread
Attended what we did. Behind, before,
Lay all the lonely pastures of the dead;
The spirit and the flesh cried out for more.
We two, together, on a darkening day
Tooks arms against our own obscurity.

Did each become the other in that play?
She laughed me out, and then she laughed me in;
In the deep middle of ourselves we lay;
When glory failed, we danced upon a pin.
The valley rocked beneath the granite hill;
Our souls looked forth, and the great day stood still.

There was a body, and it cast a spell, —
God pity those but wanton to the knees, —
The flesh can make the spirit visible;
We woke to find the moonlight on our toes.
In the rich weather of a dappled wood
We played with dark and light as children should.

What shape leaped forward at the sensual cry? —
Sea-beast or bird flung toward the ravaged shore?
Did space shake off an angel with a sigh?
We rose to meet the moon, and saw no more.
It was and was not she, a shape alone,
Impaled on light, and whirling slowly down.

IV

THE VIGIL

Dante attained the purgatorial hill,
Trembled at hidden virtue without flaw,
Shook with a mighty power beyond his will, —
Did Beatrice deny what Dante saw?

All lovers live by longing, and endure:
Summon a vision and declare it pure.

Though everything's astonishment at last,
Who leaps to heaven at a single bound?
The links were soft between us; still, we kissed;
We undid chaos to a curious sound:
The waves broke easy, cried to me in white;
Her look was morning in the dying light.

The visible obscures. But who knows when?
Things have their thought: they are the shards of me;
I thought that once, and thought comes round again;
Rapt, we leaned forth with what we could not see.
We danced to shining; mocked before the black
And shapeless night that made no answer back.

The world is for the living. Who are they?
We dared the dark to reach the white and warm.
She was the wind when wind was in my way;
Alive at noon, I perished in her form.
Who rise from flesh to spirit know the fall:
The word outleaps the world, and light is all.

The Waking

I wake to sleep, and take my waking slow.
I feel my fate in what I cannot fear.
I learn by going where I have to go.

We think by feeling. What is there to know?
I hear my being dance from ear to ear.
I wake to sleep, and take my waking slow.

Of those so close beside me, which are you?
God bless the Ground! I shall walk softly there,
And learn by going where I have to go.

Light takes the Tree; but who can tell us how?
The lowly worm climbs up a winding stair;
I wake to sleep, and take my waking slow.

Great Nature has another thing to do
To you and me; so take the lively air,
And, lovely, learn by going where to go.

This shaking keeps me steady. I should know.
What falls away is always. And is near.
I wake to sleep, and take my waking slow.
I learn by going where I have to go.

The Song

1

I met a ragged man;
He looked beyond me when
I tried to meet his eyes.
What have I done to you?
I cried, and backed away.
Dust in a corner stirred,
And the walls stretched wide.

2

I went running down a road,
In a country of bleak stone,
And shocks of ragged corn;
When I stayed for breath, I lay
With the saxifrage and fern
At the edge of a raw field.

I stared at a fissure of ground
Ringed round with crumbled clay:
The old house of a crab;
Stared, and began to sing.

3

I sang to whatever had been
Down in that watery hole:
I wooed with a low tune;
You could say I was mad.

And a wind woke in my hair,
And the sweat poured from my face,
When I heard, or thought I heard,
Another join my song
With the small voice of a child,
Close, and yet far away.

Mouth upon mouth, we sang,
My lips pressed upon stone.

Words for the Wind

I

Love, love, a lily's my care,
She's sweeter than a tree,
Loving, I use the air
Most lovingly: I breathe;
Mad in the wind I wear
Myself as I should be,
All's even with the odd,
My brother the vine is glad.

Are flower and seed the same?
What do the great dead say?
Sweet Phoebe, she's my theme:
She sways whenever I sway.
'O love me while I am,
You green thing in my way!'
I cried, and the birds came down
And made my song their own.

Motion can keep me still:
She kissed me out of thought
As a lovely substance will;
She wandered; I did not:
I stayed, and light fell
Across her pulsing throat;
I stared, and a garden stone
Slowly became the moon.

The shallow stream runs slack;
The wind creaks slowly by;
Out of a nestling's beak
Comes a tremulous cry
I cannot answer back;
A shape from deep in the eye, —
That woman I saw in a stone, —
Keeps pace when I walk alone.

II

The sun declares the earth;
The stones leap in the stream;
On a wide plain, beyond
The far stretch of a dream,
A field breaks like the sea;
The wind's white with her name,
And I walk with the wind.

The dove's my will today.
She sways, half in the sun:
Rose, easy on a stem,
One with the sighing vine,
One to be merry with,
And pleased to meet the moon.
She likes wherever I am.

Passion's enough to give
Shape to a random joy:
I cry delight: I know
The root, the core of a cry.

Swan-heart, arbutus-calm,
She moves when time is shy:
Love has a thing to do.

The loam gleams like wet coal;
The green, the springing green
Makes an intenser day
Under the rising moon;
I smile, no mineral man;
I bear, but not alone,
The burden of this joy.

III

Under a southern wind,
The birds and fishes move
North, in a single stream;
The sharp stars swing around;
I get a step beyond
The wind, and there I am;
I'm odd and full of love.

Wisdom, where is it found? —
Those who embrace, believe.
Whatever was, still is,
Says a song tied to a tree.
Below, on the ferny ground,
In rivery air, at ease,
I walk with my true love.

What time's my heart? I care.
I cherish what I have
Had of the temporal:
I am no longer young
But the winds and waters are;
What falls away will fall;
All things bring me to love.

IV

The breath of a long root,
The shy perimeter
Of the unfolding rose,
The green, the altered leaf,
The oyster's weeping foot,
And the incipient star, —
Are part of what she is.
She wakes the ends of life.

Being myself, I sing
The soul's immediate joy.
Light, light, where's my repose?
A wind wreathes round a tree.
A thing is done: a thing
Body and spirit know
When I do what she does:
Creaturely creature, she! —

I kiss her moving mouth,
Her swart hilarious skin;
She breaks my breath in half;
She frolicks like a beast;
And I dance round and round,
A fond and foolish man,
And see and suffer myself
In another being, at last.

Love's Progress

1

The possibles we dare!
O rare propinquity! —
I have considered and found
A mouth I cannot leave.
The great gods arch my bones.

2

The long veins of the vine
Journey around a tree;
Light strides the rose;
A woman's naked in water,
And I know where she is.

3

True, she can think a bird
Until it broods in her eyes.
Love me, my violence,
Light of my spirit, light
Beyond the look of love.

4

It's midnight on the mouse,
The rabbit, and the wren;
A log sings in its flame.
Father, I'm far from home,
And I have gone nowhere.

5

The close dark hugs me hard,
And all the birds are stone.
I fear for my own joy;
I fear myself in the field,
For I would drown in fire.

MURIEL RUKEYSER

Ajanta

I   THE JOURNEY

Came in my full youth to the midnight cave
Nerves ringing; and this thing I did alone.
Wanting my fulness and not a field of war,
For the world considered annihilation, a star
Called Wormwood rose and flickered, shattering
Bent light over the dead boiling up in the ground,
The biting yellow of their corrupted lives
Streaming to war, denying all our words.
Nothing was left among the tainted weather
But world-walking and shadowless Ajanta.
Hallucination and the metal laugh
In clouds, and the mountain-spectre riding storm.
Nothing was certain but a moment of peace,
A hollow behind the unbreakable waterfall.
All the way to the cave, the teeming forms of death,
And death, the price of the body, cheap as air.
I blessed my heart on the expiation journey
For it had never been unable to suffer   :
When I met the man whose face looked like the future,
When I met the whore with the dying red hair,
The child myself who is my murderer.
So came I between heaven and my grave
Past the serene smile of the voyeur, to
This cave where the myth enters the heart again.

II   THE CAVE

Space to the mind, the painted cave of dream.
This is not a womb, nothing but good emerges:
This is a stage, neither unreal nor real,
Where the walls are the world, the rocks and palaces
Stand on a borderland of blossoming ground.
If you stretch your hand, you touch the slope of the world

Reaching in interlaced gods, animals, and men.
There is no background. The figures hold their peace
In a web of movement. There is no frustration,
Every gesture is taken, everything yields connections.
The heavy sensual shoulders, the thighs, the blood-born flesh
And earth turning into color, rocks into their crystals,
Water to sound, fire to form; life flickers
Uncounted into the supple arms of love.
The space of these walls is the body's living space;
Tear open your ribs and breathe the color of time
Where nothing leads away, the world comes forward
In flaming sequences. Pillars and prisms. Riders
And horses and the figures of consciousness,
Red cow grows long, goes running through the world.
Flung into movement in carnal purity,
These bodies are sealed — warm lip and crystal hand
In a jungle of light. Color-sheeted, seductive
Foreboding eyelid lowered on the long eye,
Fluid and vulnerable. The spaces of the body
Are suddenly limitless, and riding flesh
Shapes constellations over the golden breast,
Confusion of scents and illuminated touch —
Monster touch, the throat printed with brightness,
Wide outlined gesture where the bodies ride.
Bells, and the spirit flashing. The religious bells,
Bronze under the sunlight like breasts ringing,
Bronze in the closed air, the memory of walls,
Great sensual shoulders in the web of time.

III LES TENDRESSES BESTIALES

A procession of caresses alters the ancient sky
Until new constellations are the body shining:
There's the Hand to steer by, there the horizon Breast,
And the Great Stars kindling the fluid hill.
All the rooms open into magical boxes,
Nothing is tilted, everything flickers
Sexual and exquisite.
The panther with its throat along my arm
Turns black and flows away.

Deep in all streets passes a faceless whore
And the checkered men are whispering one word.
The face I know becomes the night-black rose.
The sharp face is now an electric fan
And says one word to me.
The dice and the alcohol and the destruction
Have drunk themselves and cast.
Broken bottle of loss, and the glass
Turned bloody into the face.
Now the scene comes forward, very clear.
Dream-singing, airborne, surrenders the recalled,
The gesture arrives riding over the breast,
Singing, singing, tender atrocity,
The silver derelict wearing fur and claws.
O love, I stood under the apple branch,
I saw the whipped bay and the small dark islands,
And night sailing the river and the foghorn's word,
My life said to you   :   I want to love you well.
The wheel goes back and I shall live again,
But the wave turns, my birth arrives and spills
Over my breast the world bearing my grave.
And your eyes open in earth. You touched my life.
My life reaches the skin, moves under your smile,
And your throat and your shoulders and your face and your **thighs**
Flash.

I am haunted by interrupted acts,
Introspective as a leper, enchanted
By a repulsive clew,
A gross and fugitive movement of the limbs.
Is this the love that shook the lights to flame?
Sheeted avenues thrash in the wind,
Torn streets, the savage parks.
I am plunged deep. Must find the midnight cave.

IV   BLACK BLOOD

A habit leading to murder, smoky laughter
Hated at first, but necessary later.
Alteration of motives. To stamp in terror

Around the deserted harbor, down the hill
Until the woman laced into a harp
Screams and screams and the great clock strikes,
Swinging its giant figures past the face.
The Floating Man rides on the ragged sunset
Asking and asking. Do not say, Which loved?
Which was beloved? Only, Who most enjoyed?
Armored ghost of rage, screaming and powerless.
Only find me and touch my blood again.
Find me. A girl runs down the street
Singing   Take me,   yelling   Take me   Take
Hang me from the clapper of a bell
And you as hangman ring it sweet tonight,
For nothing clean in me is more than cloud
Unless you call it.   —   As I ran I heard
A black voice beating among all that blood:
"Try to live as if there were a God."

V   THE BROKEN WORLD

Came to Ajanta cave, the painted space of the breast,
The real world where everything is complete,
There are no shadows, the forms of incompleteness.
The great clack blows in the light, rider and horse arrive,
The shoulders turn and every gift is made.
No shadows fall. There is no source of distortion.
In our world, a tree casts the shadow of a woman,
A man the shadow of a phallus, a hand raised
The shadow of the whip.
Here everything is itself,
Here all may stand
On summer earth.
Brightness has overtaken every light,
And every myth netted itself in flesh.
New origins, and peace given entire
And the spirit alive.
In the shadowless cave
The naked arm is raised.

Animals arrive,
Interlaced, and gods
Interlaced, and men
Flame-woven.
I stand and am complete.
Crawls from the door,
Black at my two feet
The shadow of the world.

World, not yet one,
Enters the heart again.
The naked world, and the old noise of tears,
The fear, the expiation and the love,
A world of the shadowed and alone.

The journey, and the struggles of the moon.

Beast in View

Configurations of time and singing
    Bring me to a dark harbor where
    The chase is drawn to a beginning.
    And all the myths are gathered there.

I know the trees as fountains and the stars'
    Far fires fountains and your love
    A vivid fountain, and the bars
    Broken about me let me move

Among the fountains. At last seeing
    I came here by obscure preparing,
    In vigils and encounters being
    Both running hunter and fierce prey waring.

I hunted and became the followed,
    Through many lives fleeing the last me,

167

And changing fought down a far road
Through time to myself as I will be.

Chaos prepared me, and I find the track,
    Through life and darkness seek my myth —
    Move toward it, hunting grow more like,
    Draw near, and know it through our path.
    Know only that we run one path.

Boy with His Hair Cut Short

Sunday shuts down on a twentieth-century evening.
The El passes. Twilight and bulb define
the brown room, the overstuffed plum sofa,
the boy, and the girl's thin hands above his head.
A neighbor radio sings stocks, news, serenade.

He sits at the table, head down, the young clear neck exposed,
watching the drugstore sign from the tail of his eyes;
tattoo, neon, until the eye blears, while his
solicitous tall sister, simple in blue, bending
behind him, cuts his hair with her cheap shears.

The arrow's electric red always reaches its mark,
successful neon! He coughs, impressed by that precision.
His child's forehead, forever protected by his cap,
is bleached against the lamplight as he turns head
and steadies to let the snippets drop.

Erasing the failure of weeks with level fingers,
she sleeks the fine hair, combing :   "You'll look fine tomorrow!
You'll surely find something, they can't keep turning you down;
the finest gentleman's not so trim as you!" Smiling, he raises
the adolescent forehead wrinkling ironic now.

He sees his decent suit laid out, new-pressed,
his carfare on the shelf. He lets his head fall, meeting

. her earnest hopeless look, seeing the sharp blades splitting,
the darkened room, the impersonal sign, her motion,
the blue vein, bright on her temple, pitifully beating.

Chapultepec Park

The calling and the melody all night long
And then in the first stillness, morning
Leaning over the dark, over the night-park
Combing her blue hair.
After the guitars, after the tide of bells,
Surge, calls, and furious song,
Very softly the trees emerge,
A tree of light beside a tree of darkness.
And in the silent park
A girl opens her eyes and combs her hair.
Freshness of blue wavers among the lakes;
Two people wake, look at the calm forest,
Turn an iron wheelbarrow on its back
And, fanning a little fire under it,
Cook their tortillas.
Morning leans down; morning lifts out of the stone
The angry archaic statue of a god
Watching from live rock.
The Palace whitens, and all the standing fountains.
Snow is shining on the far volcanoes,
We walk smiling down the Philosopher's Footpath.
A young horse runs into the sunlight.

From the Duck-Pond to the Carousel

Playing a phonograph record of a windy morning
you gay   you imitation summer
                        let's see you slice up the Park

in green from the lake drawn bright in silver salt
while the little girl playing (in iodine and pink   )
tosses her crumbs and they all rise to catch
lifting up their white and saying Quack.

O you pastoral lighting what are you getting away with?
Wound-up lovers   fidgeting balloons   and a popsicle man
running up the road on the first day of spring.
And the baby carriages whose nurses with flat heels
(for sufferance is the badge of all their tribe   )
mark turning sunlight on far avenues
etch beacons on the grass.   You strenuous baby
rushing up to the wooden horses
with their stiff necks, their eyes,
and all their music!

Fountains!   sheepfolds!   merry-go-round!
The seal that barking slips Pacifics dark-
diving into his well until up!   with a fish!
The tiglon resembling his Siberian sire,
ice-cream and terraces and twelve o'clock.

O mister with the attractive moustache,
        How does it happen to be you?
Mademoiselle   in   cinnamon   zoo,
            Hello,   hello.

Then I Saw What the Calling Was

All the voices of the wood called "Muriel!"
But it was soon solved;   it was nothing, it was not for me.
The words were a little like Mortal and More and Endure
and a word like Real, a sound like Health or Hell.
Then I saw what the calling was   :   it was the road I travelled,
                                                            the clear
time and these colors of orchards, gold behind gold and the full
shadow behind each tree and behind each slope.   Not to me

170

the calling, but to anyone, and at last I saw : where
the road lay through sunlight and many voices and the marvel
orchard, not for me, not for me, not for me.
I came into my clear being; uncalled, alive, and sure.
Nothing was speaking to me, but I offered and all was well.

And then I arrived at the powerful green hill.

Nuns in the Wind

As I came out of the New York Public Library
you said your influence on my style would be noticed
and from now on there would be happy poems.
                    It was at that moment
the street was assaulted by a covey of nuns
going directly toward the physics textbooks.
Tragic fiascos shadowed that whole spring.
The children sang streetfuls, and I thought:
O to be the King in the carol
kissed and at peace; but recalling Costa Brava
the little blossoms in the mimosa tree
and later, the orange cliff, after they sent me out,
I knew there was no peace.
                    You smiled, saying : Take it easy.

That was the year of the five-day fall of cities.
        First day, no writers. Second, no telephones. Third,
        no venereal diseases. Fourth, no income tax. And on
        the fifth, at noon.
The nuns blocked the intersections, reading.
I used to go walking in the triangle of park,
seeing that locked face, the coarse enemy skin,
the eyes with all the virtues of a good child,
but no child was there, even when I thought, Child!
the 4 a.m. cop could never understand.
You said, not smiling, You are the future for me,
but you were the present and immediate moment

and I am empty-armed without, until to me is given
two lights to carry : my life and the light of my death.

If the wind would rise, those black throbbing umbrellas
fly downstreet, the flapping robes unfolding,
my dream would be over, poisons cannot linger
when the wind rises. . . .

All that year, the classical declaration of war was lacking.
There was a lot of lechery and disorder.
And I am queen on that island.

Well, I said suddenly in the tall and abstract room,
time to wake up.
Now make believe you can help yourself alone.
And there it was, the busy crosstown noontime
crossing, peopled with nuns.
                    Now, bragging now,
the flatfoot slambang victory,
                       thanks to a trick of wind
will you see faces blow, and though their bodies
by God's grace will never blow,
cities shake in the wind, the year's over,
calendars tear, and their clothes blow. O yes!

FROM *Ninth Elegy:* The Antagonists

Pieces of animals, pieces of all my friends
prepare assassinations while I sleep.
They shape my being, a gallery of lives
fighting within me, and all unreconciled.
Before them move my waking dreams, and ways
of the spirit, and simple action. Among these
I can be well and holy. Torn by them I am wild,
smile and revenge myself upon my friends
and find myself among my enemies.
But all these forms of incompleteness pass

out of their broken power to a place
where dream and dream meet and resolve in grace.

The closing of this conflict is the end'
of the initiation. I have known the cliff
and known the cliff-dream of the faces drowned.
Stood in the high sun, a dark girl looking down,
seeing the colors of water swaying beneath me, dense
in the flood-summer, various as my love
and like my hope enchanted. Drawn to blue
chance and horizons, and back as sea-grasses move
drawn landward slowly by incoming tides —
and then the final cancelling and choice,
not tilted as flowers under wind, but deep
blessing of root and heart, underwater swung,
wrenched, swayed, and given fully to the sea.
Heaven not of rest, but of intensity.

The forms of incompleteness in our land
pass from the eastern and western mountains where
the seas meet the dark islands, where the light
glitters white series on the snowlands, pours its wine
of lenient evening to the center. Green
on shadows of Indiana, level yellow miles . . .

The prairie emblems and the slopes of the sky
and desert stars enlarging in the frost
redeem us like our love and will not die.
All origins are here, and in this range
the changing spirit can make itself again,
continually love, continually change.

> Out of the myth the mother leaned;
> From out the mother shines the child;
> Man rises, in the mass contained;
> And from this growth creation grows.
> The fire through all the spiral flows:
> Create the creative, many-born!
> And use your love, unreconciled!

In wheels, in whirlwind, in a storm of power
alive again and over every land
the thunderbird with lightnings at his wrists.
Eclipses uncloud and show us miracle,
gleaming, our ancestors, all antagonists:
Slave and Conquistador, dead hand-to-hand,
scented fastidious Tory with his whore,
distinguished rebel and woman at the plow.
The fiery embryo umbilical
always to failure, and form developing
American out of conflict.

     Fierce dissenting ghosts,
the second Adam's fever and eagle voice
and Jackson's muscular and democratic sense.
Sprung in one birth John Brown, a mad old man
whose blood in a single broken gesture freed
many beliefs, and Lincoln's agony
condemning and confirming. O, they cry,
the oppositions cry, O fight for me!
Fight, you are bound to freedom, and be free!
When Hawthorne saw the fabulous gift, he tore
flesh from his guilt, and found more guilt; the bells
rang barter of the self, but Melville drowned.
The troubled phantoms bring to our terrible
chaos the order of a meeting-place
where the exchange is made, the agonies
lie down at last together face to face.

In the black night of blood, the forms begin
to glitter alive, fathers of constellations,
the shining and the music moving on.
We are bound by the deepest feuds to unity.
To make the connections and be born again,
create the creative, that will love the world. . . .

. . . That is what they say, who were broken off from love:
However long we were loved, it was not long enough.

We were afraid of the broad big policeman,
of lions and tigers, the dark hall and the moon.

After our father went, nothing was ever the same,
when mother did not come back, we made up a war-game.

*My cat was sitting in the doorway when the planes
went over, and my cat saw mother cry;
furry tears, fire fell, wall went down;
did my cat see mother die?*

Mother is gone away, my cat sits here coughing.
I cough and sit. I am nobody's nothing.

However long they loved us, it was not long enough.
For we have to be strong, to know what they did, and then
our people are saved in time, our houses built again.

You will not know, you have a sister and brother;
My doll is not my child, my doll is my mother.

However strong we are, it is not strong enough.
I want to grow up. To come back to love. . . .

A Charm for Cantinflas

After the lights and after the rumba and after the bourbon
      and after the beer
and after the drums and after the samba and after the
      ice cream and not long after
failure, loss, despair, and loss and despair

There was the laughter and there was Cantinflas at last
                    and his polka
doing the bumps with a hot guitar
turning unique. Slow.   Slow.   Slow. Deprecating
                shoulder up.
                Hand up.
                All the fingers tall.
Panache and rags and triumph and smile —
beggar of light in ridiculous sunlight.

All things human clumsy and fair
as graceful as loving as stupid as true.

And on this floor
the dancers, in this square the little trees,
and on this stage always the clown of our living
gives us our sunlight and our incantation
as sun does, laughing, shining, reciting dawn, noon, and down,
making all delight and healing all ills
like faraway words on jars, the labels in Protopapas' window:
marshmallow, myrtle, peppermint, pumpkin, sesame, sesame, squills.

Foghorn in Horror

I know that behind these walls is the city, over these rooftops is the
                                        sun.
But I see black clothes only and white clothes with the fog running in
and all their shadows.
Every minute the sound of the harbor
intruding on horror with a bellow of horror:
blu-a!   blu-aa!   Ao. . . .

I try to write to you, but here too I meet failure.
It has a face like mine.
Silence and in me and over the water
only the bellowing,
Niobe howling for her life and her children.

Did you think this sorrow of women was a graceful thing?
Horrible Niobe down on her knees:
Blu-a!   Blu-aa!   Ao. . . .

Thirty years, and my full strength, and all I touch has failed.
I sit and see
the black clothes on the line are beautiful, the sky drifting away.
The white clothes of the fog beyond me, beautiful, and the shadows.
Blu-aa!   Blu-aa!   AO.

The Return

An Idea ran around the world
screaming with the pain of the mind
until it met a child
who stopped it with a word.

The Idea leaned over those newborn eyes
and dreamed of the nature of things:
the nature of memory and the nature of love;
and forgave itself and all men.

Quieted in a sea of sleeping
the Idea began its long return —
renewed by the child's sea-colored eyes
remembered the flesh, smiled and said:

I see birds, spring and the birthplace
unknown by the stable stone.
I know light and I know motion
and I remember I am not alone.

The Idea voyaged nearer my breathing, saying
Come balance come
into the love of these faces and forces
find us our equilibrium.

And the child stirred, asking his question.

The Idea grew more fleshly and spoke:
Beaten down I was
Down I knew very long
Newborn I begin.

And the child went on asking his questions.

The Idea journeying into my body
returned, and I knew the nature of One,
and could forget One, and turn to the child,
and whole could turn to the world again.

Until the pain turns into answers
And all the masters become askers
And all the victims again doers
And all the sources break in light.

The child goes alive, asking his questions.

A Birth

Lately having escaped three-kinded death
Not by evasion but by coming through
I celebrate what may be true beginning.
But new begun am most without resource
Stupid and stopped. How do the newborn grow?
I am of them. Freshness has taken our hearts;
Pain strips us to the source, infants of further life
Waiting for childhood as we wait for form.

So came I into the world of all the living,
The maimed triumphant middle of my way
Where there is giving needing no forgetting.
Saw now the present that is here to say:
Nothing I wrote is what I must see written,

Nothing I did is what I now need done. —
The smile of darkness on my song and my son.

Lately emerged I have seen unfounded houses,
Have seen spirits now opened, surrounded as by sun,
And have, among limitless consensual faces
Watched all things change, an unbuilt house inherit
Materials of desire, that stone and wood and air.
Lit by a birth, I defend dark beginnings,
Waste that is never waste, most-human giving,
Declared and clear as the mortal body of grace.
Beginnings of truth-in-life, the rooms of wilderness
Where truth feeds and the ramifying heart,
Even mine, praising even the past in its pieces,
My tearflesh beckoner who brought me to this place.

Children, The Sandbar, That Summer

Sunlight the tall women may never have seen.
Men, perhaps, going headfirst into the breakers,
but certainly the children at the sandbar.
Shallow glints in the wave suspended
we knew at the breaker line, running that shore
at low tide, when it was safe. The grasses whipped
and nothing was what they said: not safety, nor the sea.
And the sand was not what they said, but various,
lion-grained, beard-gold, grey. And blue. And green.
And each grain casting its shadow down before
childhood in tide-pools where all things are food.
Behind us the shores emerged and fed on tide.
We fed on summer, the round flowers in our hands
from the snowball bush entered us, and prisoner wings,
and shells in spirals, all food.

              All keys to unlock
some world, glinting as strong as noon on the sandbar,
where men and women give each other children.

George Robinson: Blues

Gauley Bridge is a good town for Negroes, they let us stand around,
                                        they let us stand

around on the sidewalks if we're black or brown.
Vanetta's over the trestle, and that's our town.

The hill makes breathing slow, slow breathing after you row the
                                        river,
and the graveyard's on the hill, cold in the springtime blow,
the graveyard's up on high, and the town is down below.

Did you ever bury thirty-five men in a place in back of your house,
thirty-five tunnel workers the doctors didn't attend,
died in the tunnel camps, under rocks, everywhere, world without
                                        end.

When a man said I feel poorly, for any reason, any weakness or such,
letting up when he couldn't keep going barely,
the Cap and company come and run him off the job surely.

I've put them
DOWN from the tunnel camps
to the graveyard on the hill,
tin-cans all about — it fixed them! —
TUNNELITIS
hold themselves up
at the side of a tree,
I can go right now
to that cemetery.

When the blast went off the boss would call out, Come, let's go back,
when that heavy loaded blast went white, Come, let's go back,
telling us hurry, hurry, into the falling rocks and muck.

The water they would bring had dust in it, our drinking water,
the camps and their groves were colored with the dust,
we cleaned our clothes in the groves, but we always had the dust.

Looked like somebody sprinkled flour all over the parks and groves,
it stayed and the rain couldn't wash it away and it twinkled
that white dust really looked pretty down around our ankles.

As dark as I am, when I came out at morning after the tunnel at
night,
with a white man, nobody could have told which man was white.
The dust had covered us both, and the dust was white.

FROM *The Cornfield*

. . . For those given to voyages : these roads
discover gullies, invade, Where does it go now?
Now turn upstream twenty-five yards. Now road again.
Ask the man on the road. Saying, That cornfield?
Over the second hill, through the gate,
watch for the dogs. Buried, five at a time,
pine boxes, Rinehart & Dennis paid him $55
a head for burying these men in plain pine boxes.
His mother is suing him : misuse of land.
George Robinson : I knew a man
who died at four in the morning at the camp.
At seven his wife took clothes to dress her dead
husband, and at the undertaker's
they told her the husband was already buried.
— Tell me this, the men with whom you are acquainted,
the men who have this disease
have been told that sooner or later they are going to die?
— Yes, sir.
— How does that seem to affect the majority of the people?
— It don't work on anything but their wind.
— Do they seem to be living in fear
or do they wish to die?
— They are getting to breathe a little faster.

For those given to keeping their own garden:
Here is the cornfield, white and wired by thorns,

old cornstalks, snow, the planted home.
Stands bare against a line of farther field,
unmarked except for wood stakes, charred at tip,
few scratched and named (pencil or nail).
Washed-off. Under the mounds,
all the anonymous.
Abel America, calling from under the corn,
Earth, uncover my blood!
Did the undertaker know the man was married?
Uncover.
Do they seem to fear death?
Contemplate.
Does Mellon's ghost walk, povertied at last,
walking in furrows of corn, still sowing,
do apparitions come?
Voyage.
Think of your gardens. But here is corn to keep.
Marked pointed sticks to name the crop beneath.
Sowing is over, harvest is coming ripe.

— No, sir; they want to go on.
They want to live as long as they can.

JAMES SCHEVILL

The Will of Writing

The will of writing
Is to make the pen
Sound a word,
The sound neither hard nor soft
But of that balance
Which gives forth
Something surrounded
Shining and stopped.

Perhaps a Prayer

I would say a few words
Though they stumble.
Perhaps the man on the frozen corner
Will hear me and the scars
At the peak of my night vanish
And my hate change to praise.

I live in a time of unknown masses.
Over the notched fields of war
I hear only pins of voices,
Huge but not personal hate,
Unknown soldiers, idols that move
Like acolytes or an abstract sentence.

Call the kings of today administrative
Bumble-bee men with red tape
Who beat the language to its knees.
There on the impeccable standard of living

Sits a title, the anonymous name.
Our problem is one of identity.

Have I no name?
I would have this war become
Personal, she does not know me.
The man on the frozen corner
Is silent as a shelf, as a closet.
Nothing belongs to my eye.

Lament for a Man Who Loved God

I

Cobbled with stars
The night hung in its masquerade,
An awning of hallucination
Over the stone sleepers of earth,
Basalt and lignite and amethyst.
Grey moon and Milky Way were
Acids of foam, Jupiter
Wild in his zenith and Venus
Exalted her last venom of love
Over the broken body.
The man who loved God is dead,
Faith coils in a zoo of cages
And the angel is early departed
With his deadlight dream.
Sound bell and crack the lost quiet of death
For the love of God is more lonely than time.

II

From the fourteenth story
In the white silence of the clinic
He stared at the city lights,
The man who loved God
Searching for the lost vocabulary
In neon nests of banging sound.

The words answered in coarse syllables:
Dream and suffering, in the tale of time
The tree turns to coal and the milk ferments,
The tomcat kills his children and
Despair hides in the hunchbacked heart.
"Forgive me this minute of expectation" —
The prayer, with evil echo, hung in the room
And he plunged into the wizard of silence
Whose embrace is the silent sea,
The marigold and aster and demonic rose
With its thorns for the howling greed.

III

Love God in loneliness,
Beyond the lightspringing grass
Green-pointed over the suicide's body,
The fire-lilies shooting in their flame-forms
Past the humming-bird's trembling hover,
Beyond the star birds who arch
Over the foaming veins of the storm's fury
And the frontiers fanciful in peace,
Furious in war, love God in loneliness.
Seek Him beyond the night-shaken forms of art
Whose humble ends are born without humility,
Search for His unseen face beyond the hour of hate
And the myth which is the minute of expectation
That plunges always into the perilous past —
Glory is a knife drawn from the second's silence
For the love of God is more lonely than time.

Confidential Data on the Loyalty Investigation
of Herbert Ashenfoot

Until the birth of my thirtieth birthday
I sailed the wide harbors of illusion,
Wind and war of parents over my silent head

While the curse of identity tinkled
At my window like the Good Humor salesman.
Around me the black armies like bats
Lay darkly in their caves of caution
And for security I joined the Civil Service.
Rating P-3, almost a pristine pursuit plane,
I roared from basket in to basket out
And all my days were clocked and carefree.
At the dawn of thirty my reform began.
My loyalty was cleaned and prodded
And my dreams divorced from all emergencies.
Propped at my desk by aspirin I typed
Like a hermit crab in the tears of my time.

D-9

Because the Old French *chatepelose* meant hairy cat,
Caterpillar means the wormlike larva of a butterfly —

Because engineers too swing from metaphors
A caterpillar tractor moves on an endless belt —

Because of a design to tear down mountains in
Ten dervish days instead of ten years,

The latest caterpillar, the D-9, runs through tests,
Piles up ninety tons of soil in five minutes,

Slaps slantwise at an elm and treads
Lightly on eight unbroken watches.

The Death of a Dove

On the edge of a lawn where weeds
    poked through the green
A black cat with sulphur-yellow eyes
    caught a dove by the wing.

Claws raked the dove's breast
    white flesh was shredded bare
And still the dove cried and the cat
    was glad for the life of his prey.

A housewife in a Chinese dragon's coat
    rescued the dying dove and put it
In a washed-out garbage can for care.
    Enter a daughter with hoyden head
And the worry and wonder of death began;
    they fastened a sheet of glass
Over the garbage can, a two-way look
    outside at sky, inside at death.

Next morning in slotting sun through fog
    the daughter lifted the safety glass;
Shooting against his wall in a grey burst
    the dove hurled on the can a blast of will.
Daughter screamed and the dragon housecoat
    ran — they stared in the garbage can
As in the prism of a glacier tomb
    where death preens cold and clear.

A Song for Old Apis

Old Apis, old sacred bull,
Red-eyed banquet master
Chewing while the blind harpist
Sang lickerish to his lord;
Old Apis drinking from the lotus cup —
Bleary over the wine's body
While the slaves served their masters
From perfume spoons on painted floors;
Old Apis, within you Ptah
Father of Gods and men,
Chief God of Egypt's Memphis;
Now when the dumb show dictionary

Clasps you only a male animal of the
Ox family calling your Christian wife cow;
Old spirit in the threatened air
Rut for us from ancient cliffs —
Breed for us in delicate, virgin eyes,
The fleshly points of Solomon's-seal!

Seurat

Degas called him 'The Notary.'
   Dressed in black suits,
      Severe top hat,
         Pressed creases.

His only portrait shows his mistress.
   She sits in décolleté preening,
      Buxom as a barrel and we know
         He loved her flesh.

Critics crawled on knees to mock his shimmering points,
   Smeared him with the label 'Pointillism,'
     A wax-work, scientific painter,
       Jeered his dots as colored fleas.

But at the Grande Jatte, sunlit still every Sunday summer afternoon,
   Mental masters lean on formal canes like curios and
     Light gathers lemon-yellow lazily where on
       Gentle grass glide the parasol ladies.

Fabre, the Bughunter

      Only an exile, a Japanese
In France would cry Banzai to the Bughunters;
Certainly not the French ladies with green thumbs —
      Bugbear, object of dread,

Bugaboo crawls imaginary terror in the dark —
Words from bugs disdained and giddy bughunters,
     Queer men with nets and jars.

     A country bumpkin,
His parents fed him by setting fire to heath and
Gorse, where the ashes nourished oats and potatoes.
     At the age of six
He asked himself, 'How do I perceive light?'
He shut his eyes: darkness; opened them: light;
     The simple sense of vision.

     Soon a love of Latin
From Vergil's web-fingered tales of bees and crows,
Cicadas humming, the turtle dove and nanny goat.
     Born to teach
He sat as master behind a desk and for relief
Peered inside at wasps' stings, beetles' wing casings
     And snapdragons' seed vessels.

     One sweet-smelling spring day while
Teaching his class Practical Surveying by stakes and tangents,
Boys disappeared after a big black solitary bee.
     Fabre disappeared too
Into his imagination, a world of thyme honey where
History was weatherbeaten and natural if you earned the
     Title of Great Observer.

     Paris was hell.
Forced there finally to receive the Legion of Honor
He stammered and called the third Emperor Napoleon 'Monsieur.'
     Driven at last from Avignon
By the old ladies who couldn't bear his teaching
Young girls why a man breathes, how to plant flowers and seeds
     And similar subjects.

     History is indignant
But Fabre was a good seed-planter himself, eight children

And two wives who knew enough to let the dead birds
    Rot on his study table.
Everything seemed over, he was seventy-four years old,
Some fame, writer of a few celebrated monographs,
    But a seedy reputation.

    Then to Sérignan.
'The Eden of Bliss,' he called it, 'This accursed ground
Which no one would have as a gift is an earthly paradise
    For the bees and wasps.'
He grew weeds. Thistles thrived with their prickly
Stems and leaves and their tough, cylindrical heads
    Like heavy hammers.

    Couch grass too
With roots creeping through the snapping smudge
Of all wild plants reckless in their wild sense
    Thus called weeds.
He watched and wrote: 'Here come the hunters,
Carpenters boring wood, architects in pasteboard,
    Builders of clay,

    Collectors of leaf-pieces,
Plasterers mixing mortars, workers in gold-beater's skin . . .
The promptings of instinct in its highest manifestation.'
    Lived until ninety-two,
The last eighteen years at Sérignan, in seclusion,
Famous and lonely, his family dead and dispersed, while the
    Frogs yacked May into his pond.

    To the Hermit of Sérignan,
Writing for the young whom he wished to love Natural History,
Who said to the technicians, 'You rip open the little creatures,
    But I cause them to be loved;
You work in a chamber of torture and dismemberment
But I observe under the blue sky,' this Banzai
    From a Japanese in France.

The Birth of Arachne, the Spider

Idmon, a dyer in purple,
Plunger in of the white stuffs,
Transformer of old gowns,
Artificer with his hands steeped in the vats,
Lived at Colophon in Lydia
With his daughter,
Arachne,
Weaver of fine fabrics and tapestry.

Arachne, no burning beauty,
Plain as burlap used for bagging,
Skin pitted as her jute fabric,
Hair like hank, washerwoman, cook and housekeeper
To a bureaucratic father —
Master of specialization —
Compartmentalized,
Dedicated to the perfect purple.

Arachne, the homely one,
So Idmon trained her to art's service,
Art for art's sake,
A twin-faced, goggle-eyed team in their golden age;
'Daughter, no one can weave with your grace,
Challenge the Gods,
Athene,
Goddess of Female Arts and Industries.'

Athene, the machine mistress,
Also Presiding Goddess of Athens, a gavel rapper —
Sprung full-brained from Zeus's head
With all of her father's intellectual glare —
No specialist but a brainwoman,
Critic of beauty,
Analyst,
Down with the weaving fingers of intuition!

And Arachne wove like a devilfish,
Her long fingers sucking at the threads,

Unconscious of the Goddess behind her,
Perfect in daring wove patterns of such form and color
    Blacked out the Goddess,
       Brain beat into fury
         And Athene tore,
    Tore the blazing tapestry to tatters.

    Arachne, sad victor,
Unconsolable in her ruined mastery;
    Bumbled in and out, Idmon,
Muttering pulpy phrases about immortal art.
    Athene turned away in hate
      While Arachne wept for
        Art
    And hung herself with a cord from her loom.

    At the blue-faced gasp,
Guilty with shame, tense the shining cord
    With the hanging figure swaying,
Athene wove the threads to a glittering web,
    Changed Arachne to a spider,
      Gave up forever
        Weaving,
    Gone the art to the spider's grace.

    Athene, proud intellect,
Ironic Goddess of the spider's glory —
    Yielded the weaver's victory
But froze in man the fear of tiny fur.
    Through sun-lit dust weaves the spider
      And her web is fulgent form —
        Arachne
    Her name is sister to the scorpion.

Cheops

The Pharaoh Cheops lived to die
With his royal crook and his royal flail —
The crook to guide and the flail to force —

He planned to sail his Ships of Death
Through the Light of Heaven to the eastern sky,
Past the Serpent-Demon, Apophis,

Coiled in Hell's River like a scimitar.
Cheops, the Great Calf of the Great Cow
And the Great Smasher of Foreheads,

Ordered his ships built six decks high
For his retinue, one ship for day and
One for dark in the serpent realm,

Sweet with the smell of sacred sycamore —
When the Pharaoh Cheops died, priests
Pulled his cold brains through his nose

With hooks and cut out his holy viscera.
In a blood-red granite sarcophagus,
Great in his funeral garments, robbers

Despoiled his body while his Ships of Death
Sailed secretly by day and night in
Hidden chambers of his lime-stone pyramid.

A Guilty Father to His Daughter

Why are you always glad to me?
Shouts my daughter gladfully
A twist of time a tuneful word
Happy I roll into the glad gully

High father in my Morning Glory
Silk virtue violently in me
I rule my family like an old fox hound
And father my way in fancy

When I curse her she catcalls
And cancels her sparky consent

Carnal her sun foams out and her flesh
Firms between us fixed as cement

Prince of Fathers in my glad gully
Hobbledehoy in my fatherly rain
Why are you always glad to me?
Demon down the fatherly drain.

A Plea for Alias

Coleridge, they say, lived in fantasy.
   Under the name of Silas Tomkyn Comberbeck
He enlisted in a regiment of dragoons.
I too like alias, a slash of shortcutting.
   Bird of Paradise for Strelytzia — *Romanticism* —
   Quail for Colinus Virginianus — *Classicism* —
Alias I regard as a form of upper air;
When you live in the air of alias
Names fly free from their skins
Like mail to the dead letter box.
Alias of course has electric errors.
Once I knew a patriot who called his daughter
   University of Texas — *Naturalism* —
U.T. we called her for short hand,
Universal Tribulation said a secret friend.
Seldom do we find the right alias;
Young as Huck Finn we stuck our gum on
Theatre seats where W. C. Fields played
Cuthbert J. Twilly or Larson E. Whipsnade.
But the quick grass of alias still grows in the
Upper air if you strain your eye —
Alias transmuting the common metals of life,
Beating up elixirs, the golden alchemist.

Unnatural, Unusual and Unfair

Eroded beach on the bay, an empty scene,
Only an old Negro lady hunched in her coat,
Hermit-shaped, at the end of a narrow, moss-green wharf,
                                   fishing —
A bundle of fog binding her together with
Shore, sailboat, and a black buoy like a
Period mark in an unnatural sentence.

A sense of bungled weather, bullheaded sky,
But out of a ripple, action! Honeymoon of hook
And a hornpipe in her homely face,
Climbs dripping her kitchen cord line
And what she hooks is unusual —

Lean leopard shark, small, yellow lefthander
With a blasted eye at his hoity-toity family tree.
Back sinks the scene to its bungled sense,
Hollowhearted, unsuccessful and unfair.

The Coastguardsman in the Fog

To Ferdinand Schevill

I

Below my watchtower window, over the scarecrow-sticked
Masts of the fishing fleet and the pronged rocks
Pitchforking out of the surf, fog flows in with a
Soft-feather face flecked black like spattered wool.
The yellow lupin on the cliff hammered short by wind
And the purple thistle velvet-smooth in its barbed web
Flatten and disappear as the scooting white smokes in
With its sawing teeth. High I sit in the Coast Guard
Station, in my whitewashed room, white witness shacks
Pinned to the hill on bone dry rock, a guarded post
In its guarding time, hovered by skullcap hawks,

Splintering cliffs and the wink of sun before fog
Winds out its glowering dye. I loved the hunched,
Holy-stone shapes of land sheared by sea and I gave
This meeting my life to find the fortune teller, fog,
My fear, my foreshadow, the wry, soft sponge over the
Seaweed where flies and skip-jack sand fleas
Dart on the stinking green at the tide's peak.
The oyster gull with its cassock shadow stands
Mute in the mist as the drowned, smile-scoured face
Pierces again through the wagtail white at my peace.

II

Weeks ago, not once upon a time but once in all time
The alarm bell burred in its black recess and I heard
An Army plane had flamed in the sea where the cloistral
Cliffs lean like cutlery. We drove on the hardpacked beach
In a jeep past a dead sea lion's carcass hogback in the
Haze. Near an old shipwreck, bony wood veined clean and
Clear by pounding surf we stopped and cords of fog
Bound our blue uniforms in a cascading choreography.
The brown jeep stood in its shell like a snail in
Cream-thick air. I stared through high-power glasses
To see only knobs of kelp clutched by the green,
Hairy arms of seaweed. Silence harped heavy with the
Surf's twanging plunge and snap on the rocks. Then
Wind blew steppingstones in the fog and suddenly,
Far out, winding veins, I saw the rocking, floating
Veil of a parachute, but no swimming life. Wind
Warped waves from their calm and blue sky opened a
Split warmth soon twisted gray again. Two marsh-hawks
Flew hard-head over the cliff at their prey — and
Then the body pitched from the swilling surf
Headfirst on the beach, triggering my eyes.

III

Whitebait plunge on the sand, spindrift into
Stillness, taut fingers still tight in the
Swimming stretch, scraping stickpins on the shells.

White skin drained of blood like a sail, the
Hard, black inkberry eyes cracked gay as a
Sparrow shot down from his song into the filching fog.
Flapjack at our faces, over the sing-song surf,
Fog clenched this corpse for its corsair goal.
Back at the Station we packed the body in ice
To keep. Next morning from the city fifty miles in
Space and years in time came a mortician,
Bassoon voice, polished shoebill stance under a
Shipbiscuit face, eyes glittering for death,
Fingered the ankle tag, slapped the white-muscled leg,
Seeped from a setback mouth, 'Too bad. Nice boy.'

IV

Thickhead fog smothers time, not death,
Nights in my room, tossed in the wreathing net,
My flybuzzing life in that vaporous spiderweb,
Lit at the murky center by the forced glitter of
Gay eyes, a boy who died in wonder with fingers
Clutching at the net of white. What is the
Body but a softshelled coffin for the seeds of death?
The fog shed acid on such thoughts and I asked for
Leave to travel back to the coastal city where
I was born one of the halfmast lives in the
Hairtrigger towers. Walking in the shocked
Streets of sheer sun, I followed my
Shimmering memory into the City Hall —
Ponderous, prickled and ornamented as a
Hercules'-club — where my father had served as Judge.
In his old, squareset, musty courtroom, a
Murder trial neared its whirlpool end.
I stared at the flag billowing power over
Bony, brimming faces which burned alive
As veiled wicks of lamps through dirty glass.
Two dustpan lives were said to have
Smashed in a cabdriver's skull. In duplex style
Sat the law, two electric prosecution eels
Stinging with confidence, two pom-poms for defense
Waving scorn at cages locked on cipher souls.

Society ranked in a jog trot Judge with jumbo jowls
And a female jury of twelve fleshly, hard-shelled
Molluscs, their lumpy purses leaden in their laps —
And the circumstantial evidence of a year-old crime
Stammered out of memory, foamed densely, eddied and
Whirled around an invisible center of truth.
Behind the bald, bear-pit bailiff, I twisted in the
Smoky room while misty memories scratched about
Lost watches and wallets, splintered windows of
Safety glass and bloody hairs — slowly, foraging,
Fog filtered through the courtroom, the monarch's
Strands weaving their fine cords, and bolting
Bitter from my chair — a witness gaping at me
From her boggy statement and the Judge shocked from his
Sheen — I blurred out shrilling my fear: 'The memory is fog!'

V

When the bailiff learned I was a Judge's son in service
He cautioned me with clockwork words . . . 'disgrace to uniform . . .
Drunk on leave . . .' Hating the sun, afraid, a stranger to my youth,
I stayed locked in my hotel room, one leashed dream in that
Concrete tower of lost loneliness. When my leave was up,
Still caught in the searchlight shame of my courtroom scene,
I drove back to the Station. A pork-fat fog huddled the asphalt,
Millions of water drops suspended in the low-hanging cloud,
Each drop a dazzling, tiny mirror — *the memory is fog* —
Knowledge is a childish thing when evil hates or love demands.
Fog was not memory, but a hangnailed hermit of loneliness
Luring me on his lonely way, each tiny mirror flashing
My fear of the flier's death, the glaze of those gay eyes.
At the lighthouse, a glowworm tower on a forelock of land
Near the Station, I stopped the car and heard the gnarled bell
Banging slit-edged brilliance through the gathering gloom,
Hammering out its ravenous ritual. I walked to the fence and
Stared down at the veiled surf scapegrace and sibilant in the
Snagging fog. What peace was clear within that fog's dark center?
Suddenly, tearing my thoughts, the mist coiled up and a
Flock of white sea lions flowed glissando from the acorn-
Barnacled rocks. Black on that whiteness, the flier's eyes

Turned from me smiling down the flashing arch of the oiled,
Beautiful bodies and water's myths flared together in that
Gliding grace; the bell in its sea king voice was
Not my risk, my father's justice court only one scraping weed
In the sea-tangled world. Around the gamecock flier's fate,
I saw foaming the furies of sea-anchored life that form our
Deeds of death and from whose fancy we tear the wonder and
Terror of form in word or flesh. Standing with the lash of love
I stared at the white sea lions plunging peppery in the
                              plundering fog.

The Old Pilot Tunnels under
the English Channel

On fog days, early mornings wet at the mirror,
Spongy dawns misting the glass with dredger dreams,
I see her there underneath the English Channel,
Queen Victoria, stern flag of the sweepstake empire,
Riding, riding, firm her dogwood hard mouth,
Riding in a little hand-drawn car through the
        pilot tunnel towards France.

Disraeli beside her, shrewd tumbler in politics,
An oriental rug amidst the Victorian gew-gaws;
They ride ceremoniously, flunkies trundling
To the tunnel end, slap-bang against rock —
Suddenly, the empire's tuning center, the
War Office, tuned out the channel tunnel,
        enemy might sound demons through it.

Today two oldsters, one in England, one in France, still
Guard the pilot tunnels, bleary eyes for water-leaks;
I see them nodding over their lunches, the
Englishman puffs his pipe and spits, the Frenchman
Drinks his wine and the lonely tunnels wait,
Mute dinosaurs in history while channel tides
        hiss tuck-tuck on their bones.

An Astonished Listener Hears the Radio Announcer Bat Out the Long Balls of Verbs, Nouns and Adjectives

Swing on the cripple and hit the dying quail.
The roundhouse curve, the swell wrinkle, and the
Big dead fish all fail if the slugger
Rammycackles a liner over the advertising sign.
At the break of seven spasms take some of that
Good beer, for the Little Professor's at bat.
The sprayhitters are breaking out with
Five o'clock lightning and Old Casey the Cagey
Calls in a new repair man. It's Cautious Joe!
He's deep down in the barrel and has to
Swim out of it, but boy he's swimming!
Watch those fielders put on the chain,
Skid, gobble and throw. They know it's
Hang tough and root hog or die and they want the
Poke ball hit in the well. You never know in baseball.
In the last gasp or never inning the veterans can
Wield the willow and play some beautiful tunes
On ancient fiddles. Then the cripple and the
Dying quail and the big dead fish are all
    Stashed in the deep freeze.

The Turtle

"The skull of Haydn returned to his bones . . ."
And the priest in the photo held the skull high —
I was reading the paper in the rising sun
When my daughter called out: "Ants in the water!"
She came and pulled me from my mood
To the sunlit patio with the deep blue pan.
The turtle hung down in the water like a hammock,
His four feet floating in a lazy swing.

I flipped him over on his armored back
And his yellow stomach shone in the light —
(I thought of the Buddhist nun in her yellow robes,
The Buddhist renounces the world in yellow) —
The water stank and the ants in their avarice
Marched on the blue pan in frenzied lines.
Dense in the hot, yellow light through the
Oak tree, disturbed, hundreds of moths
Shook the air like tiny, grey parachutes.
Clutching the turtle, his toothless jaw
Jutting like a thorn, I hurled him to a canyon grave
Deep in the brush and the brush closed with a clunk.

The Dancers with a Hop

In that furious, final wake for Flannagan,
When they drained that booze and danced their babes,
They barreled with bulging rears; the Slang Angel
From the slum section danced with that old slick-hair,
Harry the Heel — together they performed the Hula
In honor of the Irish — the "Hula with a Hop,"
Harry explained as the Slang Angel leaped
High with flapping breasts and flopping hair . . .
While granite and grainfields away,
Flying to Arctic nesting grounds,
Soared to river-rest the sandhill cranes,
Male and female paired for life in luminous light,
Bowed to each other with brightest feathers,
Leaped in the air beating gravely their wings,
Circled again in the gracious, courtly dance and
Leaped! And the air glowed gala galore.

Dramas of the Rose

As I watched the unlikely ones at the bar
Leaning against the glow of green light,
The woman, solo, six feet tall as a tree,
Mr. Spectacles, six inches below, sizing her branches,
I saw him bewildered in the battle of fanciful flesh;
Then he moved as if muttering, "Blast me
Out of this size" — But as he moved she
Tore a rose in half out of her tinted hair
And handed him the half just as a drunk
Broke a glass with a shattering smack —
And I was blasted out of the bar
Back to the stage of intimate flesh
When in the old days of burlesque
The comic received from a chorus girl —
She of the liquid legs and untrue hair —
A rose which he sniffed with private bliss
And threw it sadly into the wings
Where it fell unseen with a crash of glass.

DELMORE SCHWARTZ

Will You Perhaps

"mentrechè il vento, come fa, si tace"

Will you perhaps consent to be
Now that a little while is still
(Ruth of sweet wind) now that a little while
My mind's continuing and unreleasing wind
Touches this single of your flowers, this one only,
Will you perhaps consent to be
My many-branchéd, small and dearest tree?

My mind's continuing and unreleasing wind
— The wind which is wild and restless, tired and asleep,
The wind which is tired, wild and still continuing,
The wind which is chill, and warm, wet, soft, in every influence,
Lusts for Paris, Crete and Pergamus,
Is suddenly off for Paris and Chicago,
Judaea, San Francisco, the Midi,
— May I perhaps return to you
Wet with an Attic dust and chill from Norway
My dear, so-many-branchéd smallest tree?

Would you perhaps consent to be
The very rack and crucifix of winter, winter's wild
Knife-edged, continuing and unreleasing,
Intent and stripping, ice-caressing wind?
My dear, most dear, so-many-branchéd tree
My mind's continuing and unreleasing wind
Touches this single of your flowers, faith in me,
Wide as the — sky! — accepting as the (air)!
— Consent, consent, consent to be
My many-branchéd, small and dearest tree.

Do They Whisper

*"As in water face answereth to face,
so the heart of man to man."*

Do they whisper behind my back? Do they speak
Of my clumsiness? Do they laugh at me,
Mimicking my gestures, retailing my shame?
I'll whirl about, denounce them, saying
That they are shameless, they are treacherous,
No more my friends, nor will I once again
Never, amid a thousand meetings in the street,
Recognize their faces, take their hands,
Not for our common love or old times' sake:
They whispered behind my back, they mimicked me.

I know the reason why, I too have done this,
Cruel for wit's sake, behind my dear friend's back,
And to amuse betrayed his private love,
His nervous shame, her habit, and their weaknesses;
I have mimicked them, I have been treacherous,
For wit's sake, to amuse, because their being weighed
Too grossly for a time, to be superior,
To flatter the listeners by this, the intimate,
Betraying the intimate, but for the intimate,
To free myself of friendship's necessity,
Fearing from time to time that they would hear,
Denounce me and reject me, say once for all
That they would never meet me, take my hands,
Speaking for old times' sake and our common love.

What an unheard-of thing it is, in fine,
To love another and equally be loved!
What sadness and what joy! How cruel it is
That pride and wit distort the heart of man,
How vain, how sad, what cruelty, what need,
For this is true and sad, that I need them
And they need me. What can we do? We need
Each other's clumsiness, each other's wit,
Each other's company and our own pride. I need

My face unshamed, I need my wit, I cannot
Denounce them once for all, they cannot
Turn away. We know our clumsiness,
Our weakness, our necessities, we cannot
Forget our pride, our faces, our common love.

The Heavy Bear

"the withness of the body"   WHITEHEAD

The heavy bear who goes with me,
A manifold honey to smear his face,
Clumsy and lumbering here and there,
The central ton of every place,
The hungry beating brutish one
In love with candy, anger, and sleep,
Crazy factotum, dishevelling all,
Climbs the building, kicks the football,
Boxes his brother in the hate-ridden city.

Breathing at my side, that heavy animal,
That heavy bear who sleeps with me,
Howls in his sleep for a world of sugar,
A sweetness intimate as the water's clasp,
Howls in his sleep because the tight-rope
Trembles and shows the darkness beneath.
— The strutting show-off is terrified,
Dressed in his dress-suit, bulging his pants,
Trembles to think that his quivering meat
Must finally wince to nothing at all.

That inescapable animal walks with me,
Has followed me since the black womb held,
Moves where I move, distorting my gesture,
A caricature, a swollen shadow,
A stupid clown of the spirit's motive,
Perplexes and affronts with his own darkness,
The secret life of belly and bone,

Opaque, too near, my private, yet unknown,
Stretches to embrace the very dear
With whom I would walk without him near,
Touches her grossly, although a word
Would bare my heart and make me clear,
Stumbles, flounders, and strives to be fed
Dragging me with him in his mouthing care,
Amid the hundred million of his kind,
The scrimmage of appetite everywhere.

For the One Who Would Take

Man's Life in His Hands

Tiger Christ unsheathed his sword,
Threw it down, became a lamb.
Swift spat upon the species, but
Took two women to his heart.
Samson who was strong as death
Paid his strength to kiss a slut.
Othello that stiff warrior
Was broken by a woman's heart.
Troy burned for a sea-tax, also for
Possession of a charming whore.
What do all examples show?
What must the finished murderer know?

You cannot sit on bayonets,
Nor can you eat among the dead.
When all are killed, you are alone,
A vacuum comes where hate has fed.
Murder's fruit is silent stone,
The gun increases poverty.
With what do these examples shine?
The soldier turned to girls and wine.
Love is the tact of every good,
The only warmth, the only peace.

"What have I said?" asked Socrates,
"Affirmed extremes, cried yes and no,
Taken all parts, denied myself,
Praised the caress, extolled the blow,
Soldier and lover quite deranged
Until their motions are exchanged.
— What do all examples show?
What can any actor know?
The contradiction in every act,
The infinite task of the human heart."

Saint, Revolutionist

Saint, revolutionist,
God and sage know well,
That there is a place
Where that much-rung bell,
The well-beloved body,
And its sensitive face
Must be sacrificed.

There is, it seems, in this
A something meaningless,
Hanging without support
And yet too dear to touch,
That life should seek its end
Where no will can descend,
Facing a gun to see
Long actuality.

What is this that is
The good of nothingness,
The death of Socrates
And that strange man on the cross
Seeking out all loss?
For men love life until
It shames both face and will.

Neither in hell nor heaven
Is the answer given,
Both are a servant's pay:
But they wish to know
How far the will can go,
Lest their infinite play
And their desires be
Shadow and mockery.

What Is to Be Given

What is to be given,
Is spirit, yet animal,
Colored, like heaven,
Blue, yellow, beautiful.

The blood is checkered by
So many stains and wishes,
Between it and the sky
You could not choose, for riches.

Yet let me now be careful
Not to give too much
To one so shy and fearful
For like a gun is touch.

In the Naked Bed, in Plato's Cave

In the naked bed, in Plato's cave,
Reflected headlights slowly slid the wall,
Carpenters hammered under the shaded window,
Wind troubled the window curtains all night long,
A fleet of trucks strained uphill, grinding,
Their freights covered, as usual.

The ceiling lightened again, the slanting diagram
Slid slowly forth.

                   Hearing the milkman's chop,
His striving up the stair, the bottle's chink,
I rose from bed, lit a cigarette,
And walked to the window. The stony street
Displayed the stillness in which buildings stand,
The street-lamp's vigil and the horse's patience.
The winter sky's pure capital
Turned me back to bed with exhausted eyes.

Strangeness grew in the motionless air. The loose
Film grayed. Shaking wagons, hooves' waterfalls,
Sounded far off, increasing, louder and nearer.
A car coughed, starting. Morning, softly
Melting the air, lifted the half-covered chair
From underseas, kindled the looking-glass,
Distinguished the dresser and the white wall.
The bird called tentatively, whistled, called,
Bubbled and whistled, so! Perplexed, still wet
With sleep, affectionate, hungry and cold. So, so,
O son of man, the ignorant night, the travail
Of early morning, the mystery of beginning
Again and again,

                while History is unforgiven.

Lincoln

"Let us go off on a candid cadenza,
For the great man still grows in the boy's mind,
All those events live in the national fable,
Expressive of America *an sich!*"

"Manic-depressive Lincoln, national hero!
How just that this great nation, being conceived
In liberty by fugitives should find
— Strange ways and plays of monstrous History —
This Hamlet-type to be the President —"

"This failure, this unwilling bridegroom,
This tricky lawyer full of black despair —"

"He grew a beard, becoming President,
And took a shawl as if he guessed his rôle,
Though with the beard he fled cartoonists' blacks,
And many laughed and were contemptuous,
And some for four years spoke of killing him —"

"He was a politician — of the heart! —
He lived from hand to mouth in moral things!
He understood quite well Grant's drunken-ness!
It was for him, before Election Day,
That at Cold Harbor Grant threw lives away
In hopeless frontal attack against Lee's breastworks!"

"O how he was the Hamlet-man, and this,
After a life of failure made him right,
After he ran away on his wedding day,
Writing a coward's letter to his bride —"

"How with his very failure, he out-tricked
The florid Douglas and the abstract Davis,
And all the vain men who, surrounding him,
Smiled in their vanity and sought his place —"

"Later, they made him out a prairie Christ
To sate the need coarse in the national heart —"

"His wife went insane, Mary Todd too often
Bought herself dresses. And his child died.
And he would not condemn young men to death
For having slept, in weakness. And he spoke
More than he knew and all that he had felt
Between outrageous joy and black despair
Before and after Gettysburg's *pure peak* —"

"He studied law, but knew in his own soul
Despair's anarchy, terror and error,
— Instruments had to be taken from his office

And from his bedroom in such days of horror,
Because some saw that he might kill himself:
When he was young, when he was middle-aged,
How just and true was he, our national hero!"

"Sometimes he could not go home to face his wife,
Sometimes he wished to hurry or end his life!"

"But do not be deceived. He did not win,
And, it is plain, the South could never win
(Despite the gifted Northern generals!)
— Capitalismus is not mocked, O no!
This stupid deity decided the War —"

"In fact, the North and South were losers both:
— Capitalismus won the Civil War —"

"— Capitalismus won the Civil War,
Yet, in the War's cruel Colosseum,
Some characters fulfilled their natures' surds,
Grant the drunkard, Lee the noble soldier,
John Brown in whom the Bible soared and cried,
Booth the unsuccessful Shakespearean,
— Each in some freedom walked and knew himself,
Then most of all when all the deities
Mixed with their barbarous stupidity
To make the rock, root, and rot of the war —"

"This is the way each only life becomes,
Tossed on History's ceaseless insane sums!"

The Masters of the Heart Touched the Unknown

For thirty years what madness I have known;
Of solitude the blankness and *longueurs*,
The nervous doubt which thought and art assure,
Causeless despair, or causeless joy alone.

But when I thought of the masters of the heart,
And of the mind and of life's long disease,
And the majesty and fury of great art,
I was renewed like April's wooden trees,

And I was *parvenu* and green with hope.
They pacified the underworld in me:
— What are we? what are we not? when touched by them —
And I rehearsed their passion's history.

His senses great palms stormed by fury,
Keats left for Italy to burn away.
Emerson lived in Eden's innocence,
Thinking the world was like a summer's day.

He did not understand Hawthorne's dark works,
His endless guilt, his passion for the snow.
Mozart knew comedy's great melancholy,
And spoke of Thermidor in Figaro.

The glib, the clever, the fluent, and the vain
Pompom chrysanthemums like Oscar Wilde
Destroyed themselves in witty drawing rooms,
By earnestness and epigrams defiled.

Hugo in Jersey like a sunset shone.
Baudelaire slumped in a deadly tiredness
And saw his own face in the tragic play
Of Poe's face which like drowned Ophelia lay.

Emily Brontë gazed awestruck to see
Passion consume her brother on the moor.
Emily Dickinson went to Washington,
Falling in love like flowers to the floor.

She learned, like heroines in Henry James,
Renunciation like a tower remains
Of Christ's great castle in the Western heart.
And sang. And made a notebook of her art.

Wordsworth on walking tours found innocence,
Harked to the mariner who talked all night
Of the real world, pure consciousness as such,
As if he understood the world of light.

The poet Dostoevsky cried and sang
Of penitence, since he was criminal,
And of forgiveness, wishing to be forgiven
The crime of making love to a little girl.

These masters used their lives like Christmas trees,
They skinned themselves alive to find the truth,
They gazed upon their vileness like excrement.
They ate their hearts to sate the need for love.
They fingered every coiled snake of the mind,
Searching for choice and chance and wish and memory.
They stood upon their heads. They thrust their hands
In furnaces to find what they could bear.
They climbed down pits and wells, and praised
The wilderness, the future, and the truth.
And in the end their separated heads
Glared from a plate and criticized this life!

She Was the Girl within the Picture Frame

Sometimes the girl on boyhood's silver screen
— The surface makes me nervous as a cat —
Sometimes the girl Vermeer once marveled at,
For there is in her face the famous queen
Who makes all other ladies seem unseen
— Sometimes the Countess in the minuet
By Mozart, hopelessly her laureate,
— Darkling, I hardly know just what I mean.

The expensive suburb has began to rot.
The latest boys and girls, full of the ache
Of being, are knocking at the gate,

As if a deathless day began to dawn,
Old immortality their natural lot:
— This news is meaningless. For she was born,
Look, in some other world! — and you were not!

"One in a Thousand of Years of the Nights"

Serene, cool and composed, and easygoing
They think you are because your smiling face
Is still, and generous, and like a growing
Summer, big and rich and luminous.
The furies and the foibles do not show,
The sickness, sorrow, weakness, and the fall,
The heartbreak of the little pensive girl.
How beautiful you are you do not know,

Because you cannot see yourself at all
Because you have been beautiful so long,
— The law and lore of jewels as blind as snow.
It is so long since it was otherwise,
— And I will never be as once I was,
Furious at the crossroads, striking at what I do not know.

I Wish I Had Great Knowledge or Great Art

I wish I had a pony or a trot
To read the obscure Latin of your heart,
Falsely I wish I were what I am not,
I would if but I could play any part
(After so many years to come to this!)
— And yet, I know, lost in this empty pass
The very shift and metamorphosis
Would merely bring me to the heart of loss.

For being what I am foists up the wish
— Once lifted from my being's element
I'd gasped with bulging eyes like a hooked fish,
Dumbfounded by my gratified intent:
Behold how in this trope, drawn from the sea,
Two worlds are separated endlessly.

"There'll Be Others but Non So for Me"

Some *bon vivant* of the heart might have come for her,
If not for me, sick in all consciousness,
Someone as rich and gay as music is,
And not like me drawn by each straining cur
Ambition and desire loose to the game,
Some being unpossessed and generous.
She would have sung and been spontaneous,
And sauntered in the summer's foam and flame.

Yet from the sadness of what has not been,
Look how there is, above unhappiness,
A certain thing which is not meaningless;
Phoenix affection rises again and again,
Beyond the harm and loss wincing in us:
A bird still chants and is magnanimous.

She Lives with the Furies of Hope and Despair

O Jan Vermeer of Delft, descend, come near
The Hudson and the West's last capital.
Here is the new Ophelia beautiful:
Only your lucid brush could make her clear
And vivid as the daughter of the Swan.
Vermeer, you too! — the early morning light
Only the sleepless see, gazing all night —
Return as faint and delicate as dawn.

Pretty and beautiful, romping and yet
Serene as statues of the classic age,
Her goodness generous in her luminous face,
Though cruel pride rack the world with rage,
Or power and vanity dance their minuet,
Her candor and her gaze are marvelous:
Marvelous shines her candor and her gaze.

Being Unused to Joyous Consciousness

Being suspicious of great happiness,
Let us a little while retreat and wait
To understand what freedom amid fate
Remains, for freedom is the sole access
To true desire. Time is most merciless
When generous. And we must hesitate;
Choose tremblingly before the deathless gate,
For this is life: nearby is nothingness.

But nonetheless, the more I think of it,
The more the promise grows, though difficult,
As in the hours when the headfirst child
Shudders amid his mother's mounting fit:
Small pain before the endless joy and guilt
With which the mind and heart will be beguiled.

The Morning Light for One with Too Much Luck

Sick and used Cambridge in the suck-
Ing sound of slow rain at dead dawn
Amid the sizzle sound of car and truck
As if continually thin cloth were torn,

Blue light, plum light, fading violet light,
And then the oyster light of the wool sky:

Is this not, after all, appropriate
Light for a long used poet such as I?

The steady juices of the rain fulfill
November, ember, ashen ageing youth:
Here, my dear poet, with weather, wit, and will,
And a long look you learned to like the truth!

The Self Unsatisfied Runs Everywhere

Sunday and sunlight ashen on the Square,
Hard wind, high blue, and clouded pennant sky,
Fifth Avenue empty in the autumn air,
As if a clear photograph of a dead day.
It was the Lord's day once, solemn and full
— Now I in an aftermath, desire spent,
Move with a will appeased and see a gull,
Then gulls drop from an arch — scythes of descent! —

Having, I think, no wish beyond the foam
Toppling to them at each fresh exercise,
Knowing success like fountains, perhaps more wise
Than one who hesitantly writes a poem
— But who, being human, wishes to be a gull,
Knows nothing much, though birds are beautiful.

The Fulfillment

"Is it a dream?" I asked. To which my fellow
Answered with a hoarse voice and dulled insistence:
"Dream? Is it a dream? What difference
Does it make or mean? If it is only a dream
It is the dream which we are. Dream or the last resort
Of reality, it is the truth of our minds:
We are condemned because this is our consciousness."

217

Where we were, if we were there, serene and shining
Each being sang and moved with the sleekness of rivers,
United in a choir, many and one, as the spires of flames in fire,
Flowing and perfected, flourishing and fulfilled forever,
Rising and falling as the carousel and palace of festival and victory.

"I was told often enough," my fellow said —
"You were told too — and you as little believed —
'Beware of all your desires. You are deceived.
(As they are deceived and deceptive, urgent and passing!)
They will be wholly fulfilled. You will be dead.
They will be gratified. And you will be dead!' "

In a fixed fascination, wonderstruck, we gazed,
Marveling at the fulfillment so long desired and praised.
There, effort was like dancing its own pleasure.
There, all things existed purely in the action of joy —
Like light, like all kinds of light, all in the domination
    of celebration existed only as the structures of joy!

Then, as we gazed in an emotion more exhausting than mountains,
Then, when at last we knew where we had come,
It was then that we saw what was lost as we knew where we
                                        had been
(Or knew where we had been as we saw all that was lost!)
And knew for the first time the richness and poverty
Of what we had been before and were no more,
The striving, the suffering, the dear dark hooded mortality
Which we had been and never known, which we had resisted,
                                        detested,
    feared and denied, the rocks and the flowers and the faces
    of the needs and the hopes which had given us our reality!

The First Morning of the Second World

after black silence

1

      Suddenly.
Suddenly and certainly, as I watched elsewhere, locked
And intent in that vigil in which the hunter is the hunted
As the mind is, seeking itself, falconer, falcon and hawk, victor and
                            victim,
Aware of the dry river beds, the droughts of the little deaths,
Sudden and overwhelming
Years rose and the damned waters of secret nature's underseas.
Where I had been before, tense and tired, was the edge of a winter
                            wood.
The gun of the mind ached in my numb and narrowed gaze,
Trembled a little, aimed at the pathless wood, and the snowclouded
                          icewhite sky,
Hearing the rush not of the birds rising from bush and thicket
                  thrashing and clacking,
But suddenly the pouring continuous sibilance of waterfalls,
Certainly and suddenly, for a moment's eternity, it was the
      ecstasy and stillness of the white
        wizard blizzard, the white god fallen, united,
        entirely whiteness
The color of forgiveness, beginning and hope.

Quickly then and certainly it was the river of summer, blue as the
                  infinite curving blueness above us,
Little boats at anchor lolled or were lapped, and a yacht slowly
                        glided.
It was wholly holiday, holiday absolute, a silk and saraband day,
                  warm and gay and
Blue and white and vibrant as the pennants buoyant on the stadium
                      near us,
White, a milk whiteness, and also all the colors flaring, melting, or
                    flowing.

There hope was, and the hopes, and the years past,
The beings I had known and forgotten and half-remembered or
        remembered too often,
Some in rowboats sunned, as on a picnic, or waiting, as before a play,
  the picnic and *the* play of eternity as summer, siesta, and
          summit
— How could I have known that the years and the hopes were
      human beings hated or loved,
Or known that I knew less and more than I supposed I supposed?
(So I questioned myself, in a voice familiar and strange)
There they were, all of them, and I was with them,
They were with me, and they were me, I was them, forever united
As we all moved forward in a consonance silent and moving
   Seated and gazing,
    Upon the beautiful river forever.

2

So we were as children on the painted wooden horses, rising and
      falling, of the carnival's carousel
Singing or smiling, at times, as the lyric of a small music tinkled
        above us
Saying: "The task is the round, the round is the task, the task and
       the round are a dance, and
There is nothing to think but drink of love and knowledge, and
       love's knowledge
When after and before are no more, and no more masks or
       unmasking,
   but only basking
(As the shining sea basks under the shining sun
In a radiance of swords and chandeliers dancing)
In the last love of knowledge, the first, when thought's abdication
   quickens thought's exaltation,
In the last blessing and sunlight of love's knowledge."

I hardly knew when my lips parted. Started to move slowly
As in the rehearsal of half-remembered memorized
   anthem, prayer, or spell
   of heartwelling gratitude and recognition.
My lips trembled, fumbled, and in the depths and death of thought

A murmur rose like the hidden humming of summer, when June
                               sleeps
In the radiant entrancings of warm light and green security.
Fumbling, feeling for what I had long supposed I had grasped and
          cast aside as worthless,
       the sparks or glitters of pleasure, trivial and transient.

— The phrases like faces came, lucid and vivid, separate, united,
                           sincere as pain
With the unity of meaning and emotion long lost, disbelieved or
                              denied,
As I sought with the words I had known a candid translation.
So I said then, in a language intimate and half-understood:
"I did not know . . . and I knew . . . surely I once knew . . .
        I must have known . . .
Surely sometimes guessed at or suspected,
Knew and did not know what love is,
The measure of pleasure, the heart of joy, the light and the heart of
                           the light
Which makes all pleasure, joy and love come to be
As light alone gives all colors being, the measure and the treasure
Of the light which unites and distinguishes the bondage and
               freedom in unity and distinction
Which is love . . . Love? . . . Is love? What is love?"

Suddenly and certainly I saw how surely the measure and treasure
              of pleasure is being as being with, belonging
Figured and touched in the experience of voices in chorus.
       Withness is ripeness,
       Ripeness is withness,
       To be is to be in love,
          Love is the fullness of being.

3

For the gratification of action by those who enact it and at once
In the enacting behold it, actual and antiphonal, *as* antiphonal in
    another and others who are with them and look to them,
                        toiling and smiling,

Know the act and their enaction and another's and others' who
                               suffer the struggling,
The effort of effort, as in the toil and ecstasy of dancing and
                               climbing,
When they know immediately within them what they see
          immediately without them, vivid in the faces,
                    lucid in the voices,
Each creating and increasing the other, as fire in fire,
And as the lover knows *yes*, knows loving and being loved, *then,*
Kissing as he is kissed: then only effort is gratitude, then toil is
                            ecstasy,
Suffering is satisfaction and both are neither but a third,
Beyond and containing the fear and the striving, the excitement and
                       the rapture:
The self is another but with and wholly the self, loving and beloved;
Is neither no more and both, passing from both beyond to the being
                    of being
Self-hooded selfhood seeks in the darkness and daylight blind and
                      lost.

Suddenly, suddenly and certainly
Then it was as waking in the waters of morning, in winter,
Certainly it was the first morning again,
Waking in the first morning to a world outside of whiteness united,
Transfigured, possessed by the blessedness of whiteness and light,
A whiteness which was light and which was more than light,
And the inner morning and meaning of all light.

Suddenly it was the awe and moment when Adam first looked upon
        another self, a self like his own self, yet an absolute
        other and newness, being the beginning of being
          and love and loving and being loved,
(Then all astonishment rippled to recognition, unbelievable,
Yet actual before him, growing with the certainty, serenity and
        majesty of morning).

Quickly and certainly it was the little moment when Lazarus
Thrusting aside the cold seated linens,
Summoned by Jesus, snow and morning,
Thrust the stone to the side, the fell conclusion,

And knew all astonishment for the first time, wonderstruck
Not that he lived again, after the wood, the stone, the closing, nails,
                and black silence empty,
But that he had ever died. Knew the illusion of death
      confused with the reality of the agony of dying,
Knowing at last that death is inconceivable among the living
(Knowing the wish, the hope, the will, the luxury and ignorance of
                the thought that man can ever die)
Hearing the thunder of the news of waking from the false dream of
                life that life can ever end.

WINFIELD TOWNLEY SCOTT

How Shall I Ever Come to Any Good?

How shall I ever come to any good
And get my works in schoolbooks if I use
A rough word here and there, but how shall I
Let you know me if I bequeath you only
The several photographs, the family letters?

There is no image of a tired mind
Tired of its own vanity for fame.
I turn in the comfort of the midnight rain
And as much for pleasure as necessity
Piss in the river beyond O'Ryan's bar.

Indian Summer — Buffalo Summer

Opened like a big new colored-picture book,
The morning took us early with the summer wind
Coming over the streets and yards from the harbor.

There was no game good enough for that morning.
By 10 o'clock my mother put on her new shirtwaist
And Aunt Essie was there in her black hat with the cherries.

I ran ahead of them, all the way to the corner
Clutching my cap pistol, ran out of the sun
And climbed a bench in the little park under the walnuts.

It must have been time: on the curbs all fathers and mothers,
Even Miss Pitman and her cane, old Mr. Kaull and his pipe,
Baby Shea, the big policeman, in the middle of Broadway.

Just then I caught my sister and pulled out her hair-ribbon
O then we stood still and amazed, hearing far off
The sweet incredible fife, the murmur of coming drums.

Every now and then a cop on a motorcycle.
But at last over the dust, out of the shade and light,
The Indians rode before us their arrogant horses.

Ah I had no genuine breath for such word made flesh —
The brown torsos, cheekbones, streaked with warpaint,
The head-dresses blowing wide like unfurled turkeys.

Then came the squaws, then came the little Indians,
And cages with buffalos, wolves, hyenas, coyotes,
An ancient stagecoach waddling, and then the scouts —

The scouts with lashed-leather gloves and buckskin jackets,
Bearing their rifles bravely across their knees,
And then just behind them an old man in an open carriage.

Old, old Buffalo Bill, bowing and smiling,
Lifting his hat from his long white hair, and riding
Right up Broadway in a little yellow-wheeled cart.

Old Talk

His mind dove down from the stars and curled in his head.
It said, We cannot know what we have no sense to know.
And the body said, Be still, take it easy; it is better so.

Mind was dizzy with space where it curved and sped
And it lay still to get warm. The body said, You are cold;
And the mind, Let us stay close together and be comforted.

The body went walking, went walking, went walking,
More or less alone the body went walking; took the tube
Rode up and down in steel, shot dry under river, felt old.

Where were you all day? asked the body; and the mind
Woke as the body would have gone to sleep. Left behind:
One of us, it said, always goes too high, or too deep.

Then while the night tossed, the cricket-mind sang and sang:
Remember — it sang — when the world was snug and small
With nothing all the morning for you to do but toss a ball
Against a sunlighted wall.
                                     And there was one street,
One house and yard changing color, spring and fall.
— Yes, said the body, that was a sweet time and neat; but.

Then the mind said, Always too high now or too deep.
What can we do about it now we're together? the body said.
Well, if it's peace we want, we can always go to sleep.

So for a time the stars flowed on, easy and unbeheld.
Even the mind drowsed in the slack, forgotten head.
Neither ever knew, in the morning, which of them rebelled.

To L. B. S.

Sometimes, tired, I imagine your death:
By childish illness, reasonless accident
Stopped still forever, gone; until I loathe
Fool dramatizations of the brain — I won't,
Though I could, write them into pictures here.

My child, outlive me! Stay beyond my times
Which — how I see now — could be worse than these,
As they are worse for many who had sons.
Death I can bear for myself once, not twice.
I am out of bed at midnight to beg this.

Baldness and the Swan

This matter of baldness: we do it badly.
We tend to be incomplete about it: obscene:
Not the semi-nude, merely the semi-clothed.
The scalp half undone, the scalp fringed
With remnants of tired hair, the scalp scalped —
All this is a weariness and a near-beer.
If baldness, then let it be full-grown,
Wonderful as first pubic hair, an attainment:
Sibelius' head, bare, virile, a completion, an
Aged and naked dome for the accomplished body.
This will be a courage against decoration, wonderful as
Where upon shadowed waters with rhymeless music a dark
                                        swan moves forth.

Green and Red and Darkness

For twenty minutes between the end of storm
And the last of sunset, green became green and
All red roses stepped forward a little and burned.

Then from all over the world like an
Indeterminate number of dusk-robed figures
Evening walked to the center and made darkness.

And then it was my ancestors, for they said
'Now you have all the stars, surer than roses.'
'Damn you,' I said: 'damn you, you dead dead.'

To Marry Strangers

Since after all we were born to marry strangers —
O child, child, child that I never knew! —
Is this photograph of a child I have begotten
And forgotten? Or is it you?

        Or is it true
Love alive is no more retroactive
Than sure of any future? But though it may
Imagine you both beautiful and gray
Cannot, the other way, return and find you?
Where would it find you? This child, this
Beloved stranger? Unconceived daughter? Who?

This is wild — this riddles reason,
This leap of leaves storming off the ground —
Their turning from gold to green is wild
Yet I love this child — would go to her, hold her —
Wherever she could be found.

        But no, but no:
The leaves are never still, they fall all seasons.
And none, none, none resumes the bough.
That alone which is lost will find what is lost,
And you are here, and I: and in this noon
Not even small ghosts run. Across the sun
No voice bends back the wind. But always the wind
Lifts your hair and all the sun is shaken,
And yet may lift it colorless in the moon,
And I — in so much blest — alone remember
The light that moves upon your strange face now.

The U.S. Sailor with the Japanese Skull

Bald-bare, bone-bare, and ivory yellow: skull
Carried by a thus two-headed U.S. sailor
Who got it from a Japanese soldier killed
At Guadalcanal in the ever-present war: our

Bluejacket, I mean, aged 20, in August strolled
Among the little bodies on the sand and hunted
Souvenirs: teeth, tags, diaries, boots; but bolder still
Hacked off this head and under a leopard tree skinned it:

Peeled with a lifting knife the jaw and cheeks, bared
The nose, ripped off the black-haired scalp and gutted
The dead eyes to these thoughtful hollows: a scarred
But bloodless job, unless it be said brains bleed.

Then, his ship underway, dragged this aft in a net
Many days and nights — the cold bone tumbling
Beneath the foaming wake, weed-worn and salt-cut
Rolling safe among fish and washed with Pacific;

Till on a warm and level-keeled day hauled in
Held to the sun and the sailor, back to a gun-rest,
Scrubbed the cured skull with lye, perfecting this:
Not foreign as he saw it first: death's familiar cast.

Bodiless, fleshless, nameless, it and the sun
Offend each other in strange fascination
As though one of the two were mocked; but nothing is in
This head, or it fills with what another imagines

As: here were love and hate and the will to deal
Death or to kneel before it, death emperor,
Recorded orders without reasons, bomb-blast, still
A child's morning, remembered moonlight on Fujiyama:

All scoured out now by the keeper of this skull
Made elemental, historic, parentless by our
Sailor boy who thinks of home, voyages laden, will
Not say, 'Alas! I did not know him at all.'

Gert Swasey

Have you ever asked yourselves — ladies, ladies —
      what it must have been like
To have been Gert Swasey?
To have a rich father,
To run away from home
To be a circus queen, and
To come back a charlady?
To come home and be old?
Dirty and old?

Few of you now can remember Gert Swasey
When she was young — how she was young:
What was it like do you suppose
To drive through town as though you thumbed your nose,
Your red hair flying, and beautiful clothes?
What was it like to want to do that
Seventy years ago — ladies, ladies?
Gert was a wild one, and when she wanted
She'd drive a pair of horses like a witch enchanted.
She'd drive them down from Mount Washington
As though she were fired out of a cannon;
And all the way along Merrimac,
Up Main, through Summer street, down Mill and back
Till she charged up the driveway of her father's mansion,
Twice around where the iron stag stared,
Then as fast to the coach-house as she dared
Which was twice as fast as anybody dared;
The horses snorting and all in lather,
But there was nothing Gert would rather
Than set the whole downtown awhirl
Gasping at that Swasey girl.

I wonder how it was to be that Swasey girl
Not a Sanders nor a Dow nor a Saltonstall,
But new-rich Irish with no family at all
Save a sporting father who kept a stable.

It must have been both mad and sweet
To thunder through leaf-filled Summer street
Disturbing the ladies at the tea table,
Disturbing the ladies in the summer house,
And all along Merrimac's shops and factories
The men's quick faces.

Then to run away — to run far away
To ride in a circus —
The colored wheels
The tights and spangles
The lights, the crowd
The wonderful horses,
The plumed, proud, wonderful white horses,
The tremendous music.
To travel like a gypsy
To dress like a queen
To see all the world that she'd never seen
That was never the world where she had been.
Not a Dow nor a Sanders nor a Saltonstall
Unless they paid to get in.
And then
After thirty-five years to come home again.

Have you ever asked yourselves what it must have been like
To be the old charlady at the B. & M. railroad station?
To clean the toilets
To mop the floors
To be greasy and gray
To be poor and alone
To be Gert Swasey?
Then there is a way — easy to learn —
Of talking to yourself,
Answering yourself,
When there is no one else
Wherever you are.
There are many stray cats, a dozen — fifty —
That will stay in your house
If you will feed them,

Lock them in to keep them safe,
Whose yowling some day wakes the neighborhood
But, at last, not you.

Have you ever asked yourselves what it must have been like
To have been Gert Swasey?
To be a rich young nobody with red restless hair?
To run away from home
To be a circus queen, and
To come back,
And to be old, and to be dirty, and to be dead —
O, ladies, ladies.

Three American Women and

a German Bayonet

Outweighing all, heavy out of the souvenir bundle
The German bayonet: grooved steel socketed in its worn wood
                                            handle,
Its detached and threatening silence.
Its gun-body lost, the great knife wrested to a personal particular
                                            violence —
Now bared shamelessly for what it is, here exposed on the American
                        kitchen table and circled with the wreath
Of his three women, the hard tool of death.

And while Mary his mother says 'I do not like it. Put it down'
Mary the young sister, her eyes gleaming and round,
Giddily giggles as, the awkward toy in her left hand,
She makes impertinent pushes toward his wife who stands
Tolerant of child's play, waiting for her to be done.
His mother says 'I wish he had not got it. It is wicked-looking. I tell
                                    you: Put it down!'
His wife says 'All right, Mary: let me have it — it is mine.'
Saucily pouting, primly frowning
The sister clangs bayonet on table; walks out
And her mother follows.

Like a live thing in not-to-be-trusted stillness,
Like a kind of engine so foreign and self-possessed
As to chill her momently between worship and terror
It lies there waiting alone in the room with her,
Oddly familiar without ever losing strangeness.
Slowly she moves along it a tentative finger
As though to measure and remember its massive, potent length:
Death-deep, tall as life,
For here prized from the enemy, wrenched away captive, his
                              dangerous escape and hers.

Mary his wife
Lifts it heavy and wonderful in her hands and with triumphant
                              tenderness.

Mrs. Severin

Mrs. Severin came home from the Methodist Encampment,
Climbed naked to the diningroom-table and lay down.
She was alone at the time but naturally told of it afterward.
'Lord! Lord!' she had called out. 'Thou seest me. Wherein is my
                              fault?'

When she heard of it, secondhand, Mrs. Bashfield laughed till she
                              cried.
'My God!' she said, 'I'd like to've watched her getting up there!'
For Mrs. Severin, you see, was a very stout old lady,
A spilling mass by buttons, shawls, pins and ribboned eyeglasses
                              held together.

The eyeglasses were a shift of drama: hoisted for reading aloud,
                              lowered for talking;
They were not interruption. Mrs. Severin's soft incessant sibilance
Through all the days she visited and rocked by the window
Braided inextricably Bible and Autobiography. Jesus was near.

'The morning Encampment began the Lord suddenly told me to go.
Ran all the way downstreet to the cars for Canobie Lake,

233

Didn't fasten my dress or tie my shoes. Left the house open. Young
                ones at the neighbors.
"Lord," I said, "I am thy servant"— and stayed the whole beautiful,
                blessed week.'

On the listening child her showers of quotation pattered a drugged
                dream.

' "Thought becomes word. Word becomes act. Act becomes
                character. Character becomes destiny,"
Remember that. And praise the Lord,' she said, giving off also
Odor of camphor, old rose jars and muttonleg sleeves. 'Amen!'

The husband long gone who wasted her inheritance; the irritable
                children
Who hated to have to have her now; the friends who took her in
                now and again: gone.
Here in her false hair and hand-me-downs, patiently talking —
                talking:
Old Mrs. Severin who once, brave on a diningroom-table, naked
           confronted her unanswering Lord.

Memento

(B. T. S. 1885-1952)

1

This is a rocksaw seacoast.
Puddingstone lugs the thud of glacial death.
Nevertheless the thin earth of the clifftops
Hedges with wild roses the summer sea,
And I say this headland is for us forever
The sheriff of the morning star.

Far down there are cave-cuts where high tide
Jets a commotion of foam.
The sterile wear is slow is
A spoon of pearled emerald from a hundred years.

Yet eastward at evening the ocean
Takes credit for the moon.

Cow-sound foreign there our bell-buoy gong
Tins and tans; off Brenton Reef
Our lightship makes a medallion.
We have chained these things and now
Would see them only if they disappeared.
We are if we touch the waters a skirl of snow.

Though I have seen navies, vicious though ours,
Soundless past these islands, out of this bay,
Curve toward Gibraltar;
I have imagined dragon-headed ships
Arriving here ten centuries out of port
Loom in marine erasure of history.

Cantilevered into surf this coast
Juts nonhuman; graves of shipwrecked were
Hurricane-gouged; but the swallows
Fly in and out of the earth, fly through
Plunges of gulls that rise
White, shadowed, and white in the dulcet sun.

And I say of these weathers I choose
A seamless afternoon — mansion of glass
As huge as childhood — sea and sky: I say
For an ancient anchor grass-grown
This wreath of roses between stone and salt air
Is breath of the dead whose memories now are mine.

2

Will you hear that I spoke these stones and trees,
These stones under trees, trees over the houses,
These streets and walks, these dooryards hedged and fenced
In the old way, this little town?
I say, without my voice this is all lost, it is nothing.
But I am the passionate marriage of memory and love
And which of you knows even my name or my voice?
How could you know today is today having forgotten

Yesterday and tomorrow.
                          Yet — whether
You hear or know — I speak: I say that here
Night pours westward off the back of the world
And the sea pours out the sun which rising
Shafts with its tiers of escalators
The moist streets of the morning;
                          and the streets
Fill with fathers, skip with schoolchildren,
They hush for cool cobbledy sound of horse and wagon
Somewhere around the corner and coming nearer;
They are lanes between lines of washing hung to dance
Over mothers and babies and sandboxes till noon.
Till I say S L E E P. It is three o'clock. The sun
Inaccessible hovers a while stilled.
No footsteps — no door — no doorbell — all is emptied.
I alone stand, a fixed dream, and watch
That piazza opening through its leafless vines
And the wind in the rockingchair.

3

This lady's memory of these things is gone.
Of us and sixty-seven years her knowledge
Is gone. While you stare down at her long-loved face
The nonexistence which shakes you is your own.

Now you have come to stare at the statue of death
Its terror is in your recognition of it and,
Unlike a real statue, its failure to change,
Its inability to respond. And this conceived you.

From what you know, from what you can bear to see
This must be buried soon. And only for you
Now and always light is everywhere altered,
All the colors of the world are otherwise.

Whom do the mourners see? A girl — a ghost —
A bride — an old and tired lady — a stranger?
They pause and make her momentary replica.
Whom do the mourners see? Themselves. Themselves.

As wave into wave, so memory into memory
Folds, falls forward, follows till some far
And unimaginable coast receives forever
The final landfall of oblivion.

You remember fright and agony were here
But pain cannot be posthumous for her.
The burial signal is thunder and rain. Say S L E E P.
SLEEP, LADY: NO LONGER REMEMBER EVEN ME.

4

Psyche whose threnodic hands
Wash the winter darkness white
Move between the stars and starlight
Where the worlds are whirled to sands
Where all music disappears,
All the answers which we know
Less than shadow less than echo,
The emolument of tears
Turned immaculate fall of snow
Turned anonymous design
Strict as stars that as they fell
Fell unrecognizable,
Now no longer think to tell
Which were hers and which were mine,
Now no further realize —
Psyche whose threnodic hands
Heal the cicatrice of years —
What had soothed her hands and eyes.
Move between the sun and sunrise.

5

Again and yet again midsummer night
Hangs the prismatic curtains of the moon
Draping as with stilled and visible winds
The ocean's quietly dancing arches, leaping
Point Judith to Brenton Reef and to Saconnet
And sweeping past Aquidneck's phosphorent roofs

Stands in this lifting light on the great bay
And all its shadowy islands: Conanicut,
Gould and Rose and north to Coddington Cove
The twisted whale of Prudence Island — fixed
As in a mindless memory of love.

The moonlight seems to shudder. It is the sea's
Intermittent pausing pulse, its flicker
Of nerves, that shudder. And even these remote
As a sleeping face watched dimly in a mirror;
Watched carefully as though it might awaken
Although I know it will only disappear
And the emptied glass swirl to blueish fog
Quick to be lost in the moon's nameless color.
Although I think that deep within these waters
Stares the figurehead of a nameless lady
Whose long farewells speak from her lidless eyes.

Now this wide glass of sea is voyageless.
The lightship blinks for nothing. The bell-buoy
Bangs for danger of emptiness and home.
At the cliffbase the tide is a caress,
Neither impersonal nor aggressive now
But in an alien armistice feigning peace.
This headland now embodied by the dead
Moves in the kinship of the moon which is
A memory of light and which is love,
And gifted with roses' wild recurrent grace
Sets forth toward day on the rugosa sea.

Bermuda Suite

5

Long. 60°50W; Lat. 32°15N

Flared down from broken cloud the calipered light
Stood strident, made exact embrace of land.
Brooched crescent upon platinum the islands

Curved gold-flecked emerald, and there was light
Only along the great bow of the islands
As though they swung burning alone in space.

Running out of the sea the man and woman
Flashed on the shore naked and beautiful,
And flung to sand as by a wave of air
They lay together breathlessly and then
They heard their hearts, and time resumed its beat.
Sand kept flickering with the ticking wind.

The sand swept high to a long wave of earth
That, wrought upon the rock, had rooted rock
Tendrilled in a gigantic grasp from air
Holding in perilous suspension
What cragged mass the sea once lifted up,
Conjoined from accident this miracle.

At its emergent line the man and woman
Stared at cloud-vexed sky, the chains of light.
They saw the flowered headlands shake and quiet
In criss-cross hammering of their sea-lashed hearts,
And remembered in wild wonder-eaten wisdom
That all the flowering was meant for them.

Exercise in Aesthetics

The lilac bushes were small with winter.
Rain-repeated, the abacus of barberries
Ran red, ran red above the smoking snow
And the green chickweed where it winked.
Low to the ground, fog hovered and blew and shifted.
The house we passed was three miles from the last
And, as it turned out, three miles from the next.
A back road between cold-blackened pines
On a cellar of a morning near December's end.
Nobody visible at the house. My question was

239

Whom were all the Christmas signals for —
The candles in the windows and the doorwreath
Ribboned to render hemlock a gay creation?
At most a stranger or two passed once a day,
Like us, in a moment passing. For us, then?
Yes, if we happened by. But of necessity
First for the mingled joy of decorations
And whoever made them. How else could it be?

Unsexed by the Cold Sea . . .

Unsexed by the cold sea, prone out of it on the beach,
Too diminished for art, I yet resolving
To write only of seasons other than the present,
To try the imagination, the larger love;
All the while the sanded wind blew over me.

Next-naked the young woman on her back
Slept brown and gold along a blue blanket,
Her children near; I spied upon her thighs
Forked open and the mount of glossy ribs and
All the while the sanded wind blew over her.

Two children small and gold who bucketed,
Built and bashed at variance, and now
Trotted with new knees to borrow some ocean,
Then peered to find if their mother still slept;
All the while the sanded wind blew past them.

Strangers, we three shared an altering patience;
I at my distance beginning to fondle a daydream
On that upturned, abandoned face, and they
Running in close to see when it would claim them,
All the while the sanded wind blew past it.

Their play dropped, sudden as fright among birds
They pounced, calling, shaking and waking her;

I closed my eyes upon her; the plunge and plunge
Of stroking ocean remotely hot and swollen,
And all the while the sanded wind blew between us.

Merrill's Brook

Sun over all and air over all and clover
Ripens with bees the summer afternoon
Where pasture right angles at the slanted oak
And swirls the narrow brook to a round brown pool.

The banks are skin-shiny with twenty boys
That flicker warm light into the shade and out,
Running. They leap to a hang of rope and swing
Above the water, let go with a shouting plunge.

The larger and skillful revolve their bald behinds
On a wheel of headover diving, and here jounce
Beginners flouncing, one foot careful in shallows,
Dog-paddlers, and ankle deep a little brother

Who stands blondly glistening, unspoken-to.
One anxious mongrel circles among the bathers
Who jump back and forth, amphibious of June:
The air's white-knived with knees and shoulder-blades.

Or loll in grass; and now and then pair off
To hide in alder thickets with hot hands,
Emerging red to dive — the hurried thud
Of racing bare-soled on bluet-bevelled earth.

So on so on a hundred summer days
Till the stranger, the stout and hairy Adam, came
With soap and a pleading smile and called to us
While we scrambled to clothes and ran and ran away.

Re-Run

I was that dancer. On the screen
Dances again who once was I
Head Grecian-curled and lean, the lean
Pectoral hardness and his hard thigh

Strident across the film in great
Loves of leaping, in whirls, in slow
Erectile pause of weightless weight
Perfected twenty years ago.

They often re-run. I save to sit
And spy upon the youth who had
Youth without its opposite,
Promise therefore that went bad.

See how he dances ignorance
Of childhood and of you and me;
Half-naked, full magnificence,
He spins before a moonlit sea

Whose tones orchestral and perverse
Whisper, snarl on the sound-track;
But all are caught around those terse
Hips and within that stallion back

To stiff finalities of strength
Feet thundering at the horn's cry,
Until the plot extrudes its length
When in the movie he must die.

Codicil for Pvt. John Hogg's Will

Gray and blue, the boy ghosts with guns are in the spring woods:
Now — a century after — they are here.
West, the Blue Ridge is a line of march along the sky and into the
      sky —

A memorial —
And those wide miles of fields roll up to it as though with love — for
      the fallacy is always pathetic;
But in these woods, poignant with April, the boys in a mist that
      makes the morning old
Rove in a haunt of spring. One can see why.

Sunshine, thin and young, burning away like mirrored light,
      probes the hepatica-broken leaves
And blankets of violets flung to the gray ground
And the windless moss furled on the cedars
And the brooks living shyly amidst embracing, stumbling, fallen
      trees; and
There's bloodwort, brief blossoming.

So youth, one knows, died here long ago.
By the five-toned mourning dove — not only, not alone; no less
Weave of sparrow, waxwing, finch, and cardinal birdsong, daylong
      birdsong,
Riddling, caroling chorus through the slowly opening day.

One, a stranger from among the victors — if there are victors — can
      see why
This could be held dearest of all and to be fought for,
Here in the willow way
Dogwood's ivory stairs to nowhere,
The deep flowering judas.

'The Hour Is Late'

It seemed to me in the night
I had no art after all.
That all I had tried to make
Was never for its own sake,
Stank with impurity,
And that what my enemies said
My kind friends left unsaid.

Then it seemed to me
I stumbled in a dark hall
In an unfamiliar house
Where I had no business to be.

Did vanity espouse
Such self-deceiving as mine?
As though not tree but vine —
As though not girl but kiss —
Were the reality.
Or had I at first some reason?
The beginning as true for me
As for some luckier men
Who quarried the light of the day
Out of such night as this?

There was nothing to which to pray
And the night was very late.
I could neither love nor hate
Who had lived so long alone
With an invented ghost
That now was utterly gone.
A naked man in a strange house
In the dark, nameless and lost.

KARL SHAPIRO

Adam and Eve

I

THE SICKNESS OF ADAM

In the beginning, at every step, he turned
As if by instinct to the East to praise
The nature of things. Now every path was learned
He lost the lifted, almost flower-like gaze

Of a temple dancer. He began to walk
Slowly, like one accustomed to be alone.
He found himself lost in the field of talk;
Thinking became a garden of its own.

In it were new things: words he had never said,
Beasts he had never seen and knew were not
In the true garden, terrors, and tears shed
Under a tree by him, for some new thought.

And the first anger. Once he flung a staff
At softly coupling sheep and struck the ram.
It broke away. And God heard Adam laugh
And for his laughter made the creature lame.

And wanderlust. He stood upon the Wall
To search the unfinished countries lying wide
And waste, where not a living thing could crawl,
And yet he would descend, as if to hide.

His thought drew down the guardian at the gate,
To whom man said, 'What danger am I in?'
And the angel, hurt in spirit, seemed to hate
The wingless thing that worried after sin,

For it said nothing but marvelously unfurled
Its wings and arched them shimmering overhead,
Which must have been the signal from the world
That the first season of our life was dead.

Adam fell down with labor in his bones,
And God approached him in the cool of day
And said, 'This sickness in your skeleton
Is longing. I will remove it from your clay.'

He said also, 'I made you strike the sheep.'
It began to rain and God sat down beside
The sinking man. When he was fast asleep
He wet his right hand deep in Adam's side

And drew the graceful rib out of his breast.
Far off, the latent streams began to flow
And birds flew out of Paradise to nest
On earth. Sadly the angel watched them go.

II

THE RECOGNITION OF EVE

Whatever it was she had so fiercely fought
Had fled back to the sky, but still she lay
With arms outspread, awaiting its assault,
Staring up through the branches of the tree,
The fig tree. Then she drew a shuddering breath
And turned her head instinctively his way.
She had fought birth as dying men fight death.

Her sigh awakened him. He turned and saw
A body swollen, as though formed of fruits,
White as the flesh of fishes, soft and raw.
He hoped she was another of the brutes
So he crawled over and looked into her eyes,
The human wells that pool all absolutes.
It was like looking into double skies.

And when she spoke the first word (it was *thou*)
He was terror-stricken, but she raised her hand
And touched his wound where it was fading now,
For he must feel the place to understand.
Then he recalled the longing that had torn
His side, and while he watched it whitely mend,
He felt it stab him suddenly like a thorn.

He thought the woman had hurt him. Was it she
Or the same sickness seeking to return;
Or was there any difference, the pain set free
And she who seized him now as hard as iron?
Her fingers bit his body. She looked old
And involuted, like the newly-born.
He let her hurt him till she loosed her hold.

Then she forgot him and she wearily stood
And went in search of water through the grove.
Adam could see her wandering through the wood,
Studying her footsteps as her body wove
In light and out of light. She found a pool
And there he followed shyly to observe.
She was already turning beautiful.

III

THE KISS

The first kiss was with stumbling fingertips.
Their bodies grazed each other as if by chance
And touched and untouched in a kind of dance.
Second, they found out touching with their lips.

Some obscure angel, pausing on his course,
Shed such a brightness on the face of Eve
That Adam in grief was ready to believe
He had lost her love. The third kiss was by force.

Their lips formed foreign, unimagined oaths
When speaking of the Tree of Guilt. So wide

Their mouths, they drank each other from inside.
A gland of honey burst within their throats.

But something rustling hideously overhead,
They jumped up from the fourth caress and hid.

IV

THE TREE OF GUILT

Why, on her way to the oracle of Love,
Did she not even glance up at the Tree
Of Life, that giant with the whitish cast
And glinting leaves and berries of dull gray,
As though covered with mold? But who would taste
The medicine of immortality,
And who would 'be as God'? And in what way?

So she came breathless to the lowlier one
And like a priestess of the cult she knelt,
Holding her breasts in token for a sign,
And prayed the spirit of the burdened bough
That the great power of the tree be seen
And lift itself out of the Tree of Guilt
Where it had hidden in the leaves till now.

Or did she know already? Had the peacock
Rattling its quills, glancing its thousand eyes
At her, the iridescence of the dove,
Stench of the he-goat, everything that joins
Told her the mystery? It was not enough,
So from the tree the snake began to rise
And dropt its head and pointed at her loins.

She fell and hid her face and still she saw
The spirit of the tree emerge and slip
Into the open sky until it stood
Straight as a standing-stone, and spilled its seed.
And all the seed were serpents of the good.
Again he seized the snake and from its lip
It spat the venomous evil of the deed.

And it was over. But the woman lay
Stricken with what she knew, ripe in her thought
Like a fresh apple fallen from the limb
And rotten, like a fruit that lies too long.
This way she rose, ripe-rotten in her prime
And spurned the cold thing coiled against her foot
And called her husband, in a kind of song.

V

THE CONFESSION

As on the first day her first word was *thou*.
He waited while she said, 'Thou art the tree.'
And while she said, almost accusingly,
Looking at nothing, 'Thou art the fruit I took.'
She seemed smaller by inches as she spoke,
And Adam wondering touched her hair and shook,
Half understanding. He answered softly, 'How?'

And for the third time, in the third way, Eve:
'The tree that rises from the middle part
Of the garden.' And almost tenderly, 'Thou art
The garden. *We.*' Then she was overcome,
And Adam coldly, lest he should succumb
To pity, standing at the edge of doom,
Comforted her like one about to leave.

She sensed departure and she stood aside
Smiling and bitter. But he asked again,
'How did you eat? With what thing did you sin?'
And Eve with body slackened and uncouth,
'Under the tree I took the fruit of truth
From an angel. I ate it with my other mouth.'
And saying so, she did not know she lied.

It was the man who suddenly released
From doubt, wept in the woman's heavy arms,
Those double serpents, subtly winding forms
That climb and drop about the manly boughs;

And dry with weeping, fiery and aroused,
Fell on her face to slake his terrible thirst
And bore her body earthward like a beast.

VI

SHAME

The hard blood falls back in the manly fount,
The soft door closes under Venus' mount,
The ovoid moon moves to the Garden's side
And dawn comes, but the lovers have not died.
They have not died but they have fallen apart
In sleep, like equal halves of the same heart.

How to teach shame? How to teach nakedness
To the already naked? How to express
Nudity? How to open innocent eyes
And separate the innocent from the wise?
And how to re-establish the guilty tree
In infinite gardens of humanity?

By marring the image, by the black device
Of the goat-god, by the clown of Paradise,
By fruits of cloth and by the navel's bud,
By itching tendrils and by strings of blood,
By ugliness, by the shadow of our fear,
By ridicule, by the fig-leaf patch of hair.

Whiter than tombs, whiter than whitest clay,
Exposed beneath the whitening eye of day,
They awoke and saw the covering that reveals.
They thought they were changing into animals.
Like animals they bellowed terrible cries
And clutched each other, hiding each other's eyes.

VII

EXILE

The one who gave the warning with his wings,
Still doubting them, held out the sword of flame
Against the Tree of Whiteness as they came
Angrily, slowly by, like exiled kings,

And watched them at the broken-open gate
Stare in the distance long and overlong,
And then, like peasants, pitiful and strong,
Take the first step toward earth and hesitate.

For Adam raised his head and called aloud,
'My Father, who has made the garden pall,
Giving me all things and then taking all,
Who with your opposite nature has endowed

Woman, give us your hand for our descent.
Needing us greatly, even in our disgrace,
Guide us, for gladly do we leave this place
For our own land and wished-for banishment.'

But woman prayed, 'Guide us to Paradise.'
Around them slunk the uneasy animals,
Strangely excited, uttering coughs and growls,
And bounded down into the wild abyss.

And overhead the last migrating birds,
Then empty sky. And when the two had gone
A slow half-dozen steps across the stone,
The angel came and stood among the shards

And called them, as though joyously, by name.
They turned in dark amazement and beheld
Eden ablaze with fires of red and gold,
The garden dressed for dying in cold flame,

And it was autumn, and the present world.

Drug Store

> *I do remember an apothecary,*
> *And hereabouts 'a dwells*

It baffles the foreigner like an idiom,
And he is right to adopt it as a form
Less serious than the living-room or bar;
    For it disestablishes the cafe,
Is a collective, and on basic country.

Not that it praises hygiene and corrupts
The ice-cream parlor and the tobacconist's
Is it a center; but that the attractive symbols
    Watch over puberty and leer
Like rubber bottles waiting for sick-use.

Youth comes to jingle nickels and crack wise;
The baseball scores are his, the magazines
Devoted to lust, the jazz, the Coca-Cola,
    The lending-library of love's latest.
He is the customer; he is heroized.

And every nook and cranny of the flesh
Is spoken to by packages with wiles.
"Buy me, buy me," they whimper and cajole;
    The hectic range of lipsticks pouts,
Revealing the wicked and the simple mouth.

With scarcely any evasion in their eye
They smoke, undress their girls, exact a stance;
But only for a moment. The clock goes round;
    Crude fellowships are made and lost;
They slump in booths like rags, not even drunk.

Haircut

O wonderful nonsense of lotions of Lucky Tiger,
Of savory soaps and oils of bottle-bright green,
The gold of liqueurs, the unguents of Newark and Niger,
Powders and balms and waters washing me clean;

In mirrors of marble and silver I see us forever
Increasing, decreasing the puzzles of luminous spaces
As I turn, am revolved and am pumped in the air on a lever,
With the backs of my heads in chorus with all of my faces.

Scissors and comb are mowing my hair into neatness,
Now pruning my ears, now smoothing my neck like a plain;
In the harvest of hair and the chaff of powdery sweetness
My snow-covered slopes grow dark with the wooly rain.

And the little boy cries, for it hurts to sever the curl,
And we too are quietly bleating to part with our coat.
Does the barber want blood in a dish? I am weak as a girl,
I desire my pendants, the fatherly chin of a goat.

I desire the pants of a bear, the nap of a monkey
Which trousers of friction have blighted down to my skin.
I am bare as a tusk, as jacketed up as a flunkey,
With the chest of a moth-eaten camel growing within.

But in death we shall flourish, you summer-dark leaves of my head,
While the flesh of the jaw ebbs away from the shores of my teeth;
You shall cover my sockets and soften the boards of my bed
And lie on the flat of my temples as proud as a wreath.

Love for a Hand

Two hands lie still, the hairy and the white,
And soon down ladders of reflected light
The sleepers climb in silence. Gradually

They separate on paths of long ago,
Each winding on his arm the unpleasant clew
That leads, live as a nerve, to memory.

But often when too steep her dream descends,
Perhaps to the grotto where her father bends
To pick her up, the husband wakes as though
He had forgotten something in the house.
Motionless he eyes the room that glows
With the little animals of light that prowl

This way and that. Soft are the beasts of light
But softer still her hand that drifts so white
Upon the whiteness. How like a water-plant
It floats upon the black canal of sleep,
Suspended upward from the distant deep
In pure achievement of its lovely want!

Quietly then he plucks it and it folds
And is again a hand, small as a child's.
He would revive it but it barely stirs
And so he carries it off a little way
And breaks it open gently. Now he can see
The sweetness of the fruit, his hand eats hers.

Mongolian Idiot

A dog that spoke, a monster born of sheep
We mercilessly kill, and kill the thought,
Yet house the parrot and let the centaur go,
These being to their nature and those not.
We laugh at apes, that never quite succeed
      At eating soup or wearing hats.

Adam had named so many but not this,
This that would name a curse when it had come,
Unfinished man, or witch, or myth, or sin,

254

Not ever father and never quite a son.
Ape had outstripped him, dog and darling lamb
      And all the kindergarten beasts.

Enter the bare room of his mind and count
His store of words with letters large and black;
See how he handles clumsily those blocks
With swans and sums; his colored picture books.
At thirty-five he squeals to see the ball
      Bounce in the air and roll away.

Pity and fear we give this innocent
Who maimed his mother's beautiful instinct;
But she would say, "My body had a dog;
I bore the ape and nursed the crying sheep.
He is my kindness and my splendid gift
      Come from all life and for all life."

October 1

That season when the leaf deserts the bole
And half-dead see-saws through the October air
Falling face-downward on the walks to print
The decalcomania of its little soul —
Hardly has the milkman's sleepy horse
On wooden shoes echoed across the blocks,
When with its back jaws open like a dredge
The van comes lumbering up the curb to someone's door
    and knocks.

And four black genii muscular and shy
Holding their shy caps enter the first room
Where someone hurriedly surrenders up
The thickset chair, the mirror half awry,
Then to their burdens stoop without a sound.
One with his bare hands rends apart the bed,
One stuffs the china-barrel with stale print,
Two bear the sofa toward the door with dark funereal tread.

The corner lamp, the safety eye of night,
Enveloped in the sun blinks and goes blind
And soon the early risers pick their way
Through kitchenware and pillows bolt upright.
The bureau on the sidewalk with bare back
And wrinkling veneer is most disgraced,
The sketch of Paris suffers in the wind,
Only the bike, its nose against the wall, does not show haste.

Two hours—the movers mop their necks and look,
Filing through dust and echoes back and forth.
The halls are hollow and all the floors are cleared
Bare to the last board, to the most secret nook;
But on the street a small chaos survives
That slowly now the leviathan ingests,
And schoolboys and stenographers stare at
The truck, the house, the husband in his hat who stands and rests.

He turns with miserable expectant face
And for the last time enters. On the wall
A picture-stain spreads from the nail-hole down.
Each object live and dead has left its trace.
He leaves his key; but as he quickly goes
This question comes behind: Did someone die?
Is someone rich or poor, better or worse?
What shall uproot a house and bring this care into his eye?

The Southerner

He entered with the authority of politeness
And the jokes died in the air. A well-made blaze
Grew round the main log in the fireplace
Spontaneously. I watched its brightness
Spread to the altered faces of my guests.
They did not like the Southerner. I did.
A liberal felt that someone should forbid
That soft voice making its soft arrests.

As when a Negro or a prince extends
His hand to an average man, and the mind
Speeds up a minute and then drops behind,
So did the conversation of my friends.
I was amused by this respectful awe
Which those hotly deny who have no prince.
I watched the frown, the stare, and the wince
Recede into attention, the arms thaw.

I saw my southern evil memories
Raped from my mind before my eyes, my youth
Practicing caste, perfecting the untruth
Of staking honor on the wish to please.
I saw my honor's paradox:
Grandpa, the saintly Jew, keeping his beard
In difficult Virginia, yet endeared
Of blacks and farmers, although orthodox.

The nonsense of the gracious lawn,
The fall of hollow columns in the pines,
Do these deceive more than the rusted signs
Of Jesus on the road? Can they go on
In the timeless manner of all gentlefolk
There in a culture rotted and unweeded
Where the black yoni of the South is seeded
By crooked men in denims thin as silk?

They do go on, denying still the fall
Of Richmond and man, who gently live
On the street above the violence, fugitive,
Graceful, and darling, who recall
The heartbroken country once about to flower,
Full of black poison, beautiful to smell,
Who know how to conform, how to compel,
And how from the best bush to receive a flower.

V-Letter

I love you first because your face is fair,
      Because your eyes Jewish and blue,
Set sweetly with the touch of foreignness
Above the cheekbones, stare rather than dream.
Often your countenance recalls a boy
      Blue-eyed and small, whose silent mischief
Tortured his parents and compelled my hate
        To wish his ugly death.
Because of this reminder, my soul's trouble,
And for your face, so often beautiful,
      I love you, wish you life.

I love you first because you wait, because
      For your own sake, I cannot write
Beyond these words. I love you for these words
That sting and creep like insects and leave filth.
I love you for the poverty you cry
      And I bend down with tears of steel
That melt your hand like wax, not for this war
        The droplets shattering
Those candle-glowing fingers of my joy,
But for your name of agony, my love,
      That cakes my mouth with salt.

And all your imperfections and perfections
      And all your magnitude of grace
And all this love explained and unexplained
Is just a breath. I see you woman-size
And this looms larger and more goddess-like
      Than silver goddesses on screens.
I see you in the ugliness of light,
      Yet you are beautiful,
And in the dark of absence your full length
Is such as meets my body to the full
      Though I am starved and huge.

You turn me from these days as from a scene
    Out of an open window far
Where lies the foreign city and the war.
You are my home and in your spacious love
I dream to march as under flaring flags
    Until the door is gently shut.
Give me the tearless lesson of your pride,
    Teach me to live and die
As one deserving anonymity,
The mere devotion of a house to keep
    A woman and a man.

Give me the free and poor inheritance
    Of our own kind, not furniture
Of education, nor the prophet's pose,
The general cause of words, the hero's stance,
The ambitions incommensurable with flesh,
    But the drab makings of a room
Where sometimes in the afternoon of thought
    The brief and blinding flash
May light the enormous chambers of your will
And show the gracious Parthenon that time
    Is ever measured by.

As groceries in a pantry gleam and smile
    Because they are important weights
Bought with the metal minutes of your pay,
So do these hours stand in solid rows,
The dowry for a use in common life.
    I love you first because your years
Lead to my matter-of-fact and simple death
    Or to our open marriage,
And I pray nothing for my safety back,
Not even luck, because our love is whole
    Whether I live or fail.

Waitress

Whoever with the compasses of his eyes
Is plotting the voyage of your steady shape
As you come laden through the room and back
And rounding your even bottom like a Cape
Crooks his first finger, whistles through his lip
Till you arrive, all motion, like a ship,

He is my friend — consider his dark pangs
And love of Niger, naked indigence,
Dance him the menu of a poem and squirm
Deep in the juke-box jungle, green and dense.
Surely he files his teeth, punctures his nose,
Carves out the god and takes off all his clothes.

For once, the token on the table's edge
Sufficing, proudly and with hair unpinned
You mounted the blueplate, stretched out and grinned
Like Christmas fish and turkey pink and skinned,
Eyes on the half-shell, loin with parsley stuck,
Thigh-bones and ribs and little toes to suck.

I speak to you, ports of the northern myth,
This dame is carved and eaten. One by one,
God knows what hour, her different parts go home,
Lastly her pants, and day or night is done;
But on the restaurant the sign of fear
Reddens and blazes — "English spoken here."

The Tingling Back

Sometimes deeply immured in white-washed tower
        quiet at ink and thinking book,
            alone with my own smoke,

the blood at rest, the body far below,
swiftly there falls an angry shower
of arrows upon my back,
like bees or electric needles run amok
between my flesh and shirt. I know
then I have touched the pain
of amour-propre, of something yesterday
I said and I should not have said,
I did and must not do.
These needles wing their insights from my brain
and through and through my flesh they play
to prick my skin with red
letters of shame and blue blurs of tattoo.
I sweat and take my medicine
for one must be sincere
and study one's sincerity like a crime:
to be the very last to smile,
the first one to begin
(when danger streaks the atmosphere) to fear,
to pocket praises like a dime,
to pet the crocodile,
to see a foreign agony as stone,
to ravel dreams in crowded room,
to let the hair grow tall,
to skin the eye and thrust it to the wind.
Yet if I stood with God alone
inside the blinding tomb
I would not feel embarrassment at all
nor those hot needles of the mind
which are so clean. I'd ask
not if I'd known the tissue of my will
and scarified my body white,
but whether, insincere,
I'd grown to the simplicity of a mask;
and if in natural error still
whether my fingers might
destroy the true and keep the error near.

Recapitulations

I

I was born downtown on a wintry day
    And under the roof where Poe expired;
Tended by nuns my mother lay
    Dark-haired and beautiful and tired.

Doctors and cousins paid their call,
    The rabbi and my father helped.
A crucifix burned on the wall
    Of the bright room where I was whelped.

At one week all my family prayed,
    Stuffed wine and cotton in my craw;
The rabbi blessed me with a blade
    According to the Mosaic Law.

The white steps blazed in Baltimore
    And cannas and white statuary.
I went home voluble and sore
    Influenced by Abraham and Mary.

II

At one the Apocalypse had spoken,
Von Moltke fell, I was housebroken.

At two how could I understand
The murder of Archduke Ferdinand?

France was involved with history,
I with my thumbs when I was three.

A sister came, we neared a war,
Paris was shelled when I was four.

I joined in our peach-kernel drive
For poison gas when I was five.

At six I cheered the big parade,
Burned sparklers and drank lemonade.

At seven I passed at school though I
Was far too young to say *Versailles*.

At eight the boom began to tire,
I tried to set our house on fire.

The Bolsheviks had drawn the line,
Lenin was stricken, I was nine.

— What evils do not retrograde
To my first odious decade?

V

My first small book was nourished in the dark,
Secretly written, published, and inscribed.
Bound in wine-red, it made no brilliant mark.
Rather impossible relatives subscribed.

The best review was one I wrote myself
Under the name of a then-dearest friend.
Two hundred volumes stood upon my shelf
Saying my golden name from end to end.

I was not proud but seriously stirred;
Sorrow was song and money poetry's maid!
Sorrow I had in many a ponderous word,
But were the piper and the printer paid?

XIII

When nuns were spitted and poets fell
And Spain the medieval hell
Became our modern one as well
    And I, a Hamlet, held my tongue,
    Tell me, conscience, was I wrong?

When matters on the Ebro failed
And Cornford died and Campbell railed
And I to my Tahiti sailed
    To ape Loti and Rupert's throng,
    Tell me, conscience, was I wrong?

When Russia smote the sledded Finn
And generals of the French let in
Germans to practice mutual sin,
    And I read Horace all night long,
    Tell me, conscience, was I wrong?

When London like the phoenix burned
And flew in fire and fire returned
And peace beneath the umbrella spurned,
    Did I to either side belong?
    Tell me, conscience, was I wrong?

When dolls in armor from their toys
Scuttled our fleet with frightful noise
And I obeyed the White House voice,
    My best friend was in a prison flung.
    Tell me, conscience, was I wrong?

ROBERT PENN WARREN

Eidolon

All night, in May, dogs barked in the hollow woods;
Hoarse, from secret huddles of no light,
By moonlit bole, hoarse, the dogs gave tongue.
In May, by moon, no moon, thus: I remember
Of their far clamor the throaty, infatuate timbre.

The boy, all night, lay in the black room,
Tick-straw, all night, harsh to the bare side.
Staring, he heard; the clotted dark swam slow.
Far off, by wind, no wind, unappeasable riot
Provoked, resurgent, the bosom's nocturnal disquiet.

What hungers kept the house? under the rooftree
The boy; the man, clod-heavy, hard hand uncurled;
The old man, eyes wide, spittle on his beard.
In dark was crushed the may-apple: plunging, the rangers
Of dark remotelier belled their unhouselled angers.

Dogs quartered the black woods: blood black on
May-apple at dawn, old beech-husk. And trails are lost
By rock, in ferns lost, by pools unlit.
I heard the hunt. Who saw, in darkness, how fled
The white eidolon from fanged commotion rude?

Revelation

Because he had spoken harshly to his mother,
The day became astonishingly bright,
The enormity of distance crept to him like a dog now,
And earth's own luminescence seemed to repel the night.

Roof was rent like loud paper tearing to admit
Sun-sulphurous splendor where had been before
But the submarine glimmer by kindly countenances lit,
As slow, phosphorescent dignities light the ocean floor.

By walls, by walks, chrysanthemum and aster,
All hairy, fat-petalled species, lean, confer,
And his ears, and heart, should burn at that insidious whisper
Which concerns him so, he knows; but he cannot make out the
                                                    words.

The peacock screamed, and his feathered fury made
Legend shake, all day, while the sky ran pale as milk;
That night, all night, the buck rabbit stamped in the moonlit glade,
And the owl's brain glowed like a coal in the grove's combustible
                                                    dark.

When Sulla smote and Rome was rent, Augustine
Recalled how Nature, shuddering, tore her gown,
And kind changed kind, and the blunt herbivorous tooth dripped
                                                    blood;
At Duncan's death, at Dunsinane, chimneys blew down.

But, oh! his mother was kinder than ever Rome,
Dearer than Duncan — no wonder, then, Nature's frame
Thrilled in voluptuous hemispheres far off from his home;
But not in terror: only as the bride, as the bride.

In separateness only does love learn definition,
Though Brahma smiles beneath the dappled shade,
Though tears, that night, wet the pillow where the boy's head was
                                                    laid

Dreamless of splendid antipodal agitation;

And though across what tide and tooth Time is,
He was to lean back toward that recalcitrant face,
He would think, than Sulla more fortunate, how once he had learned
Something important above love, and about love's grace.

Pursuit

The hunchback on the corner, with gum and shoelaces,
Has his own wisdom and pleasures, and may not be lured
To divulge them to you, for he has merely endured
Your appeal for his sympathy and your kind purchases;
And wears infirmity but as the general who turns
Apart, in his famous old greatcoat there on the hill
At dusk when the rapture and cannonade are still,
To muse withdrawn from the dead, from his gorgeous subalterns;
Or stares from the thicket of his familiar pain, like a fawn
That meets you a moment, wheels, in imperious innocence
                                        is gone.

Go to the clinic. Wait in the outer room
Where like an old possum the snag-nailed hand will hump
On its knee in murderous patience, and the pomp
Of pain swells like the Indies, or a plum.
And there you will stand, as on the Roman hill,
Stunned by each withdrawn gaze and severe shape,
The first barbarian victor stood to gape
At the sacrificial fathers, white-robed, still;
And even the feverish old Jew stares stern with authority
Till you feel like one who has come too late, or improperly
                                        clothed, to a party.

The doctor will take you now. He is burly and clean;
Listening, like lover or worshiper, bends at your heart;
But cannot make out just what it tries to impart;
So smiles; says you simply need a change of scene.
Of scene, of solace: therefore Florida,
Where Ponce de Leon clanked among the lilies,
Where white sails skit on blue and cavort like fillies,
And the shoulder gleams in the moonlit corridor.
A change of love: if love is a groping Godward, though blind,
No matter what crevice, cranny, chink, bright in dark, the pale
                                        tentacle find.

In Florida consider the flamingo
Its color passion but its neck a question;
Consider even that girl the other guests shun
On beach, at bar, in bed, for she may know
The secret you are seeking, after all;
Or the child you humbly sit by, excited and curly,
That screams on the shore at the sea's sunlit hurlyburly,
Till the mother calls its name, toward nightfall.
Till you sit alone: in the dire meridians, off Ireland, in fury
Of spume-tooth and dawnless sea-heave, salt rimes the lookout's
                                                    devout eye.

Till you sit alone — which is the beginning of error —
Behind you the music and lights of the great hotel:
Solution, perhaps, is public, despair personal,
But history held to your breath clouds like a mirror.
There are many states, and towns in them, and faces,
But meanwhile, the little old lady in black, by the wall,
Who admires all the dancers, and tells you how just last fall
Her husband died in Ohio, and damp mists her glasses;
She blinks and croaks, like a toad or a Norn, in the horrible light,
And rattles her crutch, which may put forth a small bloom,
                                                    perhaps white.

Original Sin: A Short Story

Nodding, its great head rattling like a gourd,
And locks like seaweed strung on the stinking stone,
The nightmare stumbles past, and you have heard
It fumble your door before it whimpers and is gone:
It acts like the old hound that used to snuffle your door
                                                    and moan.

You thought you had lost it when you left Omaha,
For it seemed connected then with your grandpa, who
Had a wen on his forehead and sat on the veranda

268

To finger the precious protuberance, as was his habit to do,
Which glinted in sun like rough garnet or the rich old brain
                            bulging through.

But you met it in Harvard Yard as the historic steeple
Was confirming the midnight with its hideous racket,
And you wondered how it had come, for it stood so imbecile,
With empty hands, humble, and surely nothing in pocket:
Riding the rods, perhaps — or grandpa's will paid the ticket.

You were almost kindly then, in your first homesickness,
As it tortured its stiff face to speak, but scarcely mewed;
Since then you have outlived all your homesickness,
But have met it in many another distempered latitude:
Oh, nothing is lost, ever lost! at last you understood.

But it never came in the quantum glare of sun
To shame you before your friends, and had nothing to do
With your public experience or private reformation:
But it thought no bed too narrow — it stood with lips askew
And shook its great head sadly like the abstract Jew.

Never met you in the lyric arsenical meadows
When children call and your heart goes stone in the bosom;
At the orchard anguish never, nor ovoid horror,
Which is furred like a peach or avid like the delicious plum.
It takes no part in your classic prudence or fondled axiom.

Not there when you exclaimed: "Hope is betrayed by
Disastrous glory of sea-capes, sun-torment of whitecaps
— There must be a new innocence for us to be stayed by."
But there it stood, after all the timetables, all the maps,
In the crepuscular clutter of *always, always,* or *perhaps.*

You have moved often and rarely left an address,
And hear of the deaths of friends with a sly pleasure,
A sense of cleansing and hope, which blooms from distress;
But it has not died, it comes, its hand childish, unsure,
Clutching the bribe of chocolate or a toy you used to treasure.

It tries the lock; you hear, but simply drowse:
There is nothing remarkable in that sound at the door.
Later you may hear it wander the dark house
Like a mother who rises at night to seek a childhood picture;
Or it goes to the backyard and stands like an old horse cold in the
pasture.

Variation: Ode to Fear

When the dentist adjusts his drill
And leers at the molar he's going to fill,
Murmuring softly as a mother,
"Just hold tight, it'll soon be over,"
   Timor mortis conturbat me.

When the surgeon whets his scalpel
And regards me like an apple,
And the tumor or the wart
Sings, "The best of friends must part,"
   Timor mortis conturbat me.

When flushed with morning's genial hope
I slit the crisped envelope
And read the message too oft known,
"Your account $3.00 overdrawn,"
   Timor mortis conturbat me.

When I wait on the railway platform
To say goodbye, and the friend's form,
Which was substantial, wavers there
Thinner than smoke upon the air,
   Timor mortis conturbat me.

When I think that the national debt
Will blight the children we beget,
And especially blight those of our heirs
Who have the instincts of financiers,
   Timor mortis conturbat me.

When I read in Charles A. Beard
That the Founding Fathers whom we revered
Were not above a cozy deal
And would skin a pig for the pig's squeal,
   Timor mortis conturbat me;

And read that Milton was neurotic
And Saint Joan charmingly psychotic
And Jesus in Gethsemane
Was simply sweating from T. B.,
   Timor mortis conturbat me.

When Focke-Wulf mounts, or Zero,
And my knees say I'm no hero
And manly marrow turns to soup
And lunch expertly loops the loop,
   Timor mortis conturbat me.

When in the midnight's pause I mark
The breath beside me in the dark,
And know that breath's a clock, and know
That breath's the clock that's never slow,
   Timor mortis conturbat me.

O thou, to whom the world unknown
With all its shadowy shapes is shown,
Whose foot makes no sound on the floor,
Who need no latchkey for the door
   (*Timor mortis conturbat me*),

Who gaze from out the chic dummy's gaze,
In the display window, to amaze
The yearning matron by whom you sat
At dinner last night and in her soup spat
   (*Timor mortis conturbat me*),

Who pinch the maiden's tenderest part
But warm no cockles of her heart,
Who snarl the horse's tail, who spill
The bucket fetched by Jack and Jill
   (*Timor mortis conturbat me*),

Whose sleights are slier than Houdini's
And make Puck's pranks look like a ninny's
— Though you were with me *in utero,*
Your own birthday was long ago
    (*Timor mortis conturbat me*),

And though you fawn and follow like Fido,
You'll find other master when I go.
For I'm not the first or last of men
And so I will try to remember when
    Timor mortis conturbat me

That various men in various ages
Have dispensed with heroes and with sages,
And managed without our Constitution
Or intercession and absolution
    (*Timor mortis conturbat me*),

And when they walked by grove or shore
Enjoyed the scene, not metaphor,
And when they got it in the gut
Took what comfort they could from a cigarette butt
    (*Timor mortis conturbat me*),

And though they found the going hard
Did without Jesus or the gold standard,
Or lay alone, and reaching over
Could find no hand upon the cover
    (*Timor mortis conturbat me*).

So when I wake I'll pat the head
Of the beast that sleeps beside the bed,
And put on my pants and vest, and go
Down to eat my breakfast, though
    Timor mortis conturbat me.

Mexico Is a Foreign Country

III

THE WORLD COMES GALLOPING: A TRUE STORY

By the ruined arch, where the bougainvillea bled,
And pigeons simmered and shat in the barbaric vine
And made a noise like Plato in the barbaric vine,
He stood: old.
Old, bare feet on stone, and the serape's rose
Unfolded in the garden of his rags;
Old, and all his history hung from his severe face
As from his frame the dignity of rags.

We could not see his history, we saw
Him.
And he saw us, but could not see we stood
Huddled in our history and stuck out hand for alms.

But he could give us nothing, and asked for nothing,
Whose figure, sharp against the blue lake and violet mountains,
Was under the arch, the vine, the violent blue vulgarity of sky.
He ate a peach and wiped the pulp across his gums;
His mouth was no less ruinous than the arch.

Then at the foot of that long street,
Between the pastel stucco and the feathery pepper trees,
Horse and horseman, sudden as light, and loud,
Appeared,
And up the rise, banging the cobbles like castanets,
Lashed in their fury and fever,
Plunged:
Wall-eyed and wheezing, the lurching hammer-head,
The swaying youth, and flapping from bare heels,
The great wheel-spurs of the Conquistador.
Plunged past us, and were gone:
The crow-bait mount, the fly-bit man.

So the old one, dropping his peach-pit, spat;
Regarding the street's astonishing vacancy, said:
"Viene galopando," — and spat again — "el mundo."

IV

SMALL SOLDIERS WITH DRUM IN LARGE LANDSCAPE

The little soldiers thread the hills.
Remote, the white Sierra nods
Like somnolent ice cream piled up
To tempt a tourist's taste, or God's.

I saw them in the Plaza when
They huddled there like hens, at dawn,
And forming ranks, took time to gouge
Sleep from their eyes, and spit, and yawn.

Their bearing lacked ferocity.
Their eyes were soft, their feet were splayed,
And dirt, no doubt, behind the ears
Did them no credit on parade.

They did not tell me why they march —
To give some cattle-thief a scare
Or make their captain happy or
Simply take the mountain air.

But now two hours off, they move
Across the scene, and to the eye
Give interest, and focus for
The composition's majesty.

The little drum goes rum-tum-tum,
The little hearts go rat-tat-tat,
And I am I, and they are they,
And *this* is *this*, and *that* is *that*,

And the single pine is black upon
The crag; and the buzzard, absolute
In the sun's great gold eye, hangs;
And leaf is leaf, and root is root;

And the wind has neither home nor hope;
And cause is cause, effect, effect;
And all Nature's jocund atoms bounce
In tune to keep the world intact.

And shrouded in the coats and buttons,
The atoms bounce, and under the sky,
Under the mountain's gaze, maintain
The gallant little formulae

Which sweat and march, and marching, go
On errands which I have not guessed,
Though here I stand and watch them go
From dawn to dark, from East to West,

From *what* to *what,* from *if* to *when,*
From ridge to ridge, and cross the wide
Landscape of probability.
They cross the last ridge now, and hide

In valleys where the unprinted dust
Yearns for the foot it does not know;
They march under the same sun,
Appear once more, are gone, but go

Across the high waste of the mind,
Across the distance in the breast,
And climbing hazier heights, proceed
To a bivouac in a farther West.

As I remarked, the little men
Had necks unwashed and manners rude;
They were no cloud of daffodils
As once blest William's solitude.

But when upon my couch I lie
And brood the done, and the undone,
My heart may seize its hint of pleasure
And march beside them in the sun.

To a Little Girl, One Year Old,
in Ruined Fortress

I

To a place of ruined stone we brought you, and sea-reaches.
Rocca: fortress, hawk-heel, lion-paw, set on a hill.
A hill, no. Sea-cliff, and crag-cocked, the embrasures commanding
    the beaches,
Range easy, with most fastidious mathematic and skill.

Philipus me fecit: he of Spain, the black-browed, the anguished,
For whom nothing prospered, though he loved God.
His arms, great scutcheon of stone, once at drawbridge, have now
    languished
Long in the moat, under garbage; at moat-brink, rosemary with
    blue, thistle with gold bloom, nod.

Sun-blaze and cloud tatter, it is the sirocco, the dust swirl
    is swirled
Over the bay-face, mounts air like gold gauze whirled; it
    traverses the blaze-blue of water.
We have brought you where the geometry of a military rigor
    survives its own ruined world,
And sun regilds your gilt hair, in the midst of your laughter.

Rosemary, thistle, clutch stone. Far hangs Giannutri in blue air.
    Far to that blueness the heart aches,
And on the exposed approaches the last gold of gorse-bloom, in
    the sirocco, shakes.

II

White goose by palm tree, palm ragged, among stones the white
    oleander,
And the she-goat, brown, under pink oleander, waits.
I do not think that anything in the world will move, not goat,
    not gander.
Goat-droppings are fresh in the hot dust; not yet the beetle; the
    sun beats,

And under blue shadow of mountain, over blue-braiding
    sea-shadow,
The gull hangs white; whiter than white against mountain-mass,
The gull extends motionless on the shelf of air, on substance of
    shadow.
The gull, at an eye-blink, will, into the astonishing statement
    of sun, pass.

All night, next door, the defective child cried; now squats in the
    dust where the lizard goes.
The wife of the *gobbo* sits under vine leaves, she suffers, her eyes
    glare.
The engaged ones sit in the privacy of bemusement, heads bent,
    the classic pose.
And the beetle will work, the gull comment the irrelevant
    anguish of air.

But in the moment of your laughter let the molecular dance of
    the stone-dark glimmer like joy in the stone's dream,
And in that instant of possibility, let *gobbo, gobbo's* wife, and us,
    and all, take hands and sing: redeem, redeem!

III

The child next door is defective because the mother,
Seven brats already in that purlieu of dirt,
Took a pill, or did something to herself she thought would not
    hurt,
But it did, and no good, for there came this monstrous other.

277

The sister is twelve. Is beautiful like a saint.
Sits with the monster all day with pure love, calm eyes.
Has taught it a trick, to make *ciaou*, Italian-wise.
It crooks hand in that greeting. She smiles her smile without
    taint.

I come, and her triptych beauty and joy stir hate
— Is it hate? — in my heart. Fool, doesn't she know that the
    process
Is not that joyous or simple, to bless, or unbless,
The malfeasance of nature or the filth of fate?

Can it bind or loose, that beauty in that kind,
Beauty of benediction? I trust our hope to prevail
That heart-joy in beauty be truth before beauty fail
And be gathered like air in the ruck of the world's wind!

I think of your goldness, of joy, how empires grind, stars are
    hurled.
I smile stiff, saying *ciaou*, saying *ciaou*, and think: this is the
    world.

IV

    Above the beach, the vineyard
    Terrace breaks to the seaward
    Drop, where the cliffs fail
    To a clutter of manganese shale.
    Some is purple, some powdery-pale.
    But the black lava chunks stand off
    The sea's grind, or indolent chuff.
    The lava will withstand
    The sea's beat, or insinuant hand,
    And protect our patch of sand.

    It is late. The path from the beach
    Crawls up. I take you. We reach
    The vineyard, and at that path-angle
    The hedge obtrudes a tangle
    Of leaf and green bulge and a wrangle
    Bee-drowsy and blowsy with white bloom,

Scarcely giving the passerby room.
We know that the blossomy mass
Will brush our heads as we pass,
And under our feet there's blue clover
And the blue stars of *malva* all over.
We approach, but before we get there,
If no breeze stirs that green lair,
The scent and sun-honey of air
Is too sweet comfortably to bear.

I carry you up the hill.
In my arms you are sweet and still.
We approach your special place,
And I am watching your face
To see the sweet puzzlement grow,
And then recognition glow.
Recognition explodes in delight.
You leap like spray, or like light.
Despite my arm's tightness,
You leap in gold-glitter and brightness.
You leap like a fish-flash in bright air,
And laugh with joy for the bloom there.
Yes, this is the spot, and hour,
For you to demand your flower.

When we first came this way
Up from the beach, that day
That seems now so long ago,
We moved bemused and slow
In the season's pulse and flow.
Bemused with sea, and slow
With June heat and perfume,
We paused here, and plucked you a bloom.
So here you always demand
Your flower to hold in your hand,
And the flower must be white,
For you have your own ways to compel
Observance of this ritual.
You hold it, and sing with delight,
And your mother, for our own delight,

Picks one of the blue flowers there,
To put in your yellow hair.
That done, we go on our way
Up the hill, toward the end of the day.

But the season has thinned out.
At the bay-edge below, the shout
Of a late bather reaches our ear,
But it comes to the vineyard here
By more than distance thinned.
The bay is in shadow, the wind
Nags the shore to white.
The mountain prepares the night.
By the vineyard we have found
No bloom worthily white,
And the few that we have found
Not disintegrated to the ground
Are by season and sea-salt browned.
We give the best one to you.
It is ruined, but will have to do.
Somewhat better the blue blossoms fare.
We find one for your hair,
And you sing as though human need
Were not for perfection. We proceed
Past floss-borne or sloughed-off seed,
Past curled leaf and dry pod,
And the blue blossom will nod
With your head's drowsy gold nod.

Let all seasons pace their power,
As this has to this hour.
Let season and season devise
Their possibilities.
Let the future re-assess
All past joy, and past distress,
Till we know Time's deep intent
And the last integument
Of the past shall be rent
To show how all things bent
Their energies to that hour
When you first demanded your flower.

And in that image let
Both past and future forget,
In clasped communal ease,
Their brute identities.

The path lifts up ahead
To the *rocca*, supper, bed.
We move in the mountain's shade.
But the mountain is at our back.
Ahead, climbs the coast-cliff track.
The valley between is dim.
Ahead, on the cliff-rim,
The *rocca* clasps its height.
It accepts the incipient night.
Just once we look back.
On sunset, a white gull is black.
It hangs over the mountain crest.
It hangs on the saffron west.
It makes its outcry.
It slides down the sky.
East now, it catches the light.
Its black has gone again white.
Over the *rocca's* height
It gleams in the last light.
It has sunk from our sight.
Beyond the cliff is night.

It sank on unruffled wing.
We hear the sea rustling.

You will hear it all night, darling.

V

It rained toward day. The morning came sad and white
With silver of sea-sadness and defection of season.
Our joys and convictions are sure, but in that wan light
We moved — your mother and I — in muteness of spirit past
    logical reason.

Now sun, afternoon, and again summer-glitter on sea.
As you to a bauble, the heart leaps. The heart unlocks
Joy, though we know, shamefaced, the heart's weather should not
    be
Merely a reflex to solstice, or sport of an aggrieved equinox.

No, the heart should be steadfast: I know that.
And I sit in the late-sunny lee of the watch-house,
At the fortress-point, you on my knee, and the late
White butterflies over gold thistle conduct their ritual carouse.

In whisperless carnival, in vehemence of gossamer,
Pale ghosts of pale passions of air, the white wings weave.
In tingle and tangle of arabesque, they mount light, pair by pair,
As though that tall light were eternal, not merely the summer's
    reprieve.

You leap on my knee, you exclaim at the sun-stung gyration.
And the upper air stirs, as though the vast stillness of sky
Had stirred in its sunlit sleep and made suspiration,
A luxurious languor of breath, as after love, there is a sigh.

But enough, for the highest sun-scintillant pair are gone
Seaward, past rampart and cliff borne, over blue sea-gleam.
Close to my chair, to a thistle, one butterfly sinks now, flight
    done.
On gold bloom of thistle, white wings pulse under the sky's
    dream.

The sky's dream is enormous, I lift up my eyes.
In sunlight a tatter of mist clings high on the mountain-mass.
The mountain is under the sky, and the gray scarps there rise
Past paths where on their appointed occasions men will pass.

Past grain-patch, last apron of vineyard, last terrace of olive,
Past chestnut, past cork-grove, where the last carts can go,
Past camp of the charcoal-maker, where coals glow in the black hive,
The gray scarps rise up. Above them is that place I know.

The pines are there, they are large, a deep recess,
Shelf above scarp, enclave of rock, a glade

Benched and withdrawn in the mountain-mass, under the peak's
    duress.
We came there — your mother and I — and rested in that severe
    shade.

Pine-blackness mist-tangled, the peak black above: the glade
    gives
On the empty threshold of air, the hawk-hung delight
Of distance unspooled and bright space spilled — ah, the heart
    thrives!
We stood in that shade and saw sea and land lift in far light.

Now the butterflies dance, time-tattered and disarrayed.
I watch them. I think how above that scarp's far sunlit wall
Mist threads in silence the darkness of boughs, and in that shade
Condensed moisture gathers at a needle-tip. It glitters, will fall.

I cannot interpret for you this collocation
Of memories. You will live your own life, and contrive
The language of your own heart, but let that conversation,
In the last analysis, be always of whatever truth you would live.

For fire flames but in the heart of a colder fire.
All voice is but echo to a soundless voice.
Height is not deprivation of valley, nor defect of desire,
But may define, if you are fortunate, that joy in which all your
    joys should rejoice.

Bearded Oaks

The oaks, how subtle and marine,
Bearded, and all the layered light
Above them swims; and thus the scene,
Recessed, awaits the positive night.

So, waiting, we in the grass now lie
Beneath the languorous tread of light:
The grasses, kelp-like, satisfy
The nameless motions of the air.

Upon the floor of light, and time,
Unmurmuring, of polyp made,
We rest; we are, as light withdraws,
Twin atolls on a shelf of shade.

Ages to our construction went,
Dim architecture, hour by hour:
And violence, forgot now, lent
The present stillness all its power.

The storm of noon above us rolled,
Of light the fury, furious gold,
The long drag troubling us, the depth:
Dark is unrocking, unrippling, still.

Passion and slaughter, ruth, decay
Descend, minutely whispering down,
Silted down swaying streams, to lay
Foundation for our voicelessness.

All our debate is voiceless here,
As all our rage, the rage of stone;
If hope is hopeless, then fearless fear,
And history is thus undone.

Our feet once wrought the hollow street
With echo when the lamps were dead
At windows, once our headlight glare
Disturbed the doe that, leaping, fled.

I do not love you less that now
The caged heart makes iron stroke,
Or less that all that light once gave
The graduate dark should now revoke.

We live in time so little time
And we learn all so painfully,
That we may spare this hour's term
To practice for eternity.

RICHARD WILBUR

Cicadas

You know those windless summer evenings, swollen to stasis
by too-substantial melodies, rich as a
running-down record, ground round
to full quiet. Even the leaves
have thick tongues.

And if the first crickets quicken then,
other inhabitants, at window or door
or rising from table, feel in the lungs
a slim false-freshness, by this
trick of the ear.

Chanters of miracles took for a simple sign
the Latin cicada, because of his long waiting
and sweet change in daylight, and his singing
all his life, pinched on the ash leaf,
heedless of ants.

Others made morals; all were puzzled and joyed
by this gratuitous song. Such a plain thing
morals could not surround, nor listening:
not "chirr" nor "cri-cri." There is no straight
way of approaching it.

This thin uncomprehended song it is
springs healing questions into binding air.
Fabre, by firing all the municipal cannon
under a piping tree, found out
cicadas cannot hear.

In a Bird Sanctuary

Because they could not give it too much ground
they closely planted it with fir and shrub.
A plan of pathways, voted by the Club,
contrived to lead the respiter around
a mildly wandring wood, still at no cost
to get him lost.

Now over dear Miss Drury's favored trees
they flutter (birds) and either stop or not,
as if they were unconscious that the spot
is planned for them, and meant to buy release
for one restrained department of the soul,
to "make men whole."

It's hard to tell the purpose of a bird;
for relevance it does not seem to try.
No line can trace no flute exemplify
its traveling; it darts without the word.
Who wills devoutly to absorb, contain,
birds give him pain.

Commissioners of Public Parks have won
a partial wisdom, know that birds exist.
And seeing people equally insist
on birds and statues, they go hire a man
to swab sans rancor dung from granite stare
and marble hair.

BIRDS HAVE BEEN SEEN IN TOWERS AND ON ISLES;
ALSO ON PRIVY TOPS, IN FANEUIL HALL;
BIRDS HAVE SOME OF THEM NOT BEEN SEEN AT ALL;
BIRDS, IF THEY CARE TO, WALK ALONG IN FILE.
BIRDS DO NOT FEEL ESPECIALLY GOOD IN FLIGHT:
LET'S TREAT THEM RIGHT!

The liberty of any things becomes
the liberty of all. It also brings
their abolition into anythings.

In order's name let's not turn down our thumbs
on routine visions; we must figure out
what all's about.

Lightness

    A birdsnest built on the palm of the high-
Most bough of an elm, this morning as I came by
A brute gust lifted-and-left in the midst of the air;
      Whereat the leaves went quiet, and there
      Was a moment of silence in honor of
The sweetness of danger. The chalice now bobbing above,
Of interlaid daintiest timber, began the chute
      Down forty fell feet toward stone and root
      With a drift and a sampan spin, and gripped
Loosely its fineshelled life; now viciously tipped
By a ripple of air, with an acrobat's quick not-quite-
      Lost, dipped lower to whirl upright;
      Then, with a straight-down settling, it
Descended into sunshine, and, with a hushed touch, lit
On a mesa of strenuous grass. Oh risk-hallowed eggs, oh
      Triumph of lightness! Legerity begs no
      Quarter: my Aunt Virginia, when
She'd relapsed and recovered, would sit in the garden again
Waiting, all lapped in an indigo-flowered shawl,
      In white for her "regular customers' " call;
      Whose pity she parried with very-blue-eyed
Attention, and giggled and patted their hands when they tried
To do-something-for-her; she sat in the heart of her days
      And watched with a look of peculiar praise;
      Her slight voice could catch a pleasure complete
As a gull takes a fish at the flash of his side. Her great
Heavy husband adored her, would treat with a sudden blind sally
      Of softness his "visitor from the valley";
      He called her "Birdie," which was good, for him.
And he and the others, the strong, the involved, in-the-swim,
Seeing her there in the garden, in her gay shroud

As vague and as self-possessed as a cloud,
    Requiring nothing of them any more,
And one hand lightly laid on a fatal door,
Thought of the health of the sick, and, what mocked their sighing,
    Of the strange intactness of the gladly dying.

The Beautiful Changes

One wading a Fall meadow finds on all sides
The Queen Anne's Lace lying like lilies
On water; it glides
So from the walker, it turns
Dry grass to a lake, as the slightest shade of you
Valleys my mind in fabulous blue Lucernes.

The beautiful changes as a forest is changed
By a chameleon's tuning his skin to it;
As a mantis, arranged
On a green leaf, grows
Into it, makes the leaf leafier, and proves
Any greenness is deeper than anyone knows.

Your hands hold roses always in a way that says
They are not only yours; the beautiful changes
In such kind ways,
Wishing ever to sunder
Things and things' selves for a second finding, to lose
For a moment all that it touches back to wonder.

Driftwood

In greenwoods once these relics must have known
A rapt, gradual growing,
That are cast here like slag of the old
Engine of grief;

Must have affirmed in annual increase
Their close selves, knowing
Their own nature only, and that
Bringing to leaf.

Say, for the seven cities or a war
Their solitude was taken,
They into masts shaven, or milled into
Oar and plank;

Afterward sailing long and to lost ends,
By groundless water shaken,
Well they availed their vessels till they
Smashed or sank.

Then on the great generality of waters
Floated their singleness,
And in all that deep subsumption they were
Never dissolved;

But shaped and flowingly fretted by the waves'
Ever surpassing stress,
With the gnarled swerve and tangle of tides
Finely involved.

Brought in the end where breakers dump and slew
On the glass verge of the land,
Silver they rang to the stones when the sea
Flung them and turned.

Curious crowns and scepters they look to me
Here on the gold sand,
Warped, wry, but having the beauty of
Excellence earned.

In a time of continual dry abdications
And of damp complicities,
They are fit to be taken for signs, these emblems
Royally sane,

Which have ridden to homeless wreck, and long revolved
In the lathe of all the seas,
But have saved in spite of it all their dense
Ingenerate grain.

In the Elegy Season

Haze, char, and the weather of All Souls':
A giant absence mopes upon the trees:
Leaves cast in casual potpourris
Whisper their scents from pits and cellar-holes.

Or brewed in gulleys, steeped in wells, they spend
In chilly steam their last aromas, yield
From shallow hells a revenance of field
And orchard air. And now the envious mind

Which could not hold the summer in my head
While bounded by that blazing circumstance
Parades these barrens in a golden trance,
Remembering the wealthy season dead,

And by an autumn inspiration makes
A summer all its own. Green boughs arise
Through all the boundless backward of the eyes,
And the soul bathes in warm conceptual lakes.

Less proud than this, my body leans an ear
Past cold and colder weather after wings'
Soft commotion, the sudden race of springs,
The goddess' tread heard on the dayward stair,

Longs for the brush of the freighted air, for smells
Of grass and cordial lilac, for the sight
Of green leaves building into the light
And azure water hoisting out of wells.

Juggler

A ball will bounce, but less and less. It's not
A light-hearted thing, resents its own resilience.
Falling is what it loves, and the earth falls
So in our hearts from brilliance,
Settles and is forgot.
It takes a sky-blue juggler with five red balls

To shake our gravity up. Whee, in the air
The balls roll round, wheel on his wheeling hands,
Learning the ways of lightness, alter to spheres
Grazing his finger ends,
Cling to their courses there,
Swinging a small heaven about his ears.

But a heaven is easier made of nothing at all
Than the earth regained, and still and sole within
The spin of worlds, with a gesture sure and noble
He reels that heaven in,
Landing it ball by ball,
And trades it all for a broom, a plate, a table.

Oh, on his toe the table is turning, the broom's
Balancing up on his nose, and the plate whirls
On the tip of the broom! Damn, what a show, we cry:
The boys stamp, and the girls
Shriek, and the drum booms
And all comes down, and he bows and says good-bye.

If the juggler is tired now, if the broom stands
In the dust again, if the table starts to drop
Through the daily dark again, and though the plate
Lies flat on the table top,
For him we batter our hands
Who has won for once over the world's weight.

Years-End

Now winter downs the dying of the year,
And night is all a settlement of snow;
From the soft street the rooms of houses show
A gathered light, a shapen atmosphere,
Like frozen-over lakes whose ice is thin
And still allows some stirring down within.

I've known the wind by water banks to shake
The late leaves down, which frozen where they fell
And held in ice as dancers in a spell
Fluttered all winter long into a lake;
Graved on the dark in gestures of descent,
They seemed their own most perfect monument.

There was perfection in the death of ferns
Which laid their fragile cheeks against the stone
A million years. Great mammoths overthrown
Composedly have made their long sojourns,
Like palaces of patience, in the gray
And changeless lands of ice. And at Pompeii

The little dog lay curled and did not rise
But slept the deeper as the ashes rose
And found the people incomplete, and froze
The random hands, the loose unready eyes
Of men expecting yet another sun
To do the shapely thing they had not done.

These sudden ends of time must give us pause.
We fray into the future, rarely wrought
Save in the tapestries of afterthought.
More time, more time. Barrages of applause
Come muffled from a buried radio.
The New-year bells are wrangling with the snow.

A Simile for Her Smile

Your smiling, or the hope, the thought of it,
Makes in my mind such pause and abrupt ease
As when the highway bridgegates fall,
Balking the hasty traffic, which must sit
On each side massed and staring, while
Deliberately the drawbridge starts to rise:

Then horns are hushed, the oilsmoke rarefies,
Above the idling motors one can tell
The packet's smooth approach, the slip,
Slip of the silken river past the sides,
The ringing of clear bells, the dip
And slow cascading of the paddle wheel.

Ceremony

A striped blouse in a clearing by Bazille
Is, you may say, a patroness of boughs
Too queenly kind toward nature to be kin.
But ceremony never did conceal,
Save to the silly eye, which all allows,
How much we are the woods we wander in.

Let her be some Sabrina fresh from stream,
Lucent as shallows slowed by wading sun,
Bedded on fern, the flowers' cynosure:
Then nymph and wood must nod and strive to dream
That she is airy earth, the trees, undone,
Must ape her languor natural and pure.

Ho-hum. I am for wit and wakefulness,
And love this feigning lady by Bazille.
What's lightly hid is deepest understood,

And when with social smile and formal dress
She teaches leaves to curtsey and quadrille,
I think there are most tigers in the wood.

Castles and Distances

I

From blackhearted water colder
Than Cain's blood, and aching with ice, from a gunmetal bay
  No one would dream of drowning in, rises
  The walrus: head hunched from the oxen shoulder,
    The serious face made for surprises
      Looks with a thick dismay

At the camera lens which takes
Him in, and takes him back to cities, to volleys of laughter
  In film palaces, just as another, brought
  By Jonas Poole to England for the sakes
    Of James First and his court, was thought
      Most strange, and died soon after.

So strangeness gently steels
Us, and curiosity kills, keeping us cool to go
  Sail with the hunters unseen to the walrus rock
  And stand behind their slaughter: which of us feels
    The harpoon's hurt, and the huge shock
      When the blood jumps to flow?

Oh, it is hunters alone
Regret the beastly pain, it is they who love the foe
  That quarries out their force, and every arrow
  Is feathered soft with wishes to atone;
    Even the surest sword in sorrow
      Bleeds for its spoiling blow.

Sometimes, as one can see
Carved at Amboise in a high relief, on the lintel stone
  Of the castle chapel, hunters have strangely come

294

To a mild close of the chase, bending the knee
   Instead of the bow, struck sweetly dumb
      To see from the brow bone

     Of the hounded stag a cross
Grown, and the eyes clear with grace. Perfectly still
Are the cruising dogs as well, their paws aground
   In a white hush of lichen. Beds of moss
     Spread, and the clearing wreathes around
      The dear suspense of will.

     But looking higher now
To the chapel steeple, see among points and spines of the updrawn
   Vanishing godbound stone, ringing its sped
   Thrust as a target tatters, a round row
     Of real antlers taken from dead
      Deer. The hunt goes on.

II

     They built well who made
Those palaces of hunting lords, the grounds planned
   As ruled reaches, always with a view
   Down tapered aisles of trees at last to fade
     In the world's mass. The lords so knew
      Of land beyond their land.

     If, at Versailles, outdrawn
By the stairs or the still canals, by the gradual shrink of an urn
   Or the thousand fountains, a king gave back his gaze
   To the ample balanced windows vantaged on
     The clearness near, and the far haze,
      He learned he must return.

     Seen from a palace stair
The wilderness was distance; difference; it spoke
   In the strong king's mind for mercy, while to the weak,
   To the weary of choice, it told of havens where
     The Sabbath stayed, and all were meek,
      And justice known a joke.

Some cast their crowns away
And went to live in the distance. There there was nothing seemed
Remotely strange to them, their innocence
Shone in the special features of the prey
They would not harm. The dread expense
Of golden times they dreamed

Was that their kingdoms fell
The deeper into tyranny, the more they stole
Through Ardens out to Eden isles apart,
Seeking a shore, or shelter of some spell
Where harmlessly the hidden heart
Might hold creation whole.

When to his solitude
The world became as island mists, then Prospero,
Pardoning all, and pardoned, yet aware
The full forgiveness cannot come, renewed
His reign, bidding the boat prepare
From mysteries to go

Toward masteries less sheer,
And Duke again, did rights and mercies, risking wrong,
Found advocates and enemies, and found
His bounded empire good, where he could hear
Below his walls the baying hound
And the loud hunting-song.

Winter Spring

A script of trees before the hill
Spells cold, with laden serifs; all the walls
Are battlemented still;
But winter spring is winnowing the air
Of chill, and crawls
Wet-sparkling on the gutters;
Everywhere
Walls wince, and there's the steal of waters.

Now all this proud royaume
Is Veniced. Through the drift's mined dome
One sees the rowdy rusted grass,
And we're amazed as windows stricken bright.
This too-soon spring will pass
Perhaps tonight,
And doubtless it is dangerous to love
This somersault of seasons;
But I am weary of
The winter way of loving things for reasons.

Marché aux Oiseaux

Hundreds of birds are singing in the square.
Their minor voices fountaining in air
And constant as a fountain, lightly loud,
Do not drown out the burden of the crowd.

Far from his gold Sudan, the travailleur
Lends to the noise an intermittent chirr
Which to his hearers seems more joy than rage.
He batters softly at his wooden cage.

Here are the silver-bill, the orange-cheek,
The perroquet, the dainty coral-beak
Stacked in their cages; and around them move
The buyers in their termless hunt for love.

Here are the old, the ill, the imperial child;
The lonely people, desperate and mild;
The ugly; past these faces one can read
The tyranny of one outrageous need.

We love the small, said Burke. And if the small
Be not yet small enough, why then by Hell
We'll cramp it till it knows but how to feed,
And we'll provide the water and the seed.

A World without Objects
Is a Sensible Emptiness

The tall camels of the spirit
Steer for their deserts, passing the last groves loud
With the sawmill shrill of the locust, to the whole honey of the arid
Sun. They are slow, proud,

And move with a stilted stride
To the land of sheer horizon, hunting Traherne's
Sensible emptiness, there where the brain's lantern-slide
Revels in vast returns.

O connoisseurs of thirst,
Beasts of my soul who long to learn to drink
Of pure mirage, those prosperous islands are accurst
That shimmer on the brink

Of absence; auras, lustres,
And all shinings need to be shaped and borne.
Think of those painted saints, capped by the early masters
With bright, jauntily-worn

Aureate plates, or even
Merry-go-round rings. Turn, O turn
From the fine sleights of the sand, from the long empty oven
Where flames in flamings burn

Back to the trees arrayed
In bursts of glare, to the halo-dialing run
Of the country creeks, and the hills' bracken tiaras made
Gold in the sunken sun,

Wisely watch for the sight
Of the supernova burgeoning over the barn,
Lampshine blurred in the steam of beasts, the spirit's right
Oasis, light incarnate.

Lament

Nashe's old queens who bartered young and fair
Their light tiaras for such ponderous stones:
Of them I'd think, how sunlit still their hair,
And fine as airship frames their balanced bones.

It is, I say, a most material loss.
Kept spirit is corporate; doubly the thought of you,
As air fills air, or waves together toss,
Out of my wishes and your being grew.

Water and air: such unclenched stuff can last,
But rarest things are visible and firm;
Grace falls the fastest from our failing past,
And I lament for grace's early term,

For casual dances that your body knows,
Whose spirit only sense can understand,
For times when spirit, doomed and single, flows
Into the speeches of your eye and hand.

All These Birds

Agreed that all these birds,
Hawk or heavenly lark or heard-of nightingale,
Perform upon the kite-strings of our sight
In a false distance, that the day and night
Are full of wingèd words
gone rather stale,
That nothing is so worn
As Philomel's bosom-thorn,

That it is, in fact, the male
Nightingale which sings, and that all these creatures wear
Invisible armor such as Hébert beheld
His water-ousel through, as, wrapped or shelled

In a clear bellying veil
                              or bubble of air,
        It bucked the flood to feed
        At the stream-bottom. Agreed

                That the sky is a vast claire
In which the gull, despite appearances, is not
        Less claustral than the oyster in its beak
        And dives like nothing human; that we seek
        Vainly to know the heron
                              (but can plot
        What angle of the light
        Provokes its northern flight).

        Let them be polyglot
And wordless then, those boughs that spoke with Solomon
        In Hebrew canticles, and made him wise;
        And let a clear and bitter wind arise
        To storm into the hotbeds
                              of the sun,
        And there, beyond a doubt,
        Batter the Phoenix out.

        Let us, with glass or gun,
Watch (from our clever blinds) the monsters of the sky
        Dwindle to habit, habitat, and song,
        And tell the imagination it is wrong
        Till, lest it be undone,
                              it spin a lie
        So fresh, so pure, so rare
        As to possess the air.

        Why should it be more shy
Than chimney-nesting storks, or sparrows on a wall?
        Oh, let it climb wherever it can cling
        Like some great trumpet-vine, a natural thing
        To which all birds that fly
                              come natural.
        Come, stranger, sister, dove:
        Put on the reins of love.

A Black November Turkey

Nine white chickens come
    With haunchy walk and heads
Jabbing among the chips, the chaff, the stones
        And the cornhusk-shreds,

And bit by bit infringe
    A pond of dusty light,
Spectral in shadow until they bobbingly one
        By one ignite.

Neither pale nor bright,
    The turkey-cock parades
Through radiant squalors, darkly auspicious as
        The ace of spades,

Himself his own cortège
    And puffed with the pomp of death,
Rehearsing over and over with strangled râle
        His latest breath.

The vast black body floats
    Above the crossing knees
As a cloud over thrashed branches, a calm ship
        Over choppy seas,

Shuddering its fan and feathers
    In fine soft clashes
With the cold sound that the wind makes, fondling
        Paper-ashes.

The pale-blue bony head
    Set on its shepherd's-crook
Like a saint's death-mask, turns a vague, superb
        And timeless look

Upon these clocking hens
    And the cocks that one by one,

Dawn after mortal dawn, with vulgar joy
       Acclaim the sun.

Exeunt

     Piecemeal the summer dies;
At the field's edge a daisy lives alone;
  A last shawl of burning lies
    On a gray field-stone.

     All cries are thin and terse;
The field has droned the summer's final mass;
  A cricket like a dwindled hearse
    Crawls from the dry grass.

Beasts

      Beasts in their major freedom
   Slumber in peace tonight. The gull on his ledge
Dreams in the guts of himself the moon-plucked waves below,
   And the sunfish leans on a stone, slept
     By the lyric water;

     In which the spotless feet
  Of deer make dulcet splashes, and to which
The ripped mouse, safe in the owl's talon, cries
   Concordance. Here there is no such harm
    And no such darkness

     As the selfsame moon observes
  Where, warped in window-glass, it sponsors now
The werewolf's painful change. Turning his head away
   On the sweaty bolster, he tries to remember
    The mood of manhood,

But lies at last, as always,
Letting it happen, the fierce fur soft to his face,
Hearing with sharper ears the wind's exciting minors,
The leaves' panic, and the degradation
Of the heavy streams.

Meantime, at high windows
Far from thicket and pad-fall, suitors of excellence
Sigh and turn from their work to construe again the painful
Beauty of heaven, the lucid moon
And the risen hunter,

Making such dreams for men
As told will break their hearts as always, bringing
Monsters into the city, crows on the public statues,
Navies fed to the fish in the dark
Unbridled waters.

Love Calls Us to the Things of This World

The eyes open to a cry of pulleys,
And spirited from sleep, the astounded soul
Hangs for a moment bodiless and simple
As false dawn.
                    Outside the open window
The morning air is all awash with angels.

Some are in bed-sheets, some are in blouses,
Some are in smocks: but truly there they are.
Now they are rising together in calm swells
Of halcyon feeling, filling whatever they wear
With the deep joy of their impersonal breathing;

Now they are flying in place, conveying
The terrible speed of their omnipresence, moving
And staying like white water; and now of a sudden
They swoon down into so rapt a quiet
That nobody seems to be there.
                    The soul shrinks

From all that it is about to remember,
From the punctual rape of every blessèd day,
And cries,
   'Oh, let there be nothing on earth but laundry,
Nothing but rosy hands in the rising steam
And clear dances done in the sight of heaven.'

  Yet, as the sun acknowledges
With a warm look the world's hunks and colors,
The soul descends once more in bitter love
To accept the waking body, saying now
In a changed voice as the man yawns and rises,

  'Bring them down from their ruddy gallows;
Let there be clean linen for the backs of thieves;
Let lovers go fresh and sweet to be undone,
And the heaviest nuns walk in a pure floating
Of dark habits,
    keeping their difficult balance.'

NOTES

ELIZABETH BISHOP

1911, in Worcester, Massachusetts. Reared in New England and Nova Scotia. Educated in Vassar. Among the honors she has received are the Shelley Award, a National Academy Award, and a Guggenheim Fellowship; a member of the National Institute of Arts and Letters; served as Consultant in Poetry to the Library of Congress. For some time she has made her home in Brazil.

Poetry: NORTH & SOUTH, 1946; POEMS, 1955.

Cirque d'Hiver. Winter Circus: one of two permanent circuses long established in Paris. Chirico: a twentieth-century painter.

Roosters. gallus canit: the cock crows. flet Petrus: Peter weeps.

Arrival at Santos. Santos is a port in Brazil.

RICHARD EBERHART

1904, in Austin, Minnesota. Educated in Dartmouth, Cambridge University, and Harvard. Associated with The Butcher Polish Company, Boston, since 1946, vice-president, member of the Board of Directors. Received the Shelley Memorial Prize for poetry, the Harriet Monroe Poetry Award, and a Doctor of Letters degree from Dartmouth. Has taught English at various schools and colleges: St. Mark's, University of Washington, The University of Connecticut, Wheaton College (Norton, Mass.), and, at present, Princeton.

Poetry: A BRAVERY OF EARTH, 1930; READING THE SPIRIT, 1937; SONG AND IDEA, 1942; POEMS, NEW AND SELECTED, 1944; BURR OAKS, 1947; BROTHERHOOD OF MEN, 1949; AN HERB BASKET, 1950; SELECTED POEMS, 1951; UNDERCLIFF, 1953. Co-editor, with Selden Rodman, of WAR AND THE POET, an anthology of war poetry.

RANDALL JARRELL

1914, in Nashville. Educated in Vanderbilt University and Princeton. Served for a year as literary editor of THE NATION. Has taught English at various places: Kenyon, University of Illinois, University of Texas, Sarah Lawrence, and, currently, at the Women's College of the University of North Carolina.

Poetry: BLOOD FOR A STRANGER, 1942; LITTLE FRIEND, LITTLE FRIEND, 1945; LOSSES, 1948; SEVEN-LEAGUE CRUTCHES, 1951; SELECTED POEMS, 1955. Novel: PICTURES FROM AN INSTITUTION, 1954. Criticism: POETRY AND THE AGE, 1953.

All notes are Mr. Jarrell's, from SELECTED POEMS.

A Girl in a Library is a poem about the New World and the Old: about a girl, a student of Home Economics and Physical Education, who has fallen asleep in the library of a Southern college; about a woman who looks out of one book, Pushkin's *Eugen Onegin*, at this girl asleep among so many; and about the *I* of the poem, a man somewhere between the two. A *blind date* is an unknown someone you accompany to something; if he promises to come for you and doesn't, he has *stood you up*. The Corn King and the Spring Queen went by many names; in the beginning they were the man and woman who, after ruling for a time, were torn to pieces and scattered over the fields in order that the grain might grow.

Seele im Raum is the title of one of Rilke's poems: "Soul in Space" sounded so glib that I couldn't use it instead. An eland is the largest sort of African antelope—the males are as big as a horse, and you often see people gazing at them, at the zoo, in uneasy wonder.

The Black Swan is said, long ago, by a girl whose sister is buried under the white stones of the green churchyard.

A ball turret was a plexiglass sphere set into the belly of a B-17 or B-24, and inhabited by two .50 caliber machine-guns and one man, a short small man. When this gunner tracked with his machine-guns a fighter attacking his bomber from below, he revolved with the turret; hunched upside-down in his little sphere, he looked like the foetus in the womb. The fighters which attacked him were armed with cannon firing explosive shells. The hose was a steam hose.

In *Second Air Force* the woman visiting her son remembers what she has read on the front page of her newspaper the week before, a conversation between a bomber, in flames over Germany, and one of the fighters protecting it: "Then I heard the bomber call me in: 'Little Friend, Little Friend, I got two engines on fire. Can you see me, Little Friend?' I said, 'I'm crossing right over you. Let's go home.'"

A Ward in the States: these soldiers are malaria patients home from the South Pacific, in Army hospitals.

ROBERT LOWELL

1917, in Boston, of the family which embraced James Russell and Amy Lowell. Educated in St. Mark's, Harvard, and Kenyon. Awarded a Guggenheim Fellowship and a Pulitzer Prize for Poetry; has served as Consultant in Poetry at the Library of Congress. Has been teaching English at the State University of Iowa, in the Iowa Writers' Workshop.

Poetry: LAND OF UNLIKENESS, 1944; LORD WEARY'S CASTLE, 1946; MILLS OF THE CAVANAUGHS, 1951.

Colloquy in Black Rock. Stupor Mundi: the amazement of the world. An epithet commonly given Frederick II, 13th century Holy Roman Emperor, noted for splendor.

Quaker Graveyard. Warren Winslow was a cousin of the poet's, whose ship was lost in the Atlantic during World War II. *Nantucket* is the name of an island—also of a town and a sound—south of the eastern tip of Massachusetts. *Madaket* is a harbor and *'Sconset* a town on the island; *Martha's Vineyard* is an island west of Nantucket; *Wood's Hole* is a town on the mainland nearby, on the south side of *Cape Cod.* During World War II, the U.S. Navy was important here. A century ago this area was the center of the New England whaling industry. The most famous whaling ship in literature is in Melville's MOBY DICK, the *Pequod,* whose captain is *Ahab.* To Ahab, the white whale symbolizes the malice of things; he pursues it relentlessly and to the destruction of himself, the ship, and all but one of the crew. As the ship sinks (stove in by Moby Dick) the arm of one of the crew nails the *red flag* to the *masthead* (and also accidentally nails the wing of a bird, symbolizing good).

In the Old Testament, Ahab was a wicked king of Israel; contrasting to him in part, was *Jehoshaphat,* God-fearing king of Judah. II Chronicles XX: 22–26 relates how Jehoshaphat's forces utterly destroyed their enemies, and assembled afterwards in the valley of Berachah (i.e., blessing). Mr. Lowell identifies *the ash-pits of Jehoshaphat* as the valley of judgment. "The world according to some prophets and scientists will end in fire." (From note in MODERN POETRY, Friar and Brinnin, editors.) The *rainbow* of the last line of the poem refers to God's covenant with Noah that the world will not end by floods. *Leviathan* was the Biblical name for a great sea beast. *Shiloah,* or Shiloh, was for centuries the holy place where the tabernacle of Israel was located; a stream flowed near it as near the shrine at Walsingham. *Sion,* or Zion, was the hill of Jerusalem, which came to symbolize Israel or the final gathering place. *Jonas,* or Jonah, is said by Matthew (XII:40) to have been like Jesus, the *Messias* or Messiah, because he was in the whale's belly three days and nights as Christ should be three days and nights in the heart of the earth. *Clamavimus* means "we cried out"; Psalm 130 opens, "Out of the depths I have cried to thee, O Lord." (This translation, and the forms of names from the Bible, are from the Douay Bible, used by Catholics.)

Our Lady of Walsingham was the most famous English medieval shrine of the Virgin Mary, in Norfolk; in the Reformation it was destroyed, but recently it has been restored and again attracts Catholic pilgrims. There was a saying, "When England goes to Walsingham, England will return to the Church." See pages 213–214 of CATHOLIC ART AND CULTURE by E. I. Watkin (Sheed & Ward, 1944). *Non est species, neque decor* is an elliptical quotation from Isaias LIII: 2 prophesying the Messiah: "And he shall grow up as a tender plant before him, and as a root out of a thirsty ground; *there is no beauty* in him, *nor comeliness;* and we have seen him, and there was no sightliness, that we should be desirous of him."

Children of Light. Geneva was the home of Calvin, whose arch-Protestant doctrines animated the English Pilgrims to go first to Holland and then to New England. During the Depression, the U.S. Government, to keep farm prices up, destroyed farm products—burned grain.

Between the Porch and the Altar. The title comes from the Epistle read in the Mass on Ash Wednesday (Joel II:17): "Between the porch and the altar, the priests, the Lord's ministers, shall weep, and shall say: Spare, O Lord, spare Thy people." On this verse of the Responsory is based the famous hymn sung at funerals, Dies Irae: "Dies illa, dies irae, calamitatis et miseriae, *dies* magna et *amara valde,* dum veneris judicare saeculum per ignem." "That day, a day of wrath, of bad trouble and wretchedness, *that day* great and *bitter above all* (other days) when Thou shalt come to judge the world with fire."

The visionary and apocalyptic books of the Bible, such as Ezekiel and especially Revelations, contain numerous images of great gorgeous whores and serpents, dragons, snakes, suggesting sin, worldly power, the forces of evil which imprison the sinner and deprive him of true life. *Man tasted Eve with death:* according to ancient tradition, immediately after the fall, Adam and Eve knew that they must die and they performed the sexual act, these two becoming inextricably intertwined. Sin made death; sin is a kind of dying.

According to remarks made by Mr. Lowell at a public reading at the Paul Shuster Art Gallery in Cambridge in July, 1955, the *Farmer* on the shaft is "the statue of the Minute-Man, which stands on the Concord Common." As the minute-men protected liberty, so the *Irish exiles* sought it in New England, and so St. *Patrick* brought Ireland freedom (from the serpents of sin). *Concord,* in Mr. Lowell's sonnet of that name, is the place where "ten thousand Fords" come "in search of a tradition," the main elements of which the poem identifies as the Unitarian Church (weak against "Mammon's unbridled industry"), Thoreau (who "named all the birds"), and King Philip (the echo of whose death scream "girdled this imperfect globe"). At the same reading, Mr. Lowell said that the locale at the opening of Section IV (*At the Altar*) is imagined to be "a Boston night-club in which there is an ice-skating floorshow," where the protagonist is sitting with Katherine. He is drunk, lit up like a *Christmas tree,* a *fallen* one. There follows a phantasmagoria of driving through the city and arriving at a church where a priest mumbles through his Mass; since he sprinkles Holy Water (on the corpse) it is a funeral Mass. *The Day* is the apocalyptic Day of Judgment, the last day. The region where *Lucifer* is Lord is Hell; in the Bible, harness usually means armor. A bier is the stand on which a coffin is laid before burial; in modern funerals, this *bier* is a little silver dolly which resembles a *baby carriage.*

After the Surprising Conversions. On May 30, 1735, the great New England divine, preacher, and theologian, Jonathan Edwards, wrote a letter usually referred to as "Narrative of Surprising Conversions." On June 3, he added to it a paragraph about "My Uncle Hawley," who had just committed suicide.

Noli Me Tangere. "Touch me not." Part I of a poem in two parts, entitled *The Death of the Sheriff.* tabula rasa: blank tablet (mind free from impressions).

Death from Cancer. Part I of a poem in four parts entitled *In Memory of Arthur Winslow.* Cancer in Latin means crab. resurrexit dominus: the Lord is resurrected.

Falling Asleep over the Aeneid. An old man in Concord forgets to go to morning service. He falls asleep, while reading Vergil, and dreams that he is Aeneas at the funeral of Pallas, an Italian prince [author's note]. Aeneas was a Trojan, who, in THE AENEID, allied himself with some native Italians (among them Pallas) to conquer the rest (who were led by *Turnus*). His mother was *Venus* (Latin name) or *Aphrodite* (Greek). *Mars* is the Latin of Greek *Ares.* Vergil represents Aeneas as being the founder of the Roman state. Vergil himself wrote under the patronage of the first Emperor, *Augustus. Turms* means companies of calvary.

Mother Marie Therese. The speaker is a Canadian nun stationed in New Brunswick [author's note]. Pio Nono: Pius the Ninth, Pope 1846–78. Canuck: French-Canadian. *Action Française:* the very literate newspaper of a royalist group (of the same name) in France, founded in 1898. Louis Neuvième: Louis IX of France, a saint. Frontenac: French governor of Canada in the seventeenth century. venite: come—perhaps with reference to the opening of Psalm 94: "Come, let us praise the Lord with joy." (The imperative *venite* rings through the ordinary of the Office— that section of prayers and responses which does not change from day to day—from the first Sunday of Advent to Easter.)

JOSEPHINE MILES

1911, in Chicago. Educated in University of California at Los Angeles and University of California (Berkeley); teaches English at University of California (Berkeley). Won the Shelley Award for Poetry, a Guggenheim Fellowship, and a James Phelan Award.

Poetry: LINES AT INTERSECTION, 1939; POEMS ON SEVERAL OCCASIONS, 1941; LOCAL MEASURES, 1946; PREFABRICATIONS, 1955. Scholarly criticism: VOCABULARY OF POETRY, 1946; THE CONTINUITY OF POETIC LANGUAGE, 1951.

Statute. Icarian downfall: Icarus, in the Greek myth, flew too high, so that the sun melted the wax in his wings; he fell in the sea and drowned. Ascent of F6: title of a play by Auden and Isherwood, in which those who climb the mountain F6 succeed at the cost of their lives.

The Plastic Glass. The city *Berkeley,* one of whose main streets is *Shattuck Avenue,* lies on the east side of the San Francisco Bay across from the Golden *Gate;* the city *trash flats* stretch along the shore of the Bay, between the city and the Gate.

Reason. First published under the title *Belief.*

The Savages. Miss Benedict: Ruth Benedict, American anthropologist who, in PATTERNS OF CULTURE, applied to various primitive cultures the conceptions or attitudes embodied in the Greek gods *Dionysus* and *Apollo.*

HOWARD NEMEROV

1920, in New York City. Educated in Harvard. For some years was an editor of the magazine FURIOSO. Taught English at Hamilton College and now teaches at Bennington.

Poetry: THE IMAGE AND THE LAW, 1947; GUIDE TO THE RUINS, 1950; THE SALT GARDEN, 1955. Novels: THE MELODRAMATISTS, 1949; FEDER-IGO, 1954.

The Frozen City. reefers and coke: marijuana and cocaine.

Tuba mirum spargens sonum / Per sepulcra regionum, / Coget omnes ante thronum.

"A trumpet spreading its sound through the sepulchers of the world forces all before the throne." From the "Dies Irae" sequence of the Mass for the Dead.

Quomodo ardebam, deus meus, / Revolare a terrenis ad te, / Et nescie-bam quid ageres mecum.

"How did I burn then, my God, to remount from earthly things to Thee, nor knew I what Thou wouldst do with me." From St. Augustine's CON-FESSIONS, Book III, cap. IV. (originally prose).

HYAM PLUTZIK

1911, in Brooklyn. Reared in the country in Connecticut. Educated in Trinity College and Yale. Worked on newspapers during the Depression; has taught English at University of Rochester since World War II. Received award from National Institute of Arts and Letters and shared Poetry Awards Prize with Rolfe Humphries one year.

Poetry: ASPECTS OF PROTEUS, 1949.

On the Photograph of a Man. In orthodox Jewry there must be at least ten men gathered together for a religious ceremony to be held.

For T. S. E. Only. Titus: In 70 A.D. Titus (later Emperor of Rome) laid siege to Jerusalem, captured it, and scattered the Jews. You, hypo-crite lecteur . . . : "You, hypocrite reader, my double, my brother." Like a great many other references in this poem, this line alludes to (is directly taken from) a poem of Eliot, in this case *The Wasteland.* Eliot took the line from Baudelaire.

The Road. Huey Long, as quasi-dictator of Louisiana (Governor 1928–32, U.S. Senator 1931–35), pushed through the erecting of public works, which he took credit for personally.

Portrait. a shirt by Nessus: in the Greek myth, a beautiful shirt given in apparent affection but containing a secret poison which killed whoever should wear it.

Horatio. At the outset of the poem, Horatio is imagined as talking with Bernardo the guard, on the night of Hamlet's death, and vowing to fulfill Hamlet's final wish. In addition to the ostler and Faustus he hears (over a period of years) aristocratic esthetes in Paris, a statesman of expediency back in Denmark, and a myth-making shepherd all recount their versions of the story. At the end, he is in his castle Forstness writing his account of his experiences.

> O good Horatio, what a wounded name,
> Things standing thus unknown, shall live behind me!
> If thou didst ever hold me in thy heart,
> Absent thee from felicity awhile,
> And in this harsh world draw thy breath in pain
> To tell my story.

THEODORE ROETHKE

1908, in Saginaw, Michigan. Educated in University of Michigan and Harvard. Has received a Guggenheim Fellowship, award from the American Academy of Arts and Letters, and the Pulitzer Prize in Poetry. Has taught English at Lafayette College, Penn State, Bennington, and, presently, at the University of Washington.

Poetry: OPEN HOUSE, 1941; THE LOST SON, 1948; PRAISE TO THE END, 1951; THE WAKING: POEMS 1933–1953, 1954.

The Lost Son. Ordnung: order.

Four for Sir John Davies. Davies was an Elizabethan poet.

MURIEL RUKEYSER

1913, in New York City. Educated in Vassar, Harvard Summer School, and Columbia. Lecturer, teacher, and writer by profession. Has been awarded a Guggenheim Fellowship and an award from the American Academy of Arts and Letters. Lives in New York City.

Poetry: THEORY OF FLIGHT, 1935; U. S. 1, 1938; A TURNING WIND, 1939; THE SOUL AND BODY OF JOHN BROWN, 1941; BEAST IN VIEW, 1944; THE GREEN WAVE, 1948; ELEGIES, 1949; ORPHEUS, 1949; SELECTED POEMS, 1951. Forthcoming: BODY OF WAKING (short poems) and TREE OF RIVERS (scenes and poems about Willkie). Biography: WILLARD GIBBS, 1942. Criticism: THE LIFE OF POETRY, 1949. Children's books: COME BACK PAUL, and I GO OUT.

Ajanta. The frescoes painted on the walls of the Ajanta caves, in India, by generations of painter-monks, were made according to a religious principle. This principle is an analogy between space and the space of the body. It involves an acceptance of reality which defines art as other than the changing of reality, the looking-through the wall of Western painting. The wall is accepted; the air, the space between the walls and the observer, is filled with creation [author's note]. *Les Tendresses Bestiales:* bestial endearments.

Beast in View.

> All, all of a piece throughout;
> Thy chase had a beast in view;
> Thy wars brought nothing about;
> Thy loves were all untrue.
> 'Tis well an old age is out,
> And time to begin a new.   —DRYDEN

From the Duck-Pond. tiglon: a hybrid of a tiger and a lion.

Nuns in the Wind. Costa Brava is the local name for the savage coast of Catalonia, where the train I was in was stopped for good the morning the war in Spain began [author's note].

George Robinson and *The Cornfield.* These two poems are part of a sequence called "The Book of the Dead" (from U. S. 1), dealing with workers in West Virginia who died, during the Depression, of silicosis contracted under unsafe working conditions. *Mellon* is Andrew Mellon, secretary of the U.S. Treasury during the 20's and frequently used as the type capitalist.

JAMES SCHEVILL

1920, in Berkeley, California. Educated in Harvard. Has worked in publicity and in art and music criticism for a newspaper, and has edited BERKELEY: A JOURNAL OF MODERN CULTURE. Teaches English at California College of Arts and Crafts and at University of California (Berkeley).

Poetry: TENSIONS, 1947; THE AMERICAN FANTASIES, 1951; HIGH SINNERS, LOW ANGELS (musical play), 1953; THE RIGHT TO GREET, 1955. Biography: SHERWOOD ANDERSON: HIS LIFE AND WORK, 1951.

The unusual facts in Mr. Schevill's poems are accurate. For example, Queen Victoria did in fact go down into a pilot tunnel with Disraeli under the English Channel, and the baseball phrases in *An Astonished Listener* all came from actual big league broadcasts.

Confidential Data. Good Humor Salesman: Good Humors are ice cream bars sometimes sold by men pushing carts or driving cars which tinkle tunes as they go along. P-3: a designation both for a certain civil service rating and for a kind of combat plane in World War II.

Song for Old Apis. Solomon's seal: an old mystic symbol in the shape of a six-pointed star, signifying the unity of body and mind [author's note].

DELMORE SCHWARTZ

1913, in Brooklyn. Educated in University of Wisconsin, New York University, and Harvard; taught for a time at Harvard. For several years was an editor of PARTISAN REVIEW; at present poetry editor and movie critic for NEW REPUBLIC.

Poetry (and prose mingled): IN DREAMS BEGIN RESPONSIBILITIES, 1938; SHENANDOAH (verse play), 1941; GENESIS, 1943; VAUDEVILLE FOR A PRINCESS, 1950. Short stories: THE WORLD IS A WEDDING, 1948.

Will You Perhaps. "mentrechè il vento, come fa, si tace": "while the wind, as now, is silent for us." Inferno 5, 96. Spoken by Francesca in the circle of the lustful, who are being blown by winds, in response to Dante's asking her her story. This poem and the two following are numbers 2, 6, and 9 of a sequence of eleven poems entitled *The Repetitive Heart.*

In the Naked Bed. In THE REPUBLIC, Plato develops a sort of allegory or huge metaphor to embody his notion of how far we are from apprehending reality. What we learn through the senses is compared to shadows of images cast on the wall of a cave by a fire; we think these shadows are not shadows, not shadows of images, not shadows of images of reality, but reality itself; for we are as chained men who must look only ahead at the wall of the cave, not knowing even that the light is only the flickering, faint, false light of a fire rather than the light of true knowledge.

Lincoln. This is an autonomous passage from GENESIS, Book I. *an sich:* in itself; taken from *Ding an sich*, the thing in itself, of Kant.

The Masters of the Heart. longueurs: tediums. parvenu: upstart. Thermidor: name of a month during the First French Republic. In this month in 1794 Robespierre was overthrown and the Terror brought to an end. In THE MARRIAGE OF FIGARO (1785) Mozart has Figaro denounce hereditary privileges. Hugo in Jersey: Victor Hugo spent his last years in exile on the island of Jersey, west of France.

The Morning Light. This is the Cambridge in which is located Harvard.

N. B. The titles to Mr. Schwartz's poems are of his own making, unless they are enclosed in quotation marks.

WINFIELD TOWNLEY SCOTT

1910, in Haverhill, Massachusetts. Educated in Brown University. Received the Shelley Memorial Award and worked for many years as literary editor of the PROVIDENCE JOURNAL. At present lives in Santa Fe, N.M.

Poetry: BIOGRAPHY FOR TRAMAN, 1937; WIND THE CLOCK, 1941; SWORD ON THE TABLE, 1942; TO MARRY STRANGERS, 1945; MR. WHITTIER AND OTHER POEMS, 1948.

Baldness and the Swan. Sibelius is a Finnish composer, one of whose famous compositions is "Swan of Tuonela."

Memento. The scenery is Newport, R.I., and Narragansett Bay.

Bermuda Suite. This is the fifth in a sequence of five poems.

Merrill's Brook. bluet: a plant with blue flowers.

Codicil for Pvt. John Hogg's Will. An earlier poem entitled *Pvt. John Hogg* occurs on page 39 of MR. WHITTIER AND OTHER POEMS. hepatica: a kind of herb. flowering judas: the common American name for this tree or bush is the redbud; the related European judas tree is so called because Judas was supposed to have hanged himself on one.

KARL SHAPIRO

1913, in Baltimore. Educated in University of Virginia, Johns Hopkins, and Enoch Pratt Library School. Was awarded the Pulitzer Prize for Poetry, is a member of the American Academy of Arts and Letters, served as consultant in Poetry to the Library of Congress, served as editor of POETRY: A MAGAZINE OF VERSE for some years, and has taught English at Johns Hopkins, Iowa State, University of California (Berkeley), and, currently, University of California at Davis.

Poetry: PERSON, PLACE AND THING, 1942; V-LETTER, 1944; ESSAY ON RIME, 1945; TRIAL OF A POET, 1947; POEMS 1940–1953, 1953. Also, BIBLIOGRAPHY OF MODERN PROSODY, 1948.

The Southerner. yoni: the vulva; the personification of female power in Hindu mythology.

V-Letter. during World War II, overseas soldiers and their families corresponded by means of small, microfilmed letters called V-letters.

Recapitulation I. von Moltke: German general, relieved of his command after the Battle of the Marne, 1914.

Recapitulation XIII. Second stanza: the first two lines refer to the failure of the loyalist, anti-Franco cause in the Spanish Civil War during the 1930's, the third and fourth lines to romantic-literary escapes.

ROBERT PENN WARREN

1905, in Kentucky. Educated in Vanderbilt, University of California (Berkeley), Yale, Oxford (as a Rhodes Scholar). Has been awarded the Shelley Memorial Prize, a Guggenheim Fellowship, and Pulitzer Prize for fiction. Was one of the founders and editors of THE SOUTHERN REVIEW. Has taught at Louisiana State University, University of Minnesota, and, presently, at Yale.

Poetry: THIRTY-SIX POEMS, 1936; ELEVEN POEMS ON THE SAME THEME, 1942; SELECTED POEMS, 1943; BROTHER TO DRAGONS, 1953 (a long reflective narrative). Biography: JOHN BROWN: THE MAKING OF A MARTYR, 1929. Short stories: THE CIRCUS IN THE ATTIC, 1947. Novels: NIGHT RIDER, 1939; AT HEAVEN'S GATE, 1943; ALL THE KING'S MEN, 1946 (also made into a play); WORLD ENOUGH AND TIME, 1950; BAND OF ANGELS, 1955. Editor of ANTHOLOGY OF STORIES from THE SOUTHERN REVIEW. Co-editor (with Cleanth Brooks and J. T. Purser) of APPROACH

TO LITERATURE, and (with Cleanth Brooks) of UNDERSTANDING POETRY and of UNDERSTANDING FICTION, all three texts.

Eidolon. An eidolon is an apparition.

Revelation. Sulla: A great Roman general who made himself, by force of arms and against the laws, dictator of the republic. Centuries later St. Augustine in THE CITY OF GOD speaks of Sulla as the conqueror of his fellow-citizens, and also speaks of the upset of nature during the Roman social wars. Duncan: king in "Macbeth" (see II, iii).

Ode to Fear. Timor mortis conturbat me: "the fear of death is breaking me up." This line was used as refrain in "Lament for the Makers" (or poets) by William Dunbar (a Scottish monk of the late Middle Ages). Originally the phrase is from the Seventh Lesson of the *Office of the Dead.* Focke-Wulf and Zero: German and Japanese combat planes in World War II. in utero: in the womb.

Mexico Is a Foreign Country. "Viene galopando el mundo": the world comes galloping.

To a Little Girl. rocca: tower, castle, fortress. Philipus me fecit: Philip made me. Giannutri: island off the coast of Italy, north of Rome. gobbo: hunchback. malva: mallow.

RICHARD WILBUR

1921, in New York City. Educated in Amherst and Harvard. Has taught at Harvard after a three-year membership in its Society of Fellows. Has been awarded a Guggenheim Fellowship and served as Poet in Residence at the American Academy in Rome. Now teaches at Wellesley.

Poetry: THE BEAUTIFUL CHANGES, 1947; CEREMONY, 1950; THINGS OF THIS WORLD, 1956.

Cicadas. Originally published under the title *Cigales.*

In a Bird Sanctuary. Faneuil Hall: a famous old building in Boston.

The Beautiful Changes. Lucernes: with reference to the Lake of Lucerne, in Switzerland.

Ceremony. Bazille: French impressionist painter.

Castles and Distances. Amboise: an ancient town in France, where is situated a castle long used as a royal residence. Versailles: a 17th century royal palace of pleasure not far from the capital. Ardens: in the Arden of AS YOU LIKE IT, though it was nominally the actual Forest of Arden, magical romance flourished. Prospero: the Duke in THE TEMPEST; at the end of the play he leaves the island he had ruled by magic to resume his real Dukedom in Milan.

Exeunt. Originally published under the title *Exodus.*

"A World without Objects." Traherne was a 17th-century English poet.

Lament. Nashe's old queens: see IN PLAGUE TIME by Thomas Nashe, 16th century.

Marché aux Oiseaux. Bird market.

Rinehart Editions